A History of the Laurel Brigade

A History of the Laurel Brigade

Originally
The Ashby Cavalry
of the
Army of Northern Virginia
and
Chew's Battery

by
William N. McDonald

edited by
Bushrod C. Washington

with a new introduction and index by
Eric J. Mink

The Johns Hopkins University Press
Baltimore and London

The Muster Roll of the Laurel Brigade, Seventh, Eleventh, Twelfth, and Thirty-fifth Virginia Cavalry and Chew's Battery, Army of Northern Virginia, from the original publication, is available at www.press.jhu.edu.

First published by the Sun Job Printing Office, Baltimore, Maryland, 1907
Johns Hopkins Paperbacks edition, 2002
9 8 7 6 5 4 3 2 1

The Johns Hopkins University Press
2715 North Charles Street
Baltimore, Maryland 21218-4363
www.press.jhu.edu

Library of Congress Cataloging-in-Publication Data

McDonald, William, 1834–1898.
    A history of the Laurel Brigade : originally the Ashby Cavalry of the Army of Northern Virginia and Chew's Battery / by William N. McDonald ; edited by Bushrod C. Washington ; with a new introduction and index by Eric J. Mink.
        p. cm.
    Originally published: Baltimore : Sun Job Print. Off., 1907.
    Includes bibliographical references and index.
    ISBN 0-8018-6952-8 (pbk. : alk. paper)
        1. Confederate States of America. Army. Virginia Cavalry. Laurel Brigade. 2. Virginia—History—Civil War, 1861–1865—Regimental histories. 3. United States—History—Civil War, 1861–1865—Regimental histories. 4. Virginia—History—Civil War, 1861–1865—Campaigns. 5. Shenandoah River Valley (Va. and W. Va.)—History—Civil War, 1861–1865—Campaigns. 6. United States—History—Civil War, 1861–1865—Campaigns. I. Washington, Bushrod C. (Bushrod Corbin), b. 1839. II. Title.
    E581.4 .L37 2002
    973.7'455—dc21

                                                                2001050484

A catalog record for this book is available from the British Library.

CONTENTS

CHAPTER I

Development of the Laurel Brigade from the Seventh Regiment of Virginia Cavalry, enlisted under Col. Angus W. McDonald—Border service under Colonel McDonald and Col. Turner Ashby—Heroic death of Capt. Richard Ashby—Destructive expedition against the Baltimore and Ohio Railroad and Chesapeake and Ohio Canal—Chew's Battery attached to the command—Romney winter campaign under Jackson—Battle of Kernstown

CHAPTER II

Daily skirmishes with force of Banks—Addition of new companies and recruits swell the brigade—Jackson orders it divided into two commands, and Ashby tenders his resignation—Jackson revokes the order and Ashby withdraws his resignation—Jackson marches to McDowell and defeats Fremont—Ashby screens the movement from Banks by constant skirmishing in his front—Destroys railroad and telegraph between Front Royal and Strasburg—Attack upon Federal infantry at Buckton, where Captains Sheetz and Fletcher fall—Battle of Winchester and pursuit of Banks—Ashby throws his cavalry between the converging armies of Shields and Fremont and prevents communication between them—Informs Jackson fully of their movements—Capture of Sir Percy Wyndham—Death of Ashby—Cross Keys and Port Republic

CHAPTER III

Jackson marches from Brown's Gap to the Chickahominy—His ingenious ruses to deceive Shields and Fremont—Munford screens Jackson's movement and follows him with the Second Virginia Cavalry—Genl. Beverly Robertson succeeds in command of Valley cavalry—Reorgani-

CHAPTER IV

CHAPTER V

Chapter VI

Chapter VII

Chapter VIII

Chapter XI

Chapter XII

Chapter XIII

Chapter XIV

PREFACE

This history was written by the late Capt. William N. McDonald, who was ordnance officer of the Laurel Brigade. It was written at the request of Genl. Thomas L. Rosser, its one time commander, who gave to the brigade the name "Laurel," and who by his courage, dash, and skill, in great degree contributed to win the fame which made it worthy to be known by that name.

The labor of Captain McDonald in accumulating the data and writing this history, extended through the ten years previous to his lamented death on the 4th of January, 1898. And some idea of the amount and difficulty of the labor undertaken may be gathered from his own words, below quoted, from a circular letter sent to the survivors of the brigade, in his quest for information: "This work was entered upon with the settled purpose of making it an authentic memorial of those who composed the Laurel Brigade, but with little expectation that the story of the achievements of the command would equal its measure of fame. The facts necessary to make up the record are difficult to procure. The official reports rarely give details, and after February 1st, 1864, few if any brigade or regimental reports are to be found. From that time, to the end, there was such a giving and taking of blows,—such a struggle for the means of subsistence,—that little time was left for clerical work. There is therefore a gap of more than a year full of stirring events, with small record of even the general actions of the brigade."

It was from the mass of letters received in response to his circular, Captain McDonald chiefly gathered the material for the history. While many of these were clear and explicit, many were contradictory of others, and to gather the actual facts out of multitudes of contradictions, was a labor easier to be imagined than described. While the body of the history was practically complete, the manuscript was in its first form and not yet ready for publication when it came into my hands. At the request of a committee of the survivors of the brigade, I undertook the work of reviewing the manuscript and preparing it for the hands of a publisher.

In the posthumous preparation of an author's work, there is always the temptation to the reviser, to materially alter it in some particular, and here and there to interject something suggestive of himself. Had the disposition to do this possessed me, there would hardly have been the opportunity, for the manuscript as I received it, practically covered the achievements of the brigade from Kernstown to Appomattox. My work, was rather to supply such missing links in the narrative as were to be found here and there; to make such corrections as subsequent revelations made necessary, and such additions in the way of official reports, and well-authenticated individual statements, as would add authority and verification to the history. Besides this, there was also such a general revision of the manuscript, as the author himself would have given before placing it in the hands of a publisher.

Captain McDonald having been my personal friend as well as a close comrade both in the infantry and cavalry *arms of the Confederate service, the labor of revising his work, has been mingled with a great deal of pleasure, and I have endeavored to discharge the duty in a way that would have been gratifying to him.*

It is impossible but that there will be some omissions, both regarding events, and individuals worthy of mention, and perhaps a few incidents mentioned not exactly in accord with the recollections of some. The lapse of time before undertaking the work, the lack of sources of information, and the fallibility of memory must be sufficient excuse for these. The intention of the author was to produce an authentic record, free from exaggeration and also from mere rhetorical display. It was his intention also to append as complete a roster of the officers and men as could possibly be procured. No effort has been spared to carry out this intention. Nevertheless the rolls of some companies are entirely missing and others incomplete, which is greatly to be regretted.

It has been the wish that every soldier who served in the brigade and helped to contribute to its fame, should have honorable mention. Unfortunately, the missing names are likely to be those of the killed or mortally wounded in battle and dropped from the rolls, who of all others, if possible, should be especially remembered.

To the comrades who by letters, loan of private diaries, and in other ways assisted the author and the reviser in preparing this history, whose names are too numerous to mention here, sincere thanks are given. Most of them, however, are mentioned in the body of the work.

It was at first the intention, that there should be an addendum to the work containing special mention of officers and privates who rendered conspicuous and meritorious services. But after mature consideration this was considered unadvisable and the intention abandoned, for the reason that the Laurel Brigade was composed of so many heroic men, that to single out a few for special mention, would seem in the nature of an invidious distinction.

BUSHROD C. WASHINGTON.

THE AUTHOR

The late Capt. William N. McDonald, author of this work, was born in 1834 in Romney, Virginia; was educated in his native State, taking the degree of A. M. at the University of Virginia in 1857, and was elected professor of belles-lettres in the University of Public Schools of Louisville, Kentucky, the same year; the following year he was promoted to presidency of the same, and in that capacity was acting superintendent of the schools of Louisville.

In 1859 he resigned and studied law, and in 1860 went to Europe as secretary to his father, Col. Angus W. McDonald, commissioner of Virginia, to report upon the Maryland and Virginia boundary line.

On April 19th, 1861, he enlisted as a private in Company G, Second Virginia Regiment, Stonewall Brigade, in which he served until after the reorganization of the army in 1862. He was transferred to the Laurel Brigade and served as ordnance officer upon the staff of General Rosser. He served the Confederacy with distinguished gallantry during the entire war from the day Virginia seceded to Appomattox. At the time of the surrender he was chief of ordnance of Mahone's division of Lee's army, with the rank of captain of artillery.

In 1865 he established the Cool Spring School in Clarke county, Virginia. While there he wrote, in conjunction with Prof. John S. Blackburn, the first Southern school history of the United States. It was published at their own cost, passed through about twenty editions, and still has a wide circulation.

In 1868 he left Cool Spring to accept his old place as president of the University of Public Schools of Louisville, Kentucky, at an advance of nearly double the previous salary.

In 1872 he resigned this position and established the Louisville Rugby School, which for fifteen years was the largest and most flourishing private school for boys west of the Alleghanies. While principal of the same he became editor and half proprietor of the SOUTHERN BIVOUAC, *which magazine during his connection with it greatly flourished.*

In 1887 he left Louisville and established at Berryville, Virginia, the Shenandoah University School, of which he was principal until his death on June 4th, 1898.

A History of the Laurel Brigade

INTRODUCTION TO THE
JOHNS HOPKINS EDITION

Of all the Confederate images that survive from the American Civil War, few surpass that of the Southern cavalry in its boldness, recklessness, and dash. One of the most famous mounted units to serve the Confederacy was the Laurel Brigade. Composed of horsemen who hailed mostly from the Shenandoah Valley and the mountains of northwestern Virginia (with a sprinkling of exiled Marylanders), the Laurel Brigade grew from a collection of companies that responded to Virginia's early call to arms. These companies eventually formed a regiment, and from this regiment, along with many new recruits, emerged a brigade. The western Virginia horsemen gained recognition for their determination and skill as warriors on the field, while at the same time acquiring a reputation for indifference to military discipline and organization. In time the brigade matured, due in large part to a string of commanders who instilled discipline and turned the Laurel Brigade into one of the most versatile units in the army.

The nucleus of what became known as the Laurel Brigade, the Seventh Virginia Cavalry, began to emerge in June of 1861, when Col. Angus W. McDonald, Sr., a sixty-three-year-old Winchester lawyer and West Point graduate, received permission to raise a regiment. McDonald met few obstacles in achieving this goal, receiving as his first company a group of horsemen led by Turner Ashby, a young and energetic farmer from Fauquier County. A born fighter and leader of men, Ashby soon emerged as one of the early heroes of the Confederacy. Around this company others gathered, and within a month McDonald took the field with a regimental command. Throughout the summer and autumn of 1861, the regiment's area of operations was limited to the lower (or northern) Shenandoah Valley and mountains, defending Virginia's border and guarding various lines of communication. In November, McDonald, suffering the physical hardships of active service and smarting from defeat in a small skirmish near Romney, left the cavalry for administrative duty in Winchester. Command of the regiment devolved upon the charismatic Ashby.

Turner Ashby was a natural commander of the Valley horsemen, although his detractors rightly claimed that he proved a poor administrator. The young cavalryman excelled as a troop leader, merely requesting that his men show the same selfless courage he himself displayed upon the battlefield. The young men who rode with Ashby hailed from predominantly wealthy families, were well-educated, and reflected their commander's high-spirited cavalier attitude. Used to giving orders, rather than obeying them, they often came under criticism from the more professionally trained officers in the army. Still, Ashby's men repeatedly showed that they respected his leadership and would follow him anywhere. Numerous times during Ashby's tenure as commander of the Valley cavalry—as the horsemen were known—superiors attempted to intervene and assert some control over the unit, but to no avail. Authorities feared that if they meddled in his command, it might simply fall apart. Gen. Thomas J. "Stonewall" Jackson, himself a stern disciplinarian, summed up the frustration that many of the army leaders felt. "If I persisted in my attempt to increase the efficiency of the Cavalry [by reorganizing it]," Jackson wrote, "it would produce the contrary effect, as Col. Ashby's influence, who is very popular with his men, would be thrown against me."[1] Such was the devotion the Valley horsemen felt for their commander.

The lack of discipline continued to plague the command through the winter of 1861 and into the following year, but many infantrymen sought transfers to Ashby's regiment following the expiration of their one-year enlistment. As more men poured into his camps, Ashby took very few steps to organize his growing command. He did, however, create one of the first mounted batteries in Confederate service. Under the command of Capt. Roger Preston Chew, this battery performed admirably during the war and won for itself a reputation as being second to none in the cavalry service. In the spring of 1862, during the Valley Campaign, Ashby and his companies covered Jackson's flanks and effectively screened the army's movement, keeping Union forces guessing as to Stonewall's intentions. In the end, however, Ashby's recklessness caught up to him. On June 6, while tangling with a large combined force of Union cavalry and infantry near Harrisonburg, the commander of the Valley cavalry was struck down by a bullet to his abdomen. The campaign came to a close a few days later. In his final report, Jackson devoted a few sentences as a eulogy to his fallen cavalry commander. "As a partisan officer," wrote Stonewall, "I never knew his superior; his daring was proverbial; his powers of endurance almost incredible; his tone of character heroic, and his sagacity almost intuitive in divining the purposes and movements of the enemy."[2]

---

[1]Thomas J. Jackson to Walter H. Taylor, May 5, 1862, Charles W. Dabney Papers, Southern Historical Collection, University of North Carolina, Raleigh, N.C.

[2]Report of Thomas J. Jackson, June 11, 1862, *The War of the Rebellion: A Compilation of the Official Reports of the Union and Confederate Armies*, 1st ser. (Washington, D.C.: GPO, 1880–1901), 12, pt. 1:712. (Hereafter cited as *OR*.)

While the army and Virginia were still mourning the loss of the young cavalier, authorities took steps to rectify the organizational nightmare Ashby had created. During the course of his tenure at the head of the Valley cavalry, the command had ballooned to more than twenty-five companies, nearly three times the number allotted to a regiment. On June 16, at Swift Run Gap, the long awaited reorganization finally took place. The original ten companies became the Seventh Virginia Cavalry. Chew's Battery remained intact. Ten of the remaining companies formed the new Twelfth Virginia Cavalry, while another five received designation as the Seventeenth Battalion Virginia Cavalry. Added to these were the Second and Sixth regiments, which, independent of Ashby, had previously operated with Maj. Gen. Richard S. Ewell's division of infantry. The reorganization solved only part of the problem, as military and government officials were equally concerned about a replacement for Ashby. They needed someone who could maintain the command's fighting edge while injecting some discipline into the independent spirit of the troopers. On June 18, Brig. Gen. Beverly H. Robertson, an unknown outsider, received command of Ashby's cavalry.[3]

The army could not have chosen someone more different in style to Ashby. The new commander brought with him a strong military background. A West Point graduate and officer in the prewar United States cavalry, Robertson proved to be a tough disciplinarian and unpopular replacement. Ashby had been reckless and bold; sluggishness and caution plagued Robertson. Although disliked, the new brigadier managed to keep his command together and in July led it east of the Blue Ridge to rejoin Jackson in his movement against Maj. Gen. John Pope's Army of Virginia. The men handled themselves ably under their new commander, standing up well in their debut against Yankee cavalry outside the Valley. Following the Battle of Cedar Mountain, Robertson's brigade left Jackson's command and joined Lee's celebrated force under Maj. Gen. J.E.B. Stuart.

The relationship between Stuart and Robertson was a rocky one, and the two men clashed frequently. Fortunately, Stuart's personal dislike of Robertson did not influence his impression of the latter's handling of his brigade. "General Robertson," later wrote Stuart, "had cause to be proud of the command which his superior discipline, organization, and drill had brought to the stability of veterans."[4] While the men may have chafed under Robertson's leadership, its effects were being noticed.

---

[3]Special and General Orders regarding the makeup of the brigade can be found in various volumes of the *OR*s and on microfilm, M921, roll 2, National Archives, Washington, D.C.

[4]Report of J.E.B. Stuart, February 5, 1863, *OR*, 12, pt. 2:727.

Robertson's command of Ashby's brigade, however, did not last long. Following Second Manassas, he received a transfer to North Carolina and leadership of the brigade temporarily fell to Col. Thomas T. Munford of the Second Virginia. The brigade saw rather limited service in the Maryland Campaign, and autumn found it back in the Shenandoah Valley. Once again reorganization affected its structure when Col. Munford and his Second Virginia left the brigade and were replaced by a new Valley unit, the Thirty-fifth Battalion Virginia Cavalry—which included a few more Marylanders—under Maj. Elijah V. White. On November 11, newly promoted Brig. Gen. William E. "Grumble" Jones assumed command of the Valley regiments. Like his predecessor, Jones came from a military background that included a West Point diploma and service in the prewar army. Also like Robertson, Jones considered discipline essential and harbored a strong dislike of J.E.B. Stuart and those who catered to the plumed cavalier. Something of a misfit among Stuart's regiments, Jones found a home among the Valley men and soon earned their trust and respect.

Toward the end of 1862, Jones received an independent assignment as commander of the Valley District. Under his leadership, and thanks to hours of drilling and outpost duty, the efficiency of the brigade progressed. The Seventeenth Battalion received the addition of a few new companies at this time that raised it to regimental strength and designation as the Eleventh Virginia Cavalry. Jones took advantage of his maturing brigade and conducted a number of ambitious raids into western Virginia and Maryland. Gen. Robert E. Lee was greatly impressed with the success of one these expeditions, writing that he believed "General Jones displayed sagacity and boldness in his plans and was well supported by the courage and fortitude of his officers and men."[5] The raids invigorated the Valley horsemen and further honed their martial skills. Meanwhile, the Army of Northern Virginia, east of the mountains, was basking in the aftermath of its stunning victory at Chancellorsville. In preparation for a move north, Lee recalled Jones and his brigade for duty with the army.

Jones' brigade arrived in time to participate in the Battle of Brandy Station and then embark on Lee's invasion of Pennsylvania. The Valley men participated in the spirited fighting at Middleburg and Upperville, but saw little action in Pennsylvania until Lee's defeated army began its retreat. On July 3, at Fairfield, Pennsylvania—about four miles south of Gettysburg—Jones' brigade soundly thrashed the Sixth United States

---

[5]Robert E. Lee's endorsement of William E. Jones' Report, June 15, 1863, *OR*, 25, pt. 1:121.

Cavalry before falling back to the Potomac River, skirmishing heavily with Union cavalry at Funkstown, Boonsboro, and Williamsport, Maryland. Once safely back in Virginia, Jones' regiments spent the remainder of July and August picketing the Shenandoah Valley and the upper Rappahannock River.

In late August, the tension between Stuart and Jones finally came to a head and the cavalry commander preferred charges against his subordinate. Jones was placed under arrest and the brigade now fell to the temporary leadership of Col. Lunsford L. Lomax of the Sixth Virginia. Lomax's time at the head of the brigade was short, for on September 16 he and his regiment left the brigade, and Col. Oliver R. Funsten of the Eleventh Virginia took charge of the four remaining regiments. In the midst of the Bristoe Station Campaign, word reached the brigade that Jones had been officially transferred and that newly promoted Brig. Gen. Thomas L. Rosser of the Fifth Virginia Cavalry was to assume command.

Rosser, like Jones and Robertson before him, was West Point trained. Rosser brought with him a solid reputation and ability for command. Stuart once described the young cavalryman as "a bold and dashing leader, on the march & in bivouac a rigid disciplinarian, but at the same time exacting the confidence of his entire command."[6] Of the officers who led the Valley cavalry during the war, none, with the exception of Ashby, earned the men's profound respect more than Rosser.

During the winter, the Valley regiments once again found themselves operating in the Shenandoah. Seizing the opportunity to utilize his men's knowledge of area, Rosser made numerous raids into what had now become the loyal state of West Virginia. Following the receipt of Rosser's report on one of these excursions, Stuart wrote: "The bold and successful enterprise herein reported furnishes additional proofs of General Rosser's merit as a commander, and adds fresh laurels to that veteran brigade so signalized for valor already."[7] Stuart's praise reached Rosser the first week of April, while he was encamped near Brownsburg, ten miles north of Lexington. Capitalizing on the cavalry commander's choice of words, Rosser dubbed his command the "Laurel Brigade," and called on his men to wear a badge of two laurel leaves, which was to be affixed to either their coat or hat.[8] With a renewed sense of honor and identity, the Laurel Brigade prepared for the spring offensive.

---

[6]J.E.B. Stuart to Samuel Cooper, January 13, 1863, Compiled Service Record of Thomas L. Rosser, M331, roll 215, National Archives, Washington, D.C.

[7]J.E.B. Stuart's endorsement of Thomas L. Rosser's Report, April 7, 1864, *OR*, 33:36.

[8]Andrew C. L. Gatewood to his mother, April 9, 1864, Andrew C. L. Gatewood Papers, Virginia Military Institute Archives, Lexington, Va.

On May 1, the Laurel Brigade moved east to rejoin the army near Orange Court House. Four days later, in the tangled thickets of the Wilderness, Rosser struck Union cavalry along the Catharpin Road. In one of the many charges that day, a member of the Seventh Virginia heard Lieut. Col. Thomas Marshall cry out "this is the Laurel Brig[ade] show the enemy you have won laurels and can win them again."[9] Many of the veterans later believed that this was the first usage of their nom de guerre. From the Wilderness, Rosser led his men through the battles of Haw's Shop, Ashland, and Trevilian Station. The Laurel Brigade figured prominently in each of these battles, adding to their growing reputation and extinguishing any lingering doubts about their discipline.

The Valley men enjoyed a respite once they reached Petersburg in the end of June, but the rest proved all too brief. In August, the brigade fought against Union offensives near Deep Bottom, north of the James River, and at Reams' Station, south of Petersburg. In September, the brigade participated in the successful Beef Steak Raid, which took the men behind Union lines and gained for Lee's army the capture of more than two thousand cattle. There was little time to celebrate once they returned to camp, for on September 26 Rosser received orders to march his men back across the mountains and join Jubal A. Early in the defense of the Valley.

The men of the Laurel Brigade received this order with much anticipation. The news of Philip Sheridan's depredations enraged the horsemen, who eagerly anticipated the opportunity to evict the enemy from their home country. However, the atmosphere in the Valley was anything but sympathetic to the mounted arm. Jubal Early had never been fond of his cavalry, comprised mostly of Valley regiments. Recent reversals at Third Winchester and Fisher's Hill gave him more reason to doubt the effectiveness of his troopers. In explaining his defeat at Winchester, Early blamed the cavalry for being "the cause of all my disasters."[10] The decision to return Rosser and the Laurel Brigade to the Valley was borne out of a desire to solve what army officials perceived as a lack of discipline and poor leadership among Early's horsemen. Rosser's men might stand out as an example for the other Valley regiments and thereby act as a rallying point for their fellow cavalrymen. Unfortunately, against Sheridan's superior numbers, and Early's growing criticism, poor morale among the Confederate cavalry became infectious.

Shortly after the Laurel Brigade's arrival, Sheridan and his army began to retrace their steps back down the Shenandoah. In their wake,

[9]James W. Wood, 1864 Diary, Library of Virginia, Richmond, Va.
[10]Report of Jubal A. Early, September 25, 1864, *OR*, 43:558.

homes and property fell victim to Union torches. Rosser set out in pursuit and chased the Union cavalry as far as Tom's Brook, where on October 9, Early's cavalry suffered its most disastrous defeat. Rosser's men outdistanced their infantry supports, and Sheridan's cavalry seized the opportunity to turn and attack. Although Rosser's men fought well against the superior Union horsemen, in the end the Southern cavalry broke and ran. The retreat turned into a rout and the Laurel Brigade found itself caught up in the stampede. Tom's Brook did nothing to raise Early's estimation of his cavalry, and Rosser and the Laurel Brigade were equally as culpable in their commander's eyes. Learning of Rosser's defeat, Early was heard to quip, "the laurel is a running vine."[11]

Having failed Early, Rosser soon found himself relegated to duties in which he could have little impact. A few weeks later at Cedar Creek, Rosser's troopers held the Confederate left flank and took a very limited role in the engagement. Confederate defeat at Cedar Creek marked the end of the Valley Campaign. Although Rosser continued to look for opportunities to redeem himself, he found few chances. Raids into West Virginia broke up the monotony of winter camp, but with their homes firmly within Union control, many of the Valley men took leave of their commands and desertion rates soared. In March of 1865, the fate of the Valley was sealed with a final Union victory at Waynesboro. Having swept Confederate resistance from the Shenandoah, Sheridan turned east and headed toward Petersburg.

In late March, Rosser received a promotion and was given permanent command of a cavalry division that included his Laurel Brigade. Command of the Valley regiments fell to Brig. Gen. James Dearing, who continued the tradition of a West Point–educated officer heading the brigade. Rosser reached Lee's army just in time to take part in the final act of the Petersburg Campaign, the Battle of Five Forks. Following the collapse of the Petersburg front, Dearing and the Laurel Brigade headed west with the Confederate army. On April 6, near High Bridge, the Confederate cavalry delivered for Lee the army's last victory. In the attacks upon the Union cavalry, Dearing fell mortally wounded and Lieut. Col. Elijah V. White assumed command of the brigade for its final days. While some of the Laurel Brigade surrendered three days later at Appomattox Court House, others skirted Union forces and with White safely reached Lynchburg. On April 9, White gathered the remnants of the brigade around him and informed them of Lee's surrender. Holding true to the independent nature of the command,

---

[11]Henry K. Douglas, *I Rode with Stonewall* (Chapel Hill: University of North Carolina Press, 1900), 314.

White allowed the men to make their own decision about which course they would pursue—whether to accept the terms of surrender or make their way to Gen. Joseph E. Johnston's army in North Carolina. Each man had to make the decision himself; but as a distinctive command, the Laurel Brigade officially disbanded.

Throughout its four years of service, the Laurel Brigade fought to overcome its early reputation for lacking proper discipline. The succession of commanders who followed Ashby worked diligently to mold the Valley cavalry into a well-trained and formidable mounted force. Under Ashby, the men may have become adept at outpost duty, but under Jones and Rosser they learned to be battlefield soldiers. No other brigade in Lee's army could claim to have served in such a wide variety of operations. Their selfless courage earned them praise and respect upon the battlefields of Virginia, while knowledge of the mountain region made them invaluable in operations involving the occupied areas of the state. Their versatility was unequaled by any other cavalry brigade in the army, and earned the Laurel Brigade a prominent place among the Southern horsemen who served the Confederacy.

Like so many veterans, the men of the Laurel Brigade held numerous reunions after the war to keep the memory of their daring deeds alive. At one such gathering, nearly twenty years after their return home, Rosser suggested that one of them should write a book to chronicle their service in the late war. In choosing a historian to accomplish this work, they turned to Capt. William Naylor McDonald, former brigade ordnance officer and son of the their first commander.[12] The men of the Laurel Brigade could not have found someone more appropriately suited for such a project.

William McDonald was born February 3, 1834, in Romney, Virginia (later West Virginia), the middle child of Angus W. McDonald, Sr., and Leacy Anne Naylor.[13] William's mother died in 1843, and his father remarried four years later to Miss Cornelia Peake.[14] In 1857, William graduated from the University of Virginia and then accepted an appointment as professor of belle-lettres at the public high school in Louisville, Kentucky, of which he also served as president and superintendent. He returned to his family in 1861, who were then living in

---

[12]"History of the Laurel Brigade" in *Confederate Veteran* 15 (1907): 155.

[13]McDonald Family Records, Edward McDonald Papers, Southern Historical Collection, University of North Carolina, Chapel Hill, N.C. (Hereafter cited as McDonald Papers, UNC).

[14]Cornelia Peake McDonald's wartime diary has been published under the title *A Woman's Civil War: A Diary with Reminiscences of the War, from March 1862* (Madison: University of Wisconsin Press, 1992).

Winchester, Virginia, and pursued a career in law. Although they hailed from a region that was divided on the idea of secession, with the outbreak of war, the entire McDonald clan supported the course taken by their native state. By war's end, Angus McDonald and five of his sons had served in the Confederate army.

William's military career began on April 18, 1861, with his enlistment in the "Bott's Greys," an infantry company that shortly thereafter became Company G, Second Virginia Infantry. William served in the Second Virginia through the summer of 1861, taking part in the fighting at First Manassas. His service in the infantry was brief. During November and December he was placed on special duty with his father in the Valley. The following year, he received a three-month detail to duty with the engineers, reconnoitering the Pamunkey and Chickahominy Rivers northeast of Richmond. Upon his return from detached duty, in the spring of 1862, William opted to resign from the Second Virginia and enlisted in a cavalry company commanded by his older brother Edward at New Market, Virginia.[15] Years later, William wrote about the decision of many men to leave the infantry for the mounted arm. He, like so many others, reveled in a feeling of independence in the cavalry. To leave service in the infantry behind "was to exchange servitude for freedom, and to be promoted to a sort of equestrian rank."[16] This choice was one that William would not regret, for not only would he no longer be forced "to stagger on the march beneath the burning sun," but promotion awaited him in the cavalry.

As a member of one of the companies attached to the Valley cavalry, now commanded by Ashby, William participated in the closing actions of Jackson's celebrated Valley Campaign. After the June reorganization of Ashby's companies, William became a member of Company D, Seventeenth Battalion Virginia Cavalry, and fought through the Second Manassas Campaign. He fell prey to illness that winter, having contracted a slight case of smallpox, and left his command for recovery in Harrisonburg. William returned to his regiment in February to discover an appointment to first lieutenant and duty as acting ordnance officer for his brigade, then under the command of William E. Jones. In October, his appointment became final and he was commissioned a

[15]William McDonald's military service is documented in his Compiled Service Records and can be found on microfilm, M324, rolls 112 and 277, and M331, roll 171, National Archives, Washington, D.C. For information on his detached service with the engineers, see John B. Tapscott, "Early War Incidents on the James," *Confederate Veteran* 7 (1899): 13–15.

[16]William N. McDonald, "Cavalry Versus Infantry," *Southern Bivouac* 1, no. 4 (1882): 163.

captain of artillery, remaining with the brigade and its new commander Thomas L. Rosser.

The spring of 1864 brought a brief respite for the McDonald family from the hardships and separation created by war. Rosser's brigade camped near Lexington where William's father was in command of the post, and where many of the younger members of the clan resided. There was much time for celebration and socializing among the McDonalds, for William was not the only member of the family who had recently been promoted. Edward now wore the rank of major and was in command of the Eleventh Virginia Cavalry. Edward later remembered that William made quite an impression among both soldiers and civilians around Lexington and was "a great toast with everyone."[17] This interlude, however, was quickly interrupted by the onset of the spring campaigns.

Holding a position on the brigade staff, William witnessed the engagements and campaigns from a broader perspective. That did not mean, of course, that he distanced himself from the action. On May 6, 1864, William found himself in the middle of the heated engagement along the Brock Road in the Wilderness. A shell fragment struck William in the side and inflicted a wound severe enough that he was sent to Lexington to recover. Shortly after his arrival, Union forces under Maj. Gen. David Hunter descended upon the town, but William made good his escape. His father was not so fortunate. Col. McDonald was wounded and captured near Buckhannon, while trying to evade Hunter's men, and subsequently was imprisoned in Wheeling, West Virginia. His jailers placed the elder McDonald in shackles and confined him to a small cell. He was finally released in November, but the effects of the incarceration upon the sixty-five-year-old colonel were too much, and he died the following month.

William returned to his duties with the army in August and continued to serve on Rosser's staff until November of 1864, when he received a transfer and assignment to duty as chief ordnance officer with Maj. Gen. William Mahone's division. In the final months of the war, William served on Mahone's staff in the trenches around Petersburg. On April 9, 1865, William received his parole at Appomattox. Before returning home, he sought out his brother Edward, whom he learned had been severely wounded in the clash at High Bridge. He found his brother in the

---

[17]Edward A. H. McDonald, "A Rough Sketch of the Incidents in the Experience of Major E. H. McDonald as a Confederate Soldier," McDonald Papers, UNC. This unpublished memoir contains a great deal of information concerning the McDonalds, both during and after the war, and served as the basis for Julia Davis' *Mount Up: A True Story of the Civil War* (New York: Harcourt, Brace & World, 1967).

hospital at Charlottesville. For the next six weeks he tended to Edward's needs and nursed him until he was well enough to travel. While in Charlottesville they were joined by another brother, Angus, and together the three men set off to try to put their lives, and family, back together.

With the loss of the patriarch, the war irrevocably shattered the McDonald family. The survivors returned to find their home in Winchester a shambles, uninhabitable and beyond repair. With little or no choice, William and Edward decided to apply their energies to working the land. They secured a farm outside of nearby Berryville, known as Cool Spring, where they hoped to create a new home for themselves and their family. While Edward worked the fields, William opened up the Cool Spring School, a boarding institution for boys. The farm and school prospered, and slowly the McDonalds put the pieces back together. Around Cool Spring, William and Edward built a "home or nucleus around which the family could gather."[18] Their stepmother and her children remained in Lexington, but their unmarried sisters Flora and Sue, along with their brother Angus and his family moved to the farm. On August 13, 1867, William extended his family when he wed Miss Katherine S. Gray of Loudoun County.

In the years that followed, the Cool Spring School prospered, and William found time to collaborate with John S. Blackburn, an Alexandria schoolteacher and former officer in the Sixth Virginia Cavalry, on a textbook of American history. Released in 1867, *A Southern School History of the United States of America* was praised as the first Southern school history of the United States and passed through numerous editions. The textbook sought to give the Southern point of view with regard to the causes of the Civil War and also heralded the accomplishments of Robert E. Lee and the Confederate armies. With the release of his book, and the success of his school, William in 1868 received an offer to return to Louisville and once again take up the position of president of the city's high school. Edward, who still ran the farm at Cool Spring, offered to join his older brother, and that fall the two brothers left their home in Virginia to try their luck in Kentucky.

Louisville had a rather large Confederate-veterans community, and it did not take long for the two men to make friends and integrate themselves into local society. Edward found work in the legal field and became a moving force among local former Confederates. Except for a brief return to West Virginia in 1872, William remained in Kentucky until 1887, working at the Louisville High School and establishing the Louisville Rugby School. The city's close-knit community of former

---

[18]McDonald, "A Rough Sketch of the Incidents."

Confederates gave rise to an organization in which Edward and William held prominent positions. Known as the Southern Historical Association of Louisville, this group of men began publishing solicited papers on topics dealing with the Southern struggle. Initially issued under the banner the *Bivouac,* the periodical soon changed its name to the *Southern Bivouac.* A year after its inception, William assumed the role of editor for the magazine and Edward later took control of the business end of the enterprise. Under William's control, the magazine struck a conciliatory tone with the North, while remaining true to the "lost cause" ideas on the role of slavery and the need for the Southern side of the war to be told. Articles focused on the rank and file, informing readers that "the motive which impels the privates and subordinate offices to suffer and bleed so long, demands the fullest explanation."[19] Within two years, the tireless work of the McDonald brothers increased the magazine's readership to three thousand subscribers. It soon rivaled the *Southern Historical Society Papers* and *Confederate Veteran* as a voice for former Confederates, and yet in 1885 they sold the then-ailing magazine to former Confederate Gen. Basil W. Duke. The periodical ran for another two years before the *Century*—publisher of *Battles and Leaders of the Civil War*—purchased it and circulation discontinued.

In 1887, deciding it was time to return to Virginia, William resigned his position in Louisville. Taking up residence in Berryville, he continued to ply his talents in education by establishing the Shenandoah University School, a male preparatory school (not to be confused with the college located in Winchester.) About this time, his former comrades approached him with the idea of writing a history of the Laurel Brigade. The former staff officer threw himself into the work of compiling information on the brigade's movements and activities. As a starter, William relied heavily upon the officers' reports contained within the *Official Records.* He also benefited from some previously published works, such as Frank M. Myers' *The Comanches* (a history of the Thirty-fifth Battalion Virginia Cavalry published in 1871) and James B. Avirett's *The Memoirs of Turner Ashby and His Compeers* (1867), for which William had contributed a sketch of his father. When it came to activities of the brigade during the last year of the war, he came up against a lack of reports, which proved a difficult hurdle to overcome. In a letter to Gen. Rosser, William admitted that he had already "completed a connected story . . . of the career of the brigade up to May 5

---

[19] *Southern Bivouac* no. 12 (1883): 485. In 1992, Broadfoot Publishing Company of Wilmington, North Carolina, reprinted *Southern Bivouac.* The introduction for this reprint was penned by Gary W. Gallagher and provides useful information concerning the McDonalds' involvement in the magazine.

1864" but had encountered some difficulty in obtaining reliable information from his comrades. He felt that "few men will take the trouble to write, unless they have the duties & places ready at hand and unless they for a time at least feel some of their old interest in the facts." About some of the information he received, he felt unsure of its usefulness. "[Lieut. Col. Richard H.] Dulany," he complained, "has failed to furnish me his paper as promised. [Lieut. Col. Thomas B.] Massie had written a good deal, but claims too much for the 12th . . . I feel his memory is bad."[20] On the other hand, some members of the brigade proved invaluable, such as Capt. William Baylor of the Twelfth Virginia, who provided the author with a wealth of information and in 1900 released his own memoirs under the title *Bull Run to Bull Run*. Regardless of the pitfalls William encountered in gathering the material needed to complete the history, he continued to work through the final stages of his manuscript.

William spent the last ten years of his life steeped in the history of the Laurel Brigade, reliving its battles and raids. Unfortunately he never lived to see his manuscript appear in print. On January 4, 1898, following a long bout of illness, William Naylor McDonald succumbed to heart failure and died at his home in Berryville, leaving behind his wife and nine children. The community mourned the loss of "one of its best and most highly respected citizens, and one possessed of a high order of literary attainments."[21] Two days later, friends and family gathered at Grace Episcopal Church in Berryville for his funeral. The J.E.B. Stuart Camp of the United Confederate Veterans, of which McDonald had been a standing member, provided an honor guard. Among the pallbearers were former comrades John S. Blackburn and Lieut. Robert O. Allen of the Sixth Virginia Cavalry. McDonald's body was laid to rest in Greenhill Cemetery.[22]

Just as William never forgot his fellow comrades, neither did they forget his efforts to produce an account of their wartime achievements. On August 13, 1906, at a meeting of the surviving members of Ashby's cavalry in Charles Town, West Virginia, a committee was selected for the purpose of reviving William's manuscript and providing for its publication. The committee included Roger P. Chew, James B. Avirett,

---

[20]William N. McDonald to Thomas L. Rosser, February 9, 1889, Thomas L. Rosser Papers, University of Virginia, Charlottesville, Va.

[21]*Clarke Courier,* January 5, 1898.

[22]*Clarke Courier,* January 5, 12, and 19, 1898; *Richmond Dispatch,* January 5, 1898; *Spirit of Jefferson,* January 11, 1898; *Winchester Evening Star,* January 5, 1898. These obituaries and funeral announcements proved useful in piecing together McDonald's life following the Civil War.

and William's brothers Angus and Edward. Bushrod C. Washington, who had served alongside William in the Second Virginia Infantry before joining Twelfth Virginia Cavalry, was chosen to review the manuscript, make editorial changes, and raise the necessary funds for its publication. The committee also deemed it necessary to include, as an appendix, as complete a roster as could be gathered of the brigade and Chew's Battery. They hoped to have the book in print within a year.[23] Working under such a tight schedule, Washington opted to make very few changes to the manuscript. Instead he simply added a few footnotes and inserted information that came to light following William's death. No doubt as a result of Washington's hurried editing job, the text contains numerous typographical errors and misspellings, but these do not disrupt or detract from the story. While the requested information for the rosters filled Washington's box in Charles Town, the editor worked feverishly to raise the $1,200 needed for printing the book. On July 1, 1907, Washington signed a contract with the Sun Job Printing Office of Baltimore, Maryland, for a thousand copies of McDonald's *A History of the Laurel Brigade*, with copyright to be bestowed upon William's widow, Kate.[24] After twenty years in the works, the efforts and contributions of the Laurel Brigade finally appeared in print.

A History of the Laurel Brigade stands out as one of the few brigade histories written from a Confederate perspective, and the only one that deals with service in the mounted arm. In the years following the Civil War, Confederate veterans produced numerous personal narratives and memoirs, yet they wrote few regimental or brigade histories. Historians have come to rely heavily upon McDonald's text. In his 1978 checklist of the two hundred most important Confederate books, Civil War scholar and bibliophile Richard B. Harwell referred to McDonald's work as "one of the best and best known of the brigade histories."[25] The interest in McDonald's text has kept the book alive over the last fifty years. In 1969, the small Arlington, Virginia, publishing house of R.W. Beatty printed McDonald's history in a limited run of a thousand copies, and in 1987 Olde Soldier Books of Gaithersburg, Maryland, brought forth a

---

[23]"History of the Laurel Brigade," *Confederate Veteran* 15 (1907): 155.

[24]"Memorandum of Agreement," William Thomas Leavell and Edward Allen Hitchcock McDonald Papers, Duke University, Raleigh, N.C. This collection also contains Bushrod Washington's handwritten editorial notes and many of the rosters generated by surviving officers.

[25]Richard B. Harwell, *In Tall Cotton: The 200 Most Important Confederate Books for the Reader, Researcher, and Collector* (Austin, Tex.: Jenkins Publishing & Frontier American, 1978), 42–43.

new edition. With this latest edition, the Johns Hopkins University Press includes a much needed and detailed index, an important element missing from all previous editions.

One of the true values of this book is its thoroughness. It covers the history of the brigade from its early beginnings under Angus McDonald, Sr., and Turner Ashby, through to the final engagements on the retreat to Appomattox. In the February 1908 issue of *Confederate Veteran*, the magazine heralded the history's publication as "the only book upon the war that gives an account of the cavalry campaign from the beginning to the end of the war." "There is none other," opined the editors, "that records so fully the tremendous hardships and sufferings of the cavalry . . . and which embodies a general account of the cavalry campaigns of the Army of Northern Virginia."[26] Sixty years later, historians Allan Nevins, James I. Robertson, and Bell I. Wiley offered their opinion of the sustained value of the text: "the author adroitly weaves his story from the 1861 formation of the 7th Virginia Cavalry to the 1865 disbandment of this mounted brigade."[27] Within its pages, the book fully exposes the reader to the activities of the Laurel Brigade. The minor raids into West Virginia receive no less coverage than the larger pitched cavalry battles of Brandy Station and Trevilian Station. Some of the most valuable portions of McDonald's history are those that deal with the smaller clashes and skirmishes that remain in the background of Confederate cavalry operations.

What William McDonald ultimately produced is not merely a history of the brigade's service during the Civil War; it is also a testimony to the trials and triumphs of the Valley men. Throughout the book, readers will find wonderful anecdotes and sketches of many of the men who served in this celebrated command. Their individual accomplishments often taking the forefront when describing important events. For instance, McDonald devoted an entire chapter to the daring February 1865 capture of Union Generals George Crook and Benjamin F. Kelly at Cumberland, Maryland. The Laurel Brigade did not participate in that expedition, but some of its former members played prominent roles in the successful abduction of the two Yankee officers. McDonald published, in full, a fourteen-page narrative of the episode penned by John B. Fray, a former member of the Seventh Virginia Cavalry who later rode with McNeill's Rangers. At the end of Fray's account is a list of fourteen of McNeill's men who at one time or another served in the brigade. Their exploits, felt McDonald, were a true reflection of the type

---

[26]"History of the Laurel Brigade," *Confederate Veteran* 16 (1908): 91.
[27]Allan Nevins, James I. Robertson, Jr., and Bell I. Wiley, eds., *Civil War Books: A Critical Bibliography* (Baton Rouge: Louisiana State Univ. Press, 1968), 1:125.

of soldier who evolved within the ranks of the Laurel Brigade. Maintaining McDonald's belief that the soldier was equally as important as the officer, *A History of Laurel Brigade* successfully accomplishes the author's purpose "of making it an authentic memorial of those who composed the Laurel Brigade."

ERIC J. MINK

A HISTORY OF THE LAUREL BRIGADE

CHAPTER I

June, 1861

Development of the Laurel Brigade from the Seventh Regiment of Virginia Cavalry, enlisted under Col. Angus W. McDonald—Border service under Colonel McDonald and Col. Turner Ashby—Heroic death of Capt. Richard Ashby—Destructive expedition against the Baltimore and Ohio Railroad and Chesapeake and Ohio Canal—Chew's Battery attached to the command—Romney winter campaign under Jackson—Battle of Kernstown.

Fourteen months of the War between the States had passed before the troops of Ashby possessed a brigade organization. Their gallant leader was dead and Stonewall Jackson had completed his brilliant Valley campaign. The Federal armies that had gathered from three quarters of the compass for the purpose of annihilating the army of "Stonewall" were now in full retreat; and the opportune moment was availed of to put into brigade form the twenty-six unorganized companies of border troopers which Ashby had commanded. This was effected at Swift Run Gap on the 15th and 16th of June, 1862.

Though it is purposed to confine this narrative, mainly to events that happened subsequent to this date, it is deemed not only proper but necessary, first to give a brief account of what was done by the Ashby cavalry prior to its brigade formation.

In the official reports, this body of troops, as was the rule in the Confederate service, is designated by the name of its

commanding officer at the time, and it was not until Genl.
Thomas L. Rosser became its commander that it was known
by any other name than by that of the brigadier commanding. Influenced, probably, by admiration of its prowess,
pride of commandership, and a laudable desire to increase
its *esprit du corps,* Rosser named it the Laurel Brigade.
Subsequently this name was occasionally recognized by the
division commanders when they meant to compliment the
command for gallant conduct; but by members of other
brigades, especially in the cavalry, the name was not used,
its assumption being regarded by many as a piece of
arrogance.

To what extent the name was deserved history must
determine; but the fact that it is the only name which iden-
tifies and generally describes a certain body of Confederate
troops, sufficiently justifies the use of it in these pages for
the sake of clearness and brevity.

The Laurel Brigade was certainly unique in one respect.
It was a growth and not an artificial formation. Brigades,
as a rule, were the result of an arbitrary combination of
different bodies of troops into a single group by the commanding general of the army. The Laurel Brigade had
for its nucleus a few companies which developed into a
regiment, and then into a command of brigade proportions.
The added strength that constituted the development came
from new companies that voluntarily joined, or from the
old companies whose ranks overflowing furnished the
material for other new companies. The original nucleus,
from which by natural accretions sprung the Laurel Brigade,
by happy coincidence, was Ashby's old company.

At the breaking out of the war, Col. Angus W. McDonald,[1] repairing to Harper's Ferry, offered his services in defense of his State and of the Southern Confederacy to General Harper, the commanding officer. Although then sixty-two years of age, Colonel McDonald being a West Point graduate, and having served in the army of the United States, earnestly desired to do what he could for the South. General Harper accepted his offer and committed to him the important duty of guarding the bridges and fords along the Potomac.

The troops assigned to him for this purpose was a company of cavalry commanded by Capt. Turner Ashby, from Fauquier county, Virginia. Dividing it into small detachments, he organized parties who scouted along the border, and sometimes disguised as citizens, actually entered Washington City.

This service was exacting but attractive on account of its comparative freedom from restraint, and the opportunities it afforded for personal adventure.

---

[1]Col. Angus W. McDonald, born in 1799, at Winchester, Virginia, was over sixty years old at the breaking out of the Civil War, and just returned to his home from London, whither he had gone as Commissioner of Virginia for information relative to the settlement of the disputed boundary between Maryland and Virginia. A graduate of West Point in the artillery corps, he was assigned by Gen. Kenton Harper, in command at Harper's Ferry, to the duty of guarding the fords and bridges of the Potomac below that point.

Among the troops assigned to him was the cavalry company of Capt. Turner Ashby, whose energy, daring, and soldierly traits so won the admiration of Colonel McDonald that, when authorized by President Davis to raise a regiment of cavalry, he recommended Captain Ashby as lieutenant-colonel of his command. After a few months of active service, being compelled by acute rheumatism to resign his command, Colonel McDonald was assigned by General Jackson to the command of the post at Winchester, and after its evacuation to that of Lexington, Virginia. Upon the approach of the Federal army under General

Encouraged by applications for enlistment in his command, from new companies, Colonel McDonald asked and obtained from the Confederate Government, permission to raise an independent regiment for border service.

Upon his recommendation and probably with Ashby's knowledge and consent, the latter was commissioned lieutenant-colonel, and Dr. Oliver Funsten major of the new command, that was soon afterwards known as the Seventh Regiment of Virginia Cavalry.

The necessary complement of companies was gradually obtained, and by the assiduous efforts of Colonel McDonald, the regiment was soon armed and equipped.

The organization of the Seventh was consummated on the 17th of June, 1861.

Because of the distinguished services rendered by this regiment before it was incorporated into the Laurel Brigade, a roll of the original regimental officers and company commanders is worthy of the special place here given to it.

Hunter, having no troops for its defense, he retreated with his son Harry, aged sixteen, to what he supposed a place of safety near Buckhannon, where they were captured after a gallant resistance, in which Colonel McDonald was wounded.

He was treated in the most inhuman manner by General Hunter and his officers, and compelled to ride in an ammunition wagon without springs from Lynchburg to Charleston; afterwards confined in the Atheneam Prison at Wheeling, West Virginia, handcuffed like a common felon. While there he received great kindness from the Sisters of Charity, and the picture here inserted is a copy of one he had taken for them—the basket in his hand showing their last gift to him as he was leaving to be exchanged.

Arriving in Richmond November 7th, 1864, he rapidly declined from the effects of his ill treatment, and died December 1st. He was laid to rest in Hollywood with a son, Capt. C. W. McDonald, who was killed at the battle of Cold Harbor. His only brother, Col. E. C. McDonald, died in the Confederate service, and six sons enlisted in the army, two of whom were severely wounded and in prison during the war

Regimental Officers.

Angus W. McDonald of Winchester, Va...........................Colonel.
Turner Ashby of Fauquier Co., Va.............Lieutenant-Colonel.
Oliver M. Funsten of Warren Co., Va...............................Major.
Angus W. McDonald, Jr., of Hampshire Co., Va......Adjutant.
Dr. A. P. Burns, ————, ...Surgeon.
Rev. J. B. Avirett of Frederick Co., Va.......................Chaplain.
Capt. T. P. Pendleton of Clarke Co., Va., Asst. Quartermaster.
Capt. John D. Richardson of Clarke Co., Va.........Commissary.

Captains of Companies.

Richard Ashby of Fauquier Co., Va........................Company A.
J. Q. Wingfield of Rockingham, Va........................Company B.
S. D. Myers of Shenandoah Co., Va..........................Company C.
Macon Jorden of Page Co., Va................................Company D.
Walter Bowen of Warren Co., Va.............................Company E.
George F. Sheetz of Hampshire Co., Va.................Company F.
Frank Mason of Maryland.......................................Company G.
A. Harper of Shenandoah Co., Va...........................Company H.
Shands of Rockingham Co., Va.................................Company I.
William Miller of Shenandoah Co., Va.................Company K.

The regiment engaged in active service from the day of its organization.

The headquarters of the Seventh was located at Romney, a central point from which to watch the Federal movements in West Virginia, and to operate upon the line of communication afforded by the Baltimore and Ohio Railroad. The first service engaged in was the destruction of the superstructures of this road. So thoroughly was the work done, that scarcely a bridge, culvert, or water station remained on that part of the road extending from Piedmont to the Big Cacapon, a distance of sixty miles.

As the war thickened, border duty became more onerous, and it soon devolved upon the Seventh to guard the Confederate frontier from Harper's Ferry to the head waters of the Potomac, a distance of 125 miles.

The Federal authorities had distributed numerous bodies of troops along this border; and the presence of these menaced the northern frontier with constant raids. The Union men on both sides of the line gave much trouble, carrying information to the Federals and suggesting plundering expeditions, for the purpose often, of gratifying private malice. Some of these overzealous "patriots" were particularly offensive, and their arrest and removal were deemed necessary. It was in an attempt to arrest one of these that Capt. Richard Ashby was killed. He was Col. Turner Ashby's younger brother and had succeeded him in the command of his old company.

Captain Ashby was the handsomest and most soldierly figure in his regiment, being more robust-looking and more commanding in appearance than even his elder brother. His death, especially the heroic features of it, made a profound and lasting impression upon his comrades; while the effect upon his brother Turner was transforming.

It was on the morning of the 26th of June, that Captain Ashby was ordered by his brother to take a small detachment of his company and arrest a certain obnoxious citizen, who was believed to be a spy. Failing to find the man at his home, Captain Ashby kept a path straight on, leading towards the Federal lines which extended along the track of the Baltimore and Ohio Railroad. At a place suitable for the purpose, the Federals, as if in anticipation of his further advance, had carefully prepared an ambuscade. A volley from a neighboring wood was the first intimation of the enemy's presence, and this was immediately followed by the charge of an overwhelming body of mounted Federals. Discovering his disparity of force, which consisted of only eleven men, Captain Ashby ordered a retreat. The retreat soon became disorderly, and Captain Ashby, who was some distance in the rear of his retreating command, was thrown to the ground by his horse falling in an unsuccessful attempt to leap a cattle-stop. He was soon surrounded by the enemy at close quarters, but without thought of surrender, he fought them single-handed as they swarmed around him intent only upon his destruction. At last, wounded in many places, he fell and, while prostrate, received additional wounds; one man stabbing him in the abdomen with his bayonet. Here he was left for dead, the enemy for some reason retreating.

Captain Ashby, having rallied sufficient strength, dragged himself to the shelter of a neighboring tree, where he was afterwards found.

In the meantime Col. Turner Ashby, with a detachment of his command, scouting in the neighborhood, arrived by merest accident in time to avenge his brother. Learning from a young lady that firing of small arms had been heard in the direction his brother had taken, he at once galloped to his aid. Discovering the bloody place where he had fallen and full of forebodings, he rode on in search of the foe. The Federals had retired to Kelly's Island in the Potomac. Ashby seeing them from the Virginia shore, dashed into the stream and called upon his men to charge. A volley that emptied two saddles greeted them as they pressed through the current and gained the bank.

"At them with your knives, men!" cried Ashby, whom grief for his brother had rendered furious.

The contest was most unequal, but the fiery rush of Ashby and his men made up for the lack of numbers, and after a short and bloody fight the Federals gave way before them and fled.

Among the articles captured in the fight were Captain Ashby's spurs and horse. The sight of these convinced Colonel Ashby that his brother had been killed, for it does not appear that any information was obtained from Federal prisoners, if any were taken.

Search was now made for the body, which, mangled and pierced with eight wounds, was at last found. It was soon discovered that life was not extinct, and the wounded captain was carried to the house of Col. George Washington, where, though kindly cared for, he died after seven days of intense suffering.

The fight at Kelly's Island and the death of Richard Ashby were events of no small importance, occurring as they did in the beginning of the war. The heroic example of the dead soldier in his terrific death struggle, his brutal treatment at the hands of the victors, and the subsequent punishment by Colonel Ashby, formed exhaustless topics around the camp-fires. Thoughts of vengeance were the more readily indulged in, now that the valor of Colonel Ashby had shown what true prowess might accomplish.

In a letter to his family after the death of his brother, Colonel Ashby wrote: "His country has lost the services of a brave man with a strong arm, which he proved upon his enemies in losing his life. He was buried with all the honors of war, and never was greater respect paid to the memory of one man."

About the 15th of July, 1861, the forward movement of the Federal Army under General Patterson, across the

Potomac, caused the Seventh Regiment to be ordered to Winchester.   At this point the scattered companies gathered from the Potomac frontier, on the 19th of July.   Already on the 18th fighting had begun at Manassas.

Joseph E. Johnston, who commanded the army at Winchester, secretly moved his troops by a forced march to Piedmont and thence by rail to Manassas, deceiving General Patterson, who still believed the Confederate Army to be in his front at Winchester, and by rendering timely aid to General Beauregard, gained for the Confederacy the battle of Bull Run—the first great battle of the war.

The border cavalry were ordered to co-operate in the movement, but the Seventh reached Bull Run the day after the battle.   Thence after a short rest it was ordered to Staunton, and soon back again to resume its old position along the Potomac frontier.

Colonel McDonald, with a portion of the regiment, re-established his headquarters at Romney, while Ashby, with the remainder, held the right of the border line, with his headquarters at Charles Town.

The work of destroying the Baltimore and Ohio Railroad went on, with occasional skirmishing with scouting parties of the Federals.

Early in September, General Geary, commanding the Federals near Harper's Ferry, crossed the Potomac and seemed about to march further southward.   Colonel Ashby, assisted by 400 militia and two new companies of cavalry under Captains R. W. Baylor and John Henderson, confronted the foe at Bolivar Heights near the Ferry.   After a spirited skirmish, Ashby retired to the next commanding eminence, known as School-House Hill.   During the night

Geary recrossed the Potomac and the next day Ashby took possession of Harper's Ferry.

On the 24th of September a serious brush with the enemy occurred near Romney. A Federal force gathered from Cumberland and Piedmont, making a night march, attempted to surprise Colonel McDonald's camp. The attempt was anticipated, and before the Federals reached Romney they were met in Mechanic's Gap of the South Branch Mountain and driven back. With creditable persistency, another gap further down the mountain was passed, and the enemy having crossed the South Branch River, advanced upon Romney. Their road led them through a narrow pass called Hanging Rock, where the way has the river on one side and an almost perpendicular wall of rock on the other. From the summit of the cliff, Col. E. H. McDonald, with thirteen Hampshire militiamen, threw down rocks among the Federals and created a panic among them. After firing a few volleys, the column retreated in great confusion, the cavalry, in their eagerness to escape, riding over the infantry, and forcing many into the river.

The repulse, however, did not deter the Federals from making a third attempt. Moving further down, they successfully crossed the mountain barriers and threatened the rear of the Confederates. Colonel McDonald now evacuated Romney and the Federals took possession of the town.

Next morning, having learned that the enemy were pillaging the country around Romney, and were somewhat disorganized and scattered, Colonel McDonald advanced upon them.

The Federals, apprised of his coming, hastily withdrew to the South Branch bridge, which they attempted to hold. A gallant charge of Confederate horse drove them from this position and forced them into a disorderly retreat. Assisted by the Hampshire militia, under Colonels E. H. McDonald and A. Munroe, the cavalry continued the pursuit through the gap and, following close upon the heels of the fugitives, harassed them until they reached New Creek Station (now Keyser), a fortified position on the Baltimore and Ohio Railroad, having suffered considerable loss.

About a month later, on the 26th of October, another more formidable attempt was made to occupy the South Branch Valley. Romney was considered a place of considerable strategic importance, especially to the Federals. From it as a center, fifty miles of the Baltimore and Ohio Railroad could be reached in a short day's march. Hence the small force of Confederates at Romney was regarded as a constant menace to the only direct railroad communication between Washington and the West. Its only support was at Winchester, forty miles off, while within an average distance of twenty miles along the Baltimore and Ohio Railroad were stationed considerable bodies of Federal troops. In a few hours it would have been quite easy to concentrate a force strong enough to march upon and occupy Romney. The failure of their first expedition was attributed by the Federals to lack of numbers sufficient to impress and overawe the population.

On the 24th of November, a heavy Federal force of all arms under General Kelly advanced upon Romney. Colonel McDonald was advised of its coming and of its superior strength. There was no hope of his being able to hold Romney; but he determined, in retiring, to make resistance wherever the advantages of position gave opportunity to punish and cripple the foe.

Six miles west of Romney the invading column was first confronted and opposed. Thence back through Mechanic's Gap to the South Branch bridge, the Confederates withdrew, disputing the Federal progress. On the Romney side of the bridge Colonel McDonald determined to make a stand, notwithstanding he had only a force of about 400 against more than 2,000 of the enemy. The place, however, was admirably suited for a small force to inflict a serious blow upon a large one. The high ground that, like a mountain barrier, shuts in the river valley is near to and commands the bridge and the road to Romney. About a half mile from the bridge, where the road turns and ascends through a slight defile, is Cemetery Hill, from a point on which a piece of artillery may sweep the road to the bridge.

On the high ground near the bridge a part of the command under Major Funsten was posted, with a howitzer. Colonel McDonald himself, with the reserve and a rifle gun, occupied Cemetery Hill.

At the approach of the Federals, their great superiority in numbers was plain to all. An artillery fire from both sides began, while a column of infantry attempted to force a passage through the bridge. This was driven back by a well-directed fire from Funsten's men. In the meantime a squadron of Federal cavalry had succeeded in fording the river and appeared unexpectedly on the Confederate flank. The sight of them and the formidable display of infantry coming to their support, made it apparent that further defense was futile. Major Funsten's command at once abandoned the high ground and retreated. The Federal horse, encouraged by this, charged in pursuit. The retreat soon became a rout and then a stampede. The fugitives broke through the reserve and carried it along with them. Soon the wagon trains, two miles in the rear, were reached by the Federal horse and captured, as were also both guns.

The Federal victory, though a bloodless one, was complete. Romney was taken and possessed by the Federals, and until the end of the war remained virtually in their possession.

Jackson, in the following December, retook and held it for a short time, but his expedition thither proved how untenable it was.

The logic of war is inexorable. As the commanding officer receives the most praise when a victory is gained, so he chiefly bears the penalty of defeat. Even where others are to blame, there is no difference in the result. Disaster breeds a want of confidence, and this in turn portends more calamity. The situation was painfully clear to Colonel McDonald. The good of the service demanded a change, and the majority of the men were clamorous for the leadership of Ashby.

In an interview with Jackson, Colonel McDonald asked to be relieved from the command of the Seventh. The request was acceded to, and he was placed in charge of the artillery defenses at Winchester.

It is not hard to discover why the hearts of the men of the Seventh were set upon Lieutenant-Colonel Ashby, and why they were clamorous for his leadership; for being in the flower of young manhood, he combined in the highest degree those attributes of the born soldier which ever attract men of similar mould. In person, while little above the average height, his form was well shaped, erect, sinewy, and graceful. His features were regular, clear-cut, and determined; his eyes black and rather deep-set for his age, and his swarthy complexion was almost hidden under a heavy, flowing black beard of unusual length. Harnessed in the accoutrements of a Southern cavalry officer, and mounted on his milk-white charger, which he sat with the ease of the hereditary horseman, he was a figure needing only to be seen to attract the wonder and admiration of both friend and foe. His manner in repose was modest, gentle and approachable.

It was when the duties of a soldier aroused him to action, that the transformation took place that made him the most impetuous and daring cavalry leader in the Confederate service.

His loyalty to his State and to the Southern cause was intense and almost romantic. Their enemies were his enemies, and it was his motto to attack and destroy them whenever they showed themselves; and when they did not show themselves to hunt for, locate and harass them with impetuous onsets.

Such in brief was the soldier who now succeeded to the command of the Seventh.

Ashby established his regimental headquarters near Charles Town, and continued with his troops to picket the Potomac frontier as far west as the border of Hampshire; for Romney still remained in possession of the Federals.

On the 11th of November, 1861, under special authority of the Secretary of War, there was organized a battery of artillery, which, becoming as it did a most important factor in the achievements of Ashby's command, is worthy here of special mention, as to its organization and services and subsequent assignments.

It was organized with thirty-three men and the following officers: R. P. Chew, captain; Milton Rouse, first lieutenant; J. W. McCarty and James Thompson, second lieutenants. The company had three pieces of artillery; one a rifle gun called the "Blakely," one howitzer, and one six inch rifle gun. At the suggestion of General Ashby the men were all mounted, and this was the first mounted battery of flying artillery organized in the Confederate Army. It served throughout the Valley campaign under Stonewall Jackson, and accompanied the brigade of Ashby at the front of its advances, retarding the enemy in its retreats through all that marvelous campaign.

Its officers were cadets of the Virginia Military Institute. Educated as soldiers, young and daring, it was natural enough that a battery commanded by them would render most effective service and attain a worthy distinction. So it was that "Chew's Battery" soon earned for itself a name and reputation second only to that of the Ashby command.

This company served after the death of Ashby and Jackson with the battalion of Stuart's Horse Artillery, and perhaps was engaged in more skirmishes and battles than any battery in the Confederate Army. The membership of the company increased rapidly after its first organization, and included during the war a membership of 197 men. Lieutenants Rouse and McCarty, who participated in its organization, resigned and joined the cavalry in 1862, where they distinguished themselves for gallantry, dash, and courage. Thompson was then elected first lieutenant, and James W. Williams and J. W. Carter second lieutenants. Captain Chew was in 1864 promoted to the command of Stuart's Horse Artillery, when Thompson succeeded

Chew as captain of the battery, and E. L. Yancey became the second lieutenant.

On March 1st, 1865, the Stuart Horse Artillery was reorganized into five battalions of two batteries each, when Chew was made lieutenant-colonel and Thompson was promoted to major, Carter succeeding Thompson as captain. As successive captains of Chew's Battery both these men served with great distinction.

When Jackson struck Banks' column at Middletown, this battery charged with the cavalry, and under the direction of General Ashby engaged in the close pursuit of the enemy, and it was perhaps the first battery in the service to inaugurate this peculiar and effective mode of fighting.

At Upperville, when the brigade under Genl. William E. Jones, while in marching column and without order of battle, was attacked at right angles to its line of march by the Federal cavalry, and thrown into temporary confusion, this battery under Captain Chew dashed to the front and, firing canister at close range into the head of the Federal advance, produced such havoc as to arrest it for a time, and saved the brigade from what might have been a serious disaster.

On the 6th of May, 1864, when Genl. Thomas L. Rosser attacked Wilson's division on the Catharpin Road, the beginning of the battles of the Wilderness, this battery charged with the Eleventh Cavalry, doing great execution and aiding greatly in the defeat of the enemy. Afterwards this method of fighting became a distinctive feature of the fighting of the Confederate horse artillery, the batteries being often found in the charging column of cavalry or abreast with the skirmish line.

This battery served in the Maryland and Gettysburg campaign and in the great battles between Lee and Grant from the Rapidan to Richmond, and took a conspicuous part in the battle of Trevilians and in the numerous battles of the Army of Northern Virginia around Petersburg to Appomattox.

Genl. Thomas T. Munford, who took command of the Ashby brigade at Cross Keys, after the fall of Ashby, in a letter to W. McVicar, a private of Chew's Battery, of date June 12th, 1906, says: "Chew's Battery was Ashby's pet, and under the gallant Chew it was as much Ashby's right arm as Ashby was the right arm of Jackson. Indeed the fame of this battery extended throughout the Army of Northern Virginia, and the attestations to its distinguished service are too numerous for present mention."

In the minds of the people of the Valley, the Ashby cavalry and Chew's Battery belonged to one another as by natural affinity, and they located the position of the Federals by the familiar crack of "Chew's Blakely," which awakened the echoes of the mountains and spread commotion in the encampments of the enemy ere the farmers had aroused to call and feed their hogs.

Early in December Ashby's command, including Chew's Battery, was ordered to join Jackson at Martinsburg to co-operate with him in an attempt to destroy Dam No. 5 in the Potomac. This was the most important of a succession of dams that supplied water to the Chesapeake and Ohio Canal. A Federal force on the opposite bank of the river attempted to prevent the execution of the work, but without success. Sharpshooters at points of advantage concentrated their fire on the path that led down the bank to the dam, while a brisk cannonade was kept up. The work could only be done at night, in the water, which was freezing cold.

A few days afterwards, on January 1st, 1862, Jackson, now reinforced by Loring's brigade, set out on his famous Bath and Romney expedition, the object of which was to re-occupy Romney and hold possession of the South Branch Valley. Ashby, with his command, was ordered to join him.

New Year's Day opened bright and promising, but towards evening a northwester blew, bringing storm of rain and sleet. The by-roads, which Jackson for sake of secrecy usually traveled, soon became almost impassable. Biting winter had now set in and the men suffered severely. After a weary journey of three days Bath was reached. As Ashby entered the town the Federals were moving off towards Hancock, a village three miles distant, on the opposite bank of the Potomac. Ashby followed and soon came up with their rear guard, with which he skirmished. In this affair Lieutenant Lang and three privates of Company C were badly wounded. The enemy, however, got safely across the river and halted in Hancock. Jackson sent Ashby across the river to demand a surrender, and threatening that if the town was not evacuated he would bombard it.

Says Dabney in his "Life of Jackson," "As Ashby was led blindfold up the streets, he overheard the Federal soldiers whispering the one to the other, 'That is the famous Colonel Ashby,' and soon the suppressed hum of a crowd told him that they were thronging around to catch a sight of the warrior whose name had so often carried confusion into their ranks."

The Federal general naturally refused to surrender to a hostile force on the other side of the Potomac, and declined also to evacuate the place. Upon Ashby's returning and delivering his reply, Jackson ordered the guns to open upon the town. This was done, it is said, in retaliation for the bombardment of Shepherdstown a short time before, but Jackson probably had a better reason.

Jackson began preparing to cross the river, but hearing that the enemy was reinforced, he decided to go on to Romney.

On January 7th his column left the vicinity of Hancock and marched by mountain roads sheathed with ice towards Romney. The progress was exceedingly slow. The horses, smooth-shod, continually slipped and fell; the men, ill clad, were nearly frozen; the artillery was dragged along with great difficulty. Romney was not reached until January 14th. When Capt. George Sheetz, with two companies of cavalry, was seen approaching, the Federals, supposing the main body to be near by, departed hastily, abandoning their tents and many valuable stores. Ashby pursued them, harassing their rear and taking some prisoners.

Long before Romney was reached, it was discovered that the troops under General Kelly had behaved like vandals. While in possession of Hampshire county mills, tanneries and factories had been burnt. From Blue's Gap to Romney, a distance of sixteen miles, scarcely a house had been left standing. The wayside was strewed with the carcasses of cattle and other domestic animals. In Romney the out-buildings were gone and many of the dwellings had been converted into stables, while every church save one had been foully desecrated.

The brutal treatment of the Hampshire people by the Federal soldiers appears to have been not only winked at but authorized by those in command. There were few slaveholders in the county, and the stubborn adherence of the people to the Confederate cause could not be understood from a Federal point of view. Their "treason" was regarded as of a malignant type, and deserving of the severest punishment. It was inconceivable to men believing the war to be a slaveholders' rebellion, how the yeomanry of the non-slaveholding mountains should be among the boldest and bravest defenders of secession; and consequently these "senseless rebels" were shown none of the mercies of civilized warfare. Hunted to their homes, they were shot down, and their houses burnt in many instances.

Such brutality only deepened the feeling of hostility in the hearts of the people and evoked reprisals, and the crack of the deadly rifle from wooded cover often saluted the Federal scouting parties. Sentinels were cut off, pickets captured and whole companies sometimes ambuscaded. The unconquerable mountaineers left no ground undisputed except that upon which the Federal forces camped.

Now that, after a march of nearly 100 miles through ice and snow, the South Branch Valley was occupied, the trouble of holding it began to appear. There was no danger of immediate attack. To few besides the intrepid Jackson would campaigning be thought of in the dead of winter; but spring was coming and the Federals were gathering at different points on the border. Winchester was far in the rear and a day's march nearer Harper's Ferry than Romney. Jackson therefore determined to leave General Loring with the bulk of the command at

Romney and Moorefield and return with the Stonewall Brigade to Winchester.

Ashby was sent with the larger part of his cavalry to watch the Potomac border. He established a cordon of pickets from Harper's Ferry to Hampshire. Captain Sheetz, with his company stationed near Blue's Gap, having charge of the left of the line.

On the 25th of January, the Secretary of War, learning that Loring's force was threatened with capture, ordered Jackson to recall him to Winchester. This was done on the 31st of January, and thus, after a respite of a few weeks, Romney and the South Branch Valley again fell under Federal sway.

General Loring, with his brigades, was transferred to a distant command, and Jackson was left with about 6,000 men to hold the Shenandoah Valley.

General McClellan, with a formidable army, was now threatening Richmond, and the Federal forces under Banks and Shields were now expected to co-operate in the movement.

Ashby, with scouts entering their camps and reporting their numbers, with pickets holding vigilant watch at every river crossing, kept Jackson exactly informed as to the movements of the enemy. Jackson trusted him implicitly.

Confident that Banks and Shields would soon march upon Winchester, and knowing that it was hazardous to attempt to hold the place, Jackson was busily engaged in removing his stores far up the Valley to a place of safety.

On the 25th of February Banks crossed the Potomac at Harper's Ferry, and by the 4th of March his forces and those of Shields, numbering more than 30,000, were encamped in the vicinity of Charles Town and Martinsburg.

Slowly and cautiously Banks advanced towards Winchester, Shields following with equal deliberation. Their snail-like pace was due in great measure to the fear of Jackson, and scarcely less to the fear of Ashby and to the activity of his cavalry, which, coming close up to the Federal infantry camps, beat back within their lines such bodies of cavalry as dared venture beyond them.

As the Federal main body moved forward, the head of the column from each successive hilltop was saluted by the guns of Captain Chew, and every stray squadron, discovered beyond the infantry supports, was promptly driven back by the shells of Chew and the charge of the cavalry. Ashby's force was too small to attempt serious resistance, but his sleepless vigilance and activity kept the Federals in a state of ignorance and anxiety as to the movements of Jackson.

On the 11th of March, 1862, Winchester was evacuated by Jackson and the Confederates marched slowly southward, the main body reaching Mt. Jackson on the 17th. Ashby brought up the rear, skirmishing with the Federal vanguard. Ever on the alert, he was constantly seeking points of attack, and contriving with bold ingenuity surprises and ambuscades.

At Fishers Hill, concealing a body of his men in the woods, he waited till the Federal horse was passing, and then rushed upon them. At Stony Creek, he lay in wait for some foraging parties, and swooping down from his place of concealment, took many prisoners. When there were no isolated parties to ensnare or surprise, he would make a stealthy approach to a Federal camp with one gun from Chew's Battery, and startle the inmates with a well-directed bomb. A Federal officer in Banks' army once said that he had learned to look for Ashby's shells as regularly as he did for his breakfast. This hanging hornet-like on the front and flanks of the enemy, did apparently no great damage, but the effect of it was to greatly facilitate Jackson's operations. It kept the enemy always in the dark as to the whereabouts of Jackson, and helped to create that almost superstitious dread of Jackson which possessed the minds of the Federals and which almost attributed to him the power of ubiquity.

There is no doubt that Jackson's success in the Valley was largely due to the secrecy that enveloped his movements. It was Ashby's impenetrable cordon of pickets, at the fords, crossroads, and mountain passes, and his ever aggressive demonstrations that had most to do in making Jackson's mantle of mystery, and in keeping General Banks in absolute ignorance of his movements.

On March the 19th information was received from Genl. Joseph E. Johnston, who was then retiring before McClellan towards Richmond, that a part of Banks' force was about to be recalled to aid McClellan, and that it was important to make a demonstration against Banks in order to prevent this movement.

On the 21st Ashby, who had been skirmishing with the enemy between Woodstock and Strasburg, reported that the Federals had evacuated the latter place, and that he was harassing their rear as they fell back towards Winchester.

Jackson at once prepared to pursue, ordering Ashby to press the enemy. On the 22nd the Confederate main body made a forced march to Strasburg, a distance of twenty-two miles. The same day Ashby pressed vigorously the retreating Federals, and by five o'clock P. M. had driven them into Winchester. One of his divisions, Williams', had marched that morning towards Manassas; the other, Shields', was still in camp near the town. The fugitive Federal troopers galloping through the streets and the sound of Ashby's guns startled General Banks. Shields' division was ordered under arms. An infantry brigade, two batteries of artillery and some cavalry were sent to confront Ashby. The latter had about 250 cavalry and three guns of Chew's Battery, but he did not decline the unequal combat. A spirited skirmish ensued. Chew's guns answered those of the enemy with defiant roar, while the menacing attitude of the grey squadrons, ever ready to charge, kept the Federal horse in the background and compelled the infantry to advance with great deliberation. General Shields, in command of the Federals, had his arm fractured by a piece of shell. Perchance it was a fateful hit, as it disabled and prevented him from being actively present on the field the next day.

Ashby gradually retired to Kernstown, three miles from Winchester, and took position for the night. In his report General Shields says he purposely concealed his numbers. The impression this produced upon Ashby was confirmed by some of his scouts, who in disguise had entered Winchester, and from conversation with citizens reported that only four regiments of infantry were stationed there.

This information being sent to Jackson, doubtless induced him to hurry forward from Strasburg the next day without waiting for his sore-footed stragglers to catch up.

During the night the Federals took defensive positions against further attack; but a reconnoissance in force the next morning convinced Shields and Banks that Ashby only, with some cavalry, was in their front. Ashby had misled him before by his daring strategy, but General Banks, not wishing to be outwitted again, took train and left for Washington.

It was true that Ashby only was near, but Jackson was coming, having hurried forward four companies of the Second Virginia Infantry, under Captain Naidenbousch, to support the cavalry and artillery.

In the meantime Ashby had engaged the Federals who had come out on the Strasburg turnpike to feel his strength, by opening on them with his artillery.

At ten o'clock Captain Naidenbousch arrived with his four companies, which were at once pushed forward against the Federal skirmishers, which after some resistance gave way, and Ashby's whole force advanced.

So serious did this movement appear to Colonel Kimball, who took command of the Federals after the wounding of Shields, that to check Ashby he brought up an additional force consisting of the Eighth Ohio, two companies of the Sixty-seventh Ohio, Sullivan's brigade and several batteries of artillery. Kimball's brigade and Daum's Artillery were already there, and these, together with the reinforcements mentioned, constituted more than a third of Shields' division of 9,000 men.

For nearly two hours Ashby held this force at bay, by a cunning and audacious handling of his small force. Chew's guns seizing points of advantage, with a continuous roar, fought at close range confident in the support of the grey squadrons, that at every attempt to take the guns dashed out and drove back the enemy.

The gallant Naidenbousch, with his four companies of infantry deployed as skirmishers, boldly faced the battle lines of the Federals.

Slowly, but with a steady front, Ashby fell back to the hills south of Kernstown.

When Jackson, with the main body of his army, arrived about ten o'clock "he found," says Dabney, "Ashby pressed back to the highlands south of Kernstown and confronted by heavy masses of the enemy."

Jackson's rapid march of thirty-six miles in thirty-two hours had greatly wearied his troops. Many broken down with fatigue were far in the rear. At first he thought of waiting until the next day, but fearing that Williams' division would return during the night he resolved to attack at once.

By four o'clock his men had taken position.. On the right was Ashby, with four companies of infantry and 150 cavalry, the Forty-second Virginia Infantry being in the turnpike in supporting distance.

About one-half of his troopers had been, under Major Funsten, to guard Jackson's extreme left. Next to Ashby, covering a mile in the Federal front, was the Fifth Virginia, then the rest of the infantry and artillery.

As nearly one-half of Shields' army was in front of Ashby, Jackson's plan was to threaten the Federal left and center with the small force of Ashby, while he would mass the main body of his infantry and artillery on their right, and make his chief attack there.

When his dispositions were all made, the center and left advanced, the latter being thrown continually forward.

The infantry were soon at close quarters, and for two hours there was an incessant rattle of musketry and roar of artillery. Ashby, with his handful, behaved as if a division was at his back, for his orders were to occupy the attention of the large force in his front.

Nothing but his marvelous audacity concealed the weakness of Jackson's right and prevented its being turned, and the Valley turnpike from being seized by the enemy.

As soon as Jackson's left began to go forward, Chew's[1] guns on the right drawing nearer the Federals, poured shot and shell into their dense columns; while Ashby, moving squadrons from point to point, now threatened, now charged their lines.

"On the right," says Dabney, "Colonel Ashby cannonaded the enemy continually with his three guns, with such audacity as to win ground all day from their multitudes."

The fierceness of Ashby's attack must have greatly deceived the Federal commander, for it was not until the battle had lasted nearly two hours that he withdrew a portion of the force in front of Ashby to reinforce his right. That flank was then giving way before the deadly fire and intrepid valor of Jackson's infantry, but upon the arrival at Kernstown of six regiments sent to reinforce them, soon rallied and, recovering their lost ground, became in turn the assailants.

Jackson was now sorely pressed by overwhelming numbers; already his small arms ammunition was nearly exhausted and the fire of his infantry slackening.

Soon the whole Stonewall Brigade was out of ammunition, and General Garnett ordered them to fall back. Meanwhile Jackson had ordered to the left the Fifth Virginia Regiment, that connected with Ashby, and the Forty-second Virginia, which supported him on the turnpike.

---

[1]Col. R. Preston Chew, commander of the Horse Artillery, Army of Northern Virginia.

Ashby was now left with four companies of infantry and 150 cavalry to keep back a force more than four times his own. Nearly a mile of unguarded front was between him and Jackson. Although the force in front of him had been diminished one-half, he had suffered a like diminution, and the relative strength of his adversary was the same.

The Federals, suspecting his paucity of numbers, which his menacing attitudes and constant shifting of squadrons had hitherto concealed, began to advance with confidence. It needed no courier to inform him that Jackson was powerless to send aid, for the loss of his position would probably ensure the destruction of Jackson's army. The departure of the Forty-second and Fifth regiments hurrying towards the left, the clouds of smoke over the crest of Kernstown heights, and the increasing roar of battle from that quarter, revealed the gravity of the situation and told him more plainly than words that he must do the best he could with the troops he had in hand.

Cunningly displaying his force so as to magnify it, he pushed his artillery forward and assaulted the foe.

Chew, with his dauntless gunners, secure of Ashby's support, with grape and canister kept off the Federal skirmishers, while with shot and shell they staggered the advancing battle lines.

When light detachments would approach his flank, or from under cover make a rush upon his guns, right at the auspicious moment a squadron would charge and drive them back.

Ashby was everywhere apparently, foreseeing and providing for every contingency and meeting the weight of numbers with that of skill and daring.

Evening slowly wore on; the roar of battle showed that
Jackson was giving ground. The Federals redoubled their
efforts to dislodge Ashby and seize the turnpike, but nothing
could move him until it was time to go. Naidenbousch's
four companies in skirmish order still grimly faced and
fought the foe.

Chew's guns with a furious cannonade continued to keep
the battle lines at bay.

The Federal right was victorious. The news spreading
to the Federal left inspired them to make a bolder advance.
On they came, with steady and menacing front, with bodies
of skirmishers threatening Ashby's flanks. The flanking
parties were charged and driven, but the main battle line
moved steadily forward.

At this juncture, Ashby ordered a charge of cavalry. It
was made by a squadron led by Lieutenant Thrasher. The
impetuosity of the charge broke the Federal lines, created
great disorder and quite a number of prisoners were taken.

This well-delivered blow helped much to stop the advance
of the enemy and gave Ashby opportunity to withdraw in
order, and to cover Jackson's rear as he retired, but it cost
the life of the gallant Thrasher and two privates of
Company G.

In the meantime the cavalry under Major Funsten,
stationed on Jackson's extreme left, had guarded that flank
during the fight. Towards the close when the infantry fell
back, the Federal cavalry emboldened by the retreat of the
Confederates, attempted to increase the disorder by charging their ranks. They were speedily met by the squadrons
of Funsten and held in check.

Making a circuit by the Cedarville turnpike, the Federal
horse attempted to fall suddenly upon the retreating

infantrymen; but they were confronted by Funsten and not only checked but put to flight, hurrying at breakneck speed towards their own lines.

Jackson's wearied foot soldiers, who had marched thirty-six miles to engage an enemy nearly threefold their own, and having inflicted a loss upon them nearly equal to their own fighting force, the shadows of evening rapidly falling, fell back upon Newtown, some three miles south of Kernstown, where the wagons were parked, and bivouacked for the night.

Ashby, with his undaunted handful, which had so gallantly held the right of Jackson's line, retired in good order, resisting the Federal advance, and guarding Jackson's rear, halted at Bartonsville, only a mile and a half from the scene of conflict.

While the boldness of Jackson in hurling upon the Federal right the main body of his army, which all told was less than one-third the force he was attacking, misled the Federal commander, Shields, into supposing he was supported by a large force at the center and right, yet it was Jackson's dependence and absolute confidence in the resourcefulness and boldness of Ashby, and the heroism of his men, that gave him the confidence to make such a daring movement.

Had Ashby, with his handful of cavalry, Chew's Battery, and a few skirmishers acted only on the defensive in trying to hold position, the enemy would unquestionably early in the engagement have discovered the weak spot, attacked the right in force, occupied the Valley turnpike, cutting off the only way by which Jackson could retreat, and probably have attacked him in reverse.

It was the aggressiveness of Ashby and his ingenious show of force by the incessant cannonading with the guns of Chew, the constant fusillade kept up by the skirmish line, and the activity of the cavalry, that entirely deceived the Federal commander.

CHAPTER II

March, 1862

Daily skirmishes with force of Banks—Addition of new companies and recruits swell the brigade—Jackson orders it divided into two commands, and Ashby tenders his resignation—Jackson revokes the order and Ashby withdraws his resignation—Jackson marches to McDowell and defeats Fremont—Ashby screens the movement from Banks by constant skirmishing in his front—Destroys railroad and telegraph between Front Royal and Strasburg—Attack upon Federal infantry at Buckton, where Captains Sheetz and Fletcher fall— Battle of Winchester and pursuit of Banks—Ashby throws his cavalry between the converging armies of Shields and Fremont and prevents communication between them—Informs Jackson fully of their movements—Capture of Sir Percy Wyndham—Death of Ashby—Cross Keys and Port Republic.

The day after the battle of Kernstown the Federals followed, and at Middletown the Federal cavalry advanced and endeavored to cut off Chew's Battery, which as usual in retreat was full in the rear, and now occupying the crest of a hill. The Federals had gotten on its flank and nearly in its rear, when out of a skirt of woods dashed Ashby leading a squadron and forced them to retire.

Nearly every day similar affairs occurred, and the success of Ashby's cavalry under his bold leadership, gave to both it and him, throughout the armies of friend and foe, a fame that was akin to romance.

Though beaten at Kernstown, Jackson remained in the eyes of the Confederates a real victor. The long, hard fight against a greatly superior force of the enemy was a signal proof of Southern valor. The report of the battle kindled a martial spirit. Jackson's boldness and skill inspired confidence, while Ashby's activity and personal daring made his leadership attractive.

Fresh recruits poured in to fill up the regiments of infantry. The mounted companies under Ashby began to overflow in numbers, and from the surplus new ones were formed. New companies also enlisted, and among the latter were those of Capt. Thomas Marshall of Frederick, Capt. T. B. Massie of Rappahannock, Captain Harness from Hardy, and Capt. Murat Willis from Warrenton.

By the 20th of April Ashby had twenty companies. His command, however, was unorganized. Though a brigade in size it did not have as many field officers as one regiment ordinarily has. Besides Ashby, Major Funsten was the only officer above the rank of captain.

On the 15th of April General Banks wrote to McClellan: "The progress of Fremont in the west towards Staunton has alarmed Jackson, who has moved above New Market. Ashby is still here. We have a sleepless eye upon him, and are straining every nerve to advance as quickly as possible."

The advance of Fremont was part of a concerted movement to drive Jackson out of the Valley and seize Staunton.

On the 17th of April Banks marched to Mt. Jackson. Ashby having ordered Chew's guns back to Rude's Hill, remained on a eminence north of the bridge. He had with him a small body of men. He had prepared the kindling to burn the bridge, but the cavalry of the enemy, with exceptional enterprise, charged him with a large force and drove him across the bridge, pursuing along the turnpike. A Federal cavalrymen riding up near Ashby endeavored to kill him with his pistol. Harry Hatcher of Loudoun county observing his danger, with the greatest coolness galloped forward and killed the trooper. Ashby paid little attention to this attack, being intent on getting his cavalry back to recapture and burn the bridge. His cavalry had gone so far, however, in the direction of Rude's Hill, that it was impossible to recall them in time. Ashby escaped from this conflict unscathed, but his famous white horse was shot by the enemy. He was led back beyond Rude's Hill and died near the Valley turnpike.

On this retreat Ashby fought the advance of the enemy from every hilltop, and at Edenburg, where he laid for thirty days, he was engaged with his guns and cavalry twenty-eight times.

On the 17th Jackson broke camp and retreated up the Valley. The next day he reached Harrisonburg, and there leaving the turnpike, marched in the direction of Swift Run Gap. Crossing the Shenandoah he went into camp at Conrad's Store in Elk Run Valley, and there stood at bay. The place lies between the South Fork of the Shenandoah and Swift Run Gap. A road running through the latter furnished easy communication with General Ewell, whose division of about 7,000 men lay encamped along the Rapidan River, within two days' march.

He now seemed to have abandoned the Valley and Staunton to the mercies of the Federals; but, in fact, nothing was further from his mind.

In the meanwhile Ashby, with his cavalry, confronted Banks, disputing his advance and so worrying him that he was kept in a chronic state of bewilderment as to Jackson's movements.

So completely was Banks deceived, that at one time he thought Jackson had crossed the Blue Ridge. He reports nothing to Washington except that, "Ashby is here."

Jackson, though quiet, was intensely on the alert. From his mountain perch he was watching and planning.

The road was opened to Staunton, but Banks hesitated to go forward. Perhaps he was waiting for Fremont, who, on the other side of the North Mountain, was moving slowly southward.

In the meantime Jackson, who neglected nothing, was busily engaged in reorganizing his command. The infantry recruits were distributed among the old companies and the skeleton regiments were rapidly filled up.

The mounted men were put into the cavalry, and Ashby now reported twenty-one companies. There was still no regimental formation, and his large brigade with only two field officers was an unwieldy body. There was no regimental drill, and no action as regiments in the field or elsewhere. It was more like a tribal band held together by the authority of a single chief.

Increase of numbers rather diminished than increased its efficiency as a whole, and made it more unmanageable. Jackson saw the evil and tried to correct it.

The constant demand for Ashby's presence on the enemy's front, and the absence of so many of his companies on detached service, had hitherto proved a serious obstacle to reform, but at Swift Run Gap Jackson took summary proceedings.

Eleven companies of the Ashby cavalry were ordered to report to Brigadier-General Taliaferro and to be attached to his command. The rest were ordered to report to General Winder. For Ashby was reserved the honor of commanding the advance and rear guards, with authority to call for portions of his command as necessity required. The effect of this order, was to virtually deprive Ashby of his command.   But what followed is best told in Jackson's own words.   In a letter to Colonel Taylor, Lee's assistant adjutant-general, of date May 5th, 1862, Jackson says: "I so felt the importance of having the cavalry of this district more thoroughly organized, drilled, and disciplined as to induce me to take action in the matter; but Colonel Ashby claimed that I could not interfere with his organization, as he was acting under the instructions of the late Secretary of War, Mr. Benjamin. * * * When I took steps for organizing, drilling, and disciplining the cavalry, both of its field officers sent in their resignations; and such was Colonel Ashby's influence over his command that I became well satisfied that if I persisted in my attempt to increase the efficiency of the cavalry, it would produce the contrary effect, as Colonel Ashby's influence, who is very popular with his men, would be thrown against me.   Under these circumstances, I refrained taking further action in the matter (as I was in the face of the enemy), until the War Department should have an opportunity of acting in the case.   At present there is no field officer on duty with the cavalry referred to, as Colonel Ashby and Major Funsten are both sick."

This letter, written from Staunton, explains why Jackson about ten days before had reinstated Ashby in his command.

It is true that Ashby's mode of fighting and managing his command, was quite at variance with West Point methods, but this was to be expected, both on account of the rapid increase of his force from raw recruits, and the active field service demanded, and also from the irregular nature of the service.

Jackson kept Ashby so busy fighting the enemy night and day, that he had no time to give to the details of organization.

Then, too, it may be said of Ashby's method, that it was most likely the best under the circumstances. He taught his men that war meant getting close to the enemy, and requiring him to fight for every foot of the ground he attempted to advance upon; a lesson, if choice had to be made, of far more importance than dress parades and regimental maneuvers. At any rate, his mode of fighting had the desired effect of beating the enemy in small as well as in large affairs, and at the same time of attracting the chivalry of Virginia and Maryland to his standard.

On the evening of April 30th, General Ewell arrived at Swift Run Gap with an aggregate force of 8,000 men. A few hours before Jackson had broken camp and, ascending the right bank of the Shenandoah to Port Republic, crossed the river through Brown's Gap, and thence marched to Staunton along the line of the Virginia Central Railroad.

In the meantime Ashby's cavalrymen were busy among the Federal outposts, keeping Banks in constant expectation of an attack, and acting as a screen to Jackson's movements.

But, in some way, news of Ewell's arrival and Jackson's departure reached Banks, and he felt sure that Jackson was coming by way of Thornton's Gap to attack his rear. He at once broke camp and fell back to New Market. Ashby, with eleven companies, remained to make demonstrations upon Banks' front and to mask Jackson's movement against Milroy, while the other companies went with Jackson, who was now on his way to McDowell.

Lee had directed Jackson to assume an offensive course, but his movements were left to his own discretion.

Fearing a union of Banks' and Fremont's forces, he determined to fight them in detail, and to make his first attack upon Fremont.

Leaving Ewell with 8,000 troops in the Luray Valley, on the 7th of May Jackson left Staunton, where his command had halted to rest for a day, and making a junction with Genl. Edward Johnson west of Staunton, marched against Milroy, who was at McDowell.

The cavalry that accompanied Jackson on this expedition, did little else but capture the enemy's pickets, and at different points blockade the roads leading to Jackson's rear by felling trees across them.

While Jackson was marching west in search of Milroy, Banks pushed his cavalry advance as far as Harrisonburg. Here, May 7th, quite a spirited skirmish with Ashby's horsemen occurred.

In his report of this, General Banks says: "The enemy does not show himself except by cavalry. * * * His chief object will doubtless be to prevent a junction of forces on this line with General McDowell."

Evidently he, ignorant of Jackson's designs, thought the Confederates intended to abandon the Valley. A like impression prevailed at Washington, and when Shields, with his division, was shortly afterwards ordered to cross the ridge and join the forces of General McDowell, Banks was ordered to fall back to Strasburg, so as to be able to leave the Valley on short notice and aid McDowell if necessary.

When Banks found that he might probably be left alone to confront Jackson, he began to change his opinion as to the designs of Stonewall. He made frequent requests for aid, but nothing could shake the purpose of the Federal administration.

The demonstrations on McDowell's front created alarm at Washington, and the Federal authorities might almost be accused of leaving Banks in the Valley, as a bait to keep Jackson from uniting his forces with those in front of McDowell.

Jackson, even while pursuing Milroy, feared that Banks would get away before he returned. But he defeated Milroy and then began to retrace his steps.

The fruit of Kernstown was now to be plucked by Stonewall. His audacity there in attacking a force so superior in numbers, had caused his enemies now to suspect him capable of any bold and unusual enterprise.

General McDowell (May 10th) writes that Jackson is in his front. Schenck at Franklin, nearly 100 miles distant, is positive that Jackson is trying to get in his rear, while Fremont is equally sure that Jackson is going west.

Of course, from these conflicting accounts, the authorities at Washington remained in dense ignorance and fear of Jackson's designs.

Much of Jackson's success is justly attributed to the secrecy of his movements. His rapid action and closeness of counsel, joined to a bold strategy, had much to do with the mystery that enveloped his actions, but not a little of that secrecy and mystery was due to the impenetrable veil created by the cordon of pickets maintained by Ashby, and the audacious demonstrations of his cavalry.

This was only possible where there were great activity, and sleepless vigilance on the part of the cavalry detachments, joined to their uniform successes over the foe in the numerous skirmishes.

While Jackson is away beyond the Shenandoah mountains, Ashby is busy with the companies left him in screen-
ing the movements of his chief.

May 10th Ashby writes from Lacy Springs to Maj.
James Barbour, Ewell's adjutant-general: "You will please
inform the General (Ewell) that I have moved to this
point on my way from New Market to Luray, but will wait
until my companies with General Jackson, expected today,
come up. * * * I thought it best not to leave this road
until I had followed their column as far as Strasburg, so
as to cause them to believe you were behind them upon this
road."

In the last sentence we get a glimpse of Ashby's idea of
his duty as the leader of Jackson's cavalry; namely, to so
use it that the movement of the main body should be
effectually hidden from the enemy.

Whatever he did was without reference to selfish ends.

We find him never attempting a brilliant raid for personal
glory.   Though always close to the foe and worrying them
in a thousand ways, it is solely to further what he conceives
to be the plan of his commanding officer.

On Sunday morning, May 18th, Jackson rested after his
long march from Franklin at Mt. Solon.   Ewell rode across
the Valley and joined him here.   In the interview that
occurred between them it was resolved to go quickly and
assail General Banks' army.

Fearing, if they attacked him by marching down the
Valley turnpike, he would retreat to Strasburg and thence
to McDowell's army, they determined to head him off by
delivering the first blow at Front Royal.

Success depended on secrecy, and secrecy on the activity
and faithfulness of the cavalry in front of Banks.

So well was the movement hid by Ashby's cavalry that Jackson had reached Front Royal, routed and captured the force there before General Banks heard a word about it. And when a messenger in hot haste brought him the news, it was not credited, so confident was the Federal general that Jackson was on his front.

Jackson, with his division and that of Genl. Edward Johnson, followed the Valley turnpike to New Market. Here he turned to the right and, passing through New Market Gap in Massanutton Mountain, crossed the Shenandoah River at Columbia bridge and united his column with Ewell's, that had marched down the Luray Valley.

The Confederates went from Columbia bridge straight towards Front Royal, until within four and a half miles of the town, when they turned from the main road and followed one that approached the place from the south. At Spangler's crossroads the cavalry under Ashby and Flournoy were sent to destroy communications between Strasburg and Front Royal.

A short distance beyond the river Ashby and Flournoy separated, the former taking a more western course, while Flournoy kept on so as to strike the railroad near Front Royal and come around in the rear of the Federal garrison.

Ashby moved towards Buckton Station, between Front Royal and Strasburg, a point of importance, and guarded by three companies of Federal infantry.

Upon discovering his approach, the Federals quickly took shelter in the depot building and the outhouses of a Mr. Jenkins.

Thus protected they made a spirited defense. Their musket volleys poured into the ranks of the grey horsemen were not without effect, but the continued persistence of the mounted men finally ended all resistance. The station was taken and the Federals were captured or driven off.

The victory, however, was dearly bought, for two of Ashby's best captains fell mortally wounded—Fletcher and Sheetz.

In the meantime Front Royal had been taken by Jackson.

The Federal garrison, consisting of Colonel Kenly's First Maryland Infantry and two companies of the New York cavalry, retreated across the North and South Forks of the Shenandoah. A short distance beyond the latter, they were overtaken by Colonel Flournoy's cavalry. The rear guard made but a feeble resistance, then broke and fled. The infantry made a brief stand, but upon Flournoy's men charging among them, they also soon gave way.

Company B, Captain Grimsly, charged directly up the turnpike supported by Company E; Colonel Flournoy on the left, and Companies A and K on the right.

Colonel Kenly made a gallant effort to rally his men in an orchard. Here for a few minutes stout resistance was made, but the progress of the Confederates was not stopped. Charging boldly among the infantry they attacked them furiously with sabre and pistol, Stonewall himself near the front urging them on.

Colonel Kenly fell badly wounded; his men broke and fled and the retreat of the Federals soon became a wild rout.

As the result of this day's fight 750 prisoners were captured; also two parrot guns and nearly all the enemy's wagon train.

Jackson camped at Cedarville that night and waited for the rest of his forces. Ewell's division arrived about dark. Jackson's old division and that of Genl. Edward Johnson, weary with their long march from Franklin, 120 miles distant, got no further than Front Royal.

Banks was still at Strasburg. A courier despatched from Front Royal had ridden around the cavalry pickets of the Confederates and carried the information that Jackson in heavy force was at Front Royal.

Banks refused to believe the messenger.

Firmly convinced that Jackson's main body was still in his front on the turnpike, and that the attacking force at Front Royal was only a raiding body of cavalry, he took no steps to retreat until despatches were received from Winchester from fugitives who had come from Front Royal.

His persistence in believing that the Confederate main body was south of him was probably due to a demonstration made in that quarter by a small body of the Ashby cavalry under Capt. Sam Myers. With his own company and those of Capt. E. H. McDonald and Capt. William Harness, he had boldly driven in the Federal pickets and erected breastworks on the hills near Strasburg in sight of Banks' army. Moving his troops about from point to point partly in view of the Federals, he created the impression that he was supported by a large force.

That the demonstration had the effect intended is shown by the fact that even after hearing from Winchester General Banks did not abandon Strasburg until he had sent out a cavalry force towards Woodstock and learned that the driving in of his pickets and the bold display of the Ashby cavalry was a "take in."

After resting all night at Cedarville, Jackson in the morning set out to find and assail the foe.

Not knowing which way General Banks would retreat, whether by Strasburg or Winchester, Jackson planned to intercept him by either road. In his official report he says: "In order to watch both directions and at the same time advance upon him if he remained in Strasburg, I determined with the main body of the army to strike the Valley turnpike near Middletown, a village five miles north of Strasburg and thirteen south of Winchester."

As the column moved towards Middletown, Ashby led the advance supported by skirmishers from Taylor's brigade, with Chew's Battery and two parrot guns from the Rockbridge Artillery.

Ashby was directed to keep scouts on his left in order to prevent Banks from passing unobserved to Front Royal.

Some time before Genl. George Stuart, temporarily in command of the Sixth and Second Virginia Cavalry, had been sent to Newtown, a village five miles north of Middletown, to observe the movements of the enemy.

While Jackson was thus preparing to confront Banks, the latter, whom Jackson describes in one of his letters as a "cautious" man, was making great speed down the turnpike. It was a race between the fresh troops of the Federals and the footsore Confederates; a race, too, in which the Federals had several hours' start.

General Banks was long in making up his mind, but the conclusion once formed he acted promptly, and his retreating column moved rapidly.

By the time Jackson's advance reached Middletown all the Federal infantry had passed and were nearly to Winchester.

When near Middletown Ashby discovered that the enemy's cavalry, 2,000 strong, was rapidly retreating, only trains and a large body of cavalry being seen.

Ashby, with a small body of cavalry, ordering three guns of Chew's Battery to follow him, swooped down on their right like an eagle. The guns moved with the cavalry, and unlimbered within a few hundred feet of the retreating column, and opened on them with canister. Soon the road was so blockaded with dead men and horses that those in rear could not pass, and an indescribable scene of carnage and confusion ensued. The main body of the Federals escaped in detachments across the fields westward.

General Jackson, in his official report referring to this incident, says: "In a few moments the turnpike, which just before had teemed with life, presented a most appalling spectacle of carnage and destruction. The road was literally obstructed with the mingled and confused mass of struggling and dying horses and riders. Amongst the survivors the wildest confusion ensued, and they scattered in disorder in various directions, leaving some 200 prisoners in the hands of the Confederates."

Ashby then pursued the enemy with the utmost vigor to Newtown, fighting his guns upon the skirmish line, and with the greatest boldness and audacity he pressed the enemy through the whole night. The morning following, he was at the head of Jackson's column, and after the battle of Winchester, followed the enemy on the turnpike until dark.

Dabney, in his "Life of Jackson," says Ashby went off on an independent expedition towards Berryville, and subsequent historians, including Henderson, have fallen into this error. It is thoroughly attested by soldiers who were with him at the time, that, at no time was Ashby anywhere during this particular conflict, except at the head of Jackson's army on the Valley turnpike.

The Federal column was effectually sundered, the rear retiring towards Strasburg, though not until after a gallant effort was made to cut its way through towards Winchester.

Jackson halted his force at Middletown until he could ascertain whether the Federal main body had passed or not. Upon learning that it had he pressed on towards Winchester.

In the battle of Winchester, which occurred May 25th, Ashby, with the few cavalry with him, took position on Jackson's left.

It has been claimed that the small number of the Ashby cavalry present for duty at this battle was due to the fact that they stopped the pursuit in order to plunder the captured trains.

This was in part true, but the same may be said of many of the infantry, as Jackson bears witness in his report.

The true reason was, that Ashby had only a small part of his command with him when he reached Middletown, the greater number of his men being engaged in picketing the roads leading to Jackson's line of march from McDowell, and many were detailed to guard prisoners. After the battle at Winchester, Ashby, notwithstanding his small force, kept up the pursuit to Martinsburg.

It would seem that a vindication is due to Ashby as to the commonly accepted statement contained in Dabney's "Life of Jackson," and quoted later by Henderson in his "Stonewall Jackson and the American Civil War," that at the time of Banks' defeat at Winchester, Ashby was off on an independent expedition, and not present on the turnpike in pursuit, and also as to the alleged plundering of the wagon trains by his cavalrymen.   Such vindication is amply found in a letter of Col. R. P. Chew to Rev. Jas. B. Avirett, found in his "Ashby and His Compeers," page 269, here quoted in part by permission of the author—

"CHARLES TOWN, W. VA., Jan. 18th, 1867.

REV. J. B. AVIRETT.

DEAR SIR:— * * * With reference to the affair referred to by Dr. Dabney, I will give you a statement of the facts as far as my observation and knowledge extend. General Ashby followed the infantry of General Jackson with a detachment of his cavalry, a portion of it having been sent down the Shenandoah Valley to confront the enemy at Strasburg. I accompanied him with my guns. He diverged from the Front Royal and Luray Road, and struck the railroad, as you know, at Buckton. I was not with him until I rejoined the head of the army near Cedarville. Here General Ashby, with his cavalry, my battery, two guns of Poague's Battery and some infantry skirmishers, left the turnpike and pushed for Middletown. * * * After a short delay, to enable his force to reach its destination at the proper time, he formed his skirmishers and advanced rapidly across the fields to the lower part of the town. Here he encountered a considerable force of cavalry, and running up his artillery to within 100 yards opened on the Federals with artillery and small arms. The enemy crowded in the turnpike, gave way and retreated in all directions. Ashby dashed in among them, pistol in hand, and captured himself many prisoners. Major Funsten in the meantime had reached the turnpike below Middletown, perhaps two miles, and forced the retreating cavalry of the enemy towards the Back Road, besides capturing a large wagon train. It was here that our cavalry became dispersed, and the reasons why Ashby failed to have his cavalry in hand next morning, as I have understood them, were these: The cavalry we defeated at Middletown retreated towards North Mountain and Winchester, scattered, in fact completely routed. Major Funsten prevented those going towards Winchester from pursuing their retreat in that direction, and forced them to retire across the hills, as I said before, towards the Back Road. Our cavalry of course pursued, and in following a scattered foe became dispersed themselves.

Ashby pushed on with my guns towards Winchester, and when we reached the point where Funsten struck the turnpike, we threw the guns into position, and Ashby with about forty men charged a line of the enemy's infantry between us and Christman's house.

General Ashby had started from New Market with but a part of his cavalry. They had marched until the horses were exhausted,—without rest day or night; and when the enemy became dispersed, and fled in the greatest confusion, our cavalry scattered *in pursuit of them.* Major Funsten had but a very small detachment when he reached him, and we had passed the wagon train where the plundering was reported to have occurred, and the cavalry were not there, and unless they returned to the wagon train after we passed it, it was the infantry and not the cavalry who got the benefit of the spoils. General Ashby pushed the enemy with his small force of cavalry and my guns through Newtown, and until dark, when we went into camp to feed our exhausted horses, having pushed the enemy from hill to hill between Middletown and Newtown.

General Jackson now pressed forward and night found him before the enemy at Winchester. * * * General Ashby was with General Jackson on the morning of the battle of Winchester, while the latter was engaged in planting his batteries.

I know nothing of his subsequent action until after the battle.

I overtook him below Stephenson's depot, dashing upon the enemy whenever an opportunity offered, with a handful of his men.

I never heard of any *independent enterprise* of General Ashby, nor do I believe he was anywhere but at the front of the army with a small force of his cavalry.

The rapidity of General Jackson's movements added to the confusion attending the march of a large army, and prevented our cavalry from re-forming quickly after they had scattered in pursuit of the enemy on different roads and across country.

I always believed that the matter was misrepresented to General Jackson, and hence his severe criticism of the cavalry.

It was certainly unfortunate for Ashby as well as the cause, that more of his men were not with him on that day, as an excellent opportunity was afforded to dash upon and pursue the enemy. Yet I do not believe he was to blame for their absence.

It was then popular to say that Ashby exercised no control over his men beyond personal influence, and that there was no discipline in his command. It was said that his successes were gained, not by skillful maneuver, but by the reckless dash and courage of himself and men; but I will do him the justice to say that he could always command more men for duty from the same muster-roll than any cavalry commander under whom I have sinced served. * * * I have served at different times during the war, with almost all the prominent cavalry leaders of the Army of Northern Virginia, and I have never seen one who possessed the ability to inspire troops under fire with the courage and enthusiasm that Ashby's presence always excited.

He adopted in the beginning of the war the tactics with cavalry by which, later in the war, other cavalry commanders could only secure success; namely, always to meet the enemy with bold and determined charges, and when they were defeated to press them with the utmost vigor."

Jackson had ventured far and the Federals were gathering for his destruction. It was necessary to retrace his steps somewhat hurriedly if he wished to save the spoils of victory and avoid defeat, if not destruction.

The object of the movement which was to arrest the advance on Richmond had been accomplished. Besides, Banks had been badly beaten, and with a loss of one-third of his army had been driven across the Potomac.

The retreat was more full of peril to Jackson's army than the advance had been, for from the west and east armies were marching to cut off his retreat, while from the north his rear would be threatened by a force superior to his own.

Jackson did not hurry. Four days after the battle of Winchester, on the 29th of May, he laid siege to Harper's Ferry, and occupied the Loudoun heights as if he had concluded to move on Washington.

Next day, on the 30th, he began to retire and was followed as far as Charles Town by Banks and Saxton with 14,000 Federals. By the evening of the 31st, his main body was in Strasburg, where he halted for the rear of his column to close up.

Fremont, marching from Wardensville and making for the same point, had encountered Ashby. Whatever fault Jackson might find with his cavalry for plundering, he always placed them on guard at the point of greatest danger.

Ashby was soon supported by Ewell, and the advance of Fremont was arrested.

Meantime, Jackson's rear column was closed up, and he fell back to Harrisonburg. From that point Jackson retired to Port Republic, which was twelve miles eastward. In this march, it was Ashby's command which, picketing and scouting in all directions, kept Jackson informed as to the movements of the enemy. On Shields' front towards Front Royal hung Ashby's men. In the path too, of Fremont, as we have seen, were they. And in the rear of Jackson nearly all the time.

On the 20th of June the Sixth and Second Virginia Cavalry were transferred to Ashby's command, and for more than a year the Sixth remained a part of the Ashby brigade.

On Monday, June the 2nd, Jackson retreated to Mt. Jackson, closely followed by Fremont. The cavalry under Ashby protected the rear, engaging almost constantly in skirmishes with the enemy.

The Federals evidently wanted vengeance for Banks' disaster, and frequently with great gallantry charged the Confederate rear guard.

On the afternoon of the 2nd, Jackson crossed the North Fork of the Shenandoah, the cavalry burning the bridge in spite of the efforts of the Federals to prevent it.

On the 5th Jackson reached Harrisonburg. The next day Fremont, who had been delayed by the burning of the bridge across the North Fork, was close at hand.

Jackson withdrew towards Port Republic as the head of the Federal column approached. The same evening Ashby was attacked by the Federal cavalry under Percy Wyndham, an English adventurer and soldier of fortune, commanding the First New Jersey Cavalry, who, greedy of Ashby's fame, wished

> "To pluck the budding honors on his crest
> To weave them on his own."

He openly avowed his intention of capturing Ashby, and was said to be watching an opportunity to make a successful dash for that purpose.

Ashby was, however, prepared for them, and as they approached his line of battle drawn up across the road and extending into the fields, some dismounted men in a wheatfield, stationed there for that purpose, fired into the flank of the Federal column. In the confusion which followed in their ranks, Ashby's men charged, capturing Wyndham and the colors of the First New Jersey Regiment, and inflicting an acknowledged loss of thirty-six killed and wounded upon the Federals.

This repulse caused the Federals under General Bayard to come forward with reinforcements of all arms. Ashby anticipating him, asked and received from General Ewell the support of the First Maryland and Fifty-eighth Virginia regiments of infantry.

In the hotly contested fight which ensued the skirmish line of the Fifty-eighth Virginia was forced back, and Ashby while rallying them, having ordered in the reserve, had his horse shot under him, and rising and leading on foot fell himself, pierced by a bullet, and died almost instantly. His death at the morning tide of his fame, with his face to the foe, and in defense of his beloved country, was such as he would have wished it to be, and in perfect keeping with his heroic ideal.

Beloved and idolized by his command, the news of his death, which quickly spread among the men, produced general and profound sorrow, which was mingled with a resolve for vengeance.

While the admiration of Ashby's prowess had extended even to the enemy, yet the news of his death encouraged greatly the opposing Federal cavalry, and was hailed by the Federal authorities as a distinctive loss to the Confederate cause, and, as to the Union side, equal to a Federal victory.

On June 7th the armies of both Jackson and Fremont remained comparatively quiet. The latter having been roughly handled the day before, its commander was disposed to even more than his usual caution and characteristic indecision, and his slowness of motion gave to the wearied Confederates a moment of enjoyable repose.

But Shields was approaching Port Republic from Luray by a road on the east side of the South Fork of the Shenandoah, skirting the foothills of the Blue Ridge.

He seems to have believed that Jackson was in full retreat before Fremont, and accordingly moved his forces as rapidly as the unfavorable condition of the road would permit, having Tyler's brigade attended by considerable cavalry, far in advance of his main body. His purpose was to make a dash across the river at Port Republic and destroy the bridge before Jackson could reach there, and thus intercept his retreat eastward across the mountain through Brown's Gap.

The plan was well conceived, and that the execution of it was not a success was more due to the blundering good luck on the part of the Confederates than to a lack of enterprise and dash on the part of the Federals.

The cavalry of Shields, with one gun of a light battery, actually had possession of the eastern end of the bridge, Jackson himself having dashed across it in advance of them, leaving most of his staff behind and escaping capture himself only by a hairbreadth.

The Federals were driven back by the timely arrival of one gun of a battery near at hand and a battalion of infantry.

Colonel Munford, who with the Ashby brigade had been operating upon the flanks of Fremont, now arrived and pursued the retreating Federals some distance in the direction of Conrad's Store, capturing many prisoners and much plunder, and occupied the rest of the day in arresting Shields' advance, though the nature of the country did not favor cavalry operations.[1]

---

[1] Account by Genl. T. T. Munford.

Fremont had heard the sound of the brief cannonade at Port Republic on the 7th, and supposing Shields had arrived there, on the morning of the 8th put his army in motion and cautiously advanced in that direction, but soon found his progress arrested by the pickets of Ewell's division.

Jackson had planned that Ewell should hold Fremont in check on the west side of the Shenandoah, while he with his own division would deal with Shields on the east side of the river.

Ewell, with about 6,000 infantry, five batteries of artillery, and 500 cavalry, was opposing his adversary, whose army numbered 10,000 infantry, with eight batteries of artillery, and 2,000 cavalry.[2]

In an all-day battle near Cross Keys, at times fought with great fierceness, Ewell was victorious, having driven back Fremont and camped upon the field. The losses on both sides, killed, wounded, and missing, were 972, of which the Federal loss was 684.

The cavalry does not appear to have been heavily engaged.

The next day, June the 9th, was fought perhaps the most hotly contested battle of the Valley campaign, at Port Republic, which, says Henderson (Vol. I, page 385), was the most costly to the army of the Valley during the whole campaign. Out of 5,900 Confederates engaged 804 were disabled. The Federal losses were heavier, being 1,001 killed, wounded, and missing.

The ground was of such nature, being heavily wooded on both sides of the road, that the cavalry could not operate except in pursuit. But the battery of Chew, which always

---

[2] Figures given by Henderson, Vol. I, page 368.

accompanied the Ashby cavalry, did fine service. Being ordered from the field of Cross Keys on the morning of the 9th, it crossed the river at Port Republic, and came upon the field just as the Stonewall Brigade was being driven back with heavy loss by Tyler's Federal brigade, and under the heavy fire of a Federal battery well and strongly posted on an eminence near the Lewis house.

The gunners of Chew's Battery promptly got the range of this battery and poured upon it a terrific enfilading fire, crippling the enemy's guns, just at the time that Taylor's brigade of infantry had moved around through the forest and attacked it and its infantry support in front and flank.

Taylor's brigade charged through the battery and captured it.

Chew's Battery then moved rapidly to a position near the Lewis house, and opened upon the retreating columns of the enemy, producing great havoc amongst them, and joined in the pursuit for about two miles.

The cavalry led by Munford now dashed upon the retreating Federals and pursued them for nine miles, when the pursuit was arrested near Conrad's Store by the presence of Shields, who had arrived there with his main force of two brigades, which were deployed in line of battle.

Fremont, after an ineffectual attempt to aid Shields by throwing a few shells from his batteries east of the river, and witnessing Shields' discomfiture, retired to a point north of Harrisonburg. Shields withdrew to Luray.

The cavalry brigade continued to watch both armies, the large part with Chew's Battery crossing to the east side of the river for the purpose of observing Fremont.

CHAPTER III

June, 1862

Jackson marches from Brown's Gap to the Chickahominy—His ingenious ruses to deceive Shields and Fremont—Munford screens Jackson's movement and follows him with the Second Virginia Cavalry—Genl. Beverly Robertson succeeds in command of Valley cavalry—Reorganization of the Ashby cavalry—Robertson an organizer and disciplinarian—Brigade leaves Valley and joins Jackson near Richmond, July 10th, Company B of Twelfth Virginia Cavalry being left in the Valley—Fighting at Gordonsville and Cedar Run—Genl. J. E. B. Stuart leads cavalry in a reconnoissance—Brandy Station—Catlett's Station—Thoroughfare Gap—Sudley Road fight and death of Major Patrick—Second Manassas campaign—Advance into Maryland—Robertson assigned to Department of North Carolina, and Munford again commands the brigade—Poolesville and Crampton's Gap—Affair at Darksville—Capture of Harper's Ferry—Brigade covers Lee's recrossing of Potomac—Raid into Pennsylvania—Col. William E. Jones takes command—Various skirmishes in the Valley—White's Battalion attached to brigade—Snickers Gap and Castleman's Ferry—Company D of the Eleventh at Romney, and capture of Capt. E. H. McDonald—General Jones in command of the Valley District—Expedition to Moorefield—Scarcity of forage—Midwinter diversions in the Valley.

After defeating Shields at Port Republic, Jackson withdrew into Brown's Gap in the Blue Ridge Mountains, and there rested his footsore and battle-worn soldiers until June 17th. On that day, receiving orders from General Lee, he broke camp and marched towards the Chickahominy, where he arrived in time to join the commander-in-chief in the famous Seven Days' Battles before Richmond, in which McClellan and his myriads were beaten and driven with great loss to the cover of 'his gunboats.

So successfully was the movement of Jackson screened from the doughty Federal generals in the Shenandoah Valley that between the 17th and 28th of June he had made the march from Brown's Gap to near Richmond, 130 miles, and had been successfully participating in the defeat of McClellan for two days before either Shields, Fremont, Banks, or even the authorities at Washington were aware that he had moved from the scene of his late victory over Shields near Port Republic.

The success of this movement depended primarily upon its being hidden from the observation and knowledge of the enemy. That duty devolved upon the cavalry and was performed with eminent skill and resourcefulness by Col. Thomas T. Munford, who succeeded to the command of Jackson's cavalry after the death of the lamented Ashby.

Referring to this, says Henderson in his "Stonewall Jackson and the American Civil War": "The cavalry, though far from support, was ordered to maneuver boldly to prevent all information reaching the Federals, and to follow Fremont as long as he retreated.

"The bearers of flags of truce were impressed with the idea that the Southerners were advancing with great strength. The outpost line was made as close as possible; no civilians were allowed to pass, and the Confederate troopers, in order that they should have nothing to tell if they were captured, were kept in ignorance of the position of the infantry.

"Jackson's real intention was concealed from every one except Colonel Munford. The officers of his staff fared worse than the remainder of the army. Not only were they debarred from their commander's confidence, but they became the unconscious instruments whereby false intelligence was spread. The engineers were directed to prepare a

series of maps of the Valley; and all who acquired a knowledge of this carefully divulged order told their friends in
confidence that Jackson was going in pursuit of Fremont.
As these friends told their friends without loss of time, it
was soon the well-settled conviction of everybody that nothing was further from Jackson's intention than an evacuation
of the Valley."

After masking Jackson's eastward movement, Colonel
Munford returned from the pursuit of Shields, and receiving
orders from Jackson to follow him to the Chickahominy
with his regiment, the Second Virginia Cavalry, he turned
over command of the Ashby brigade, which had just been
reorganized, to Col. Beverly Robertson, a West Pointer,
who undertook to inaugurate for it a discipline more in keeping with West Point ideals than it had heretofore known.
No curtailment of personal liberty either of civilian or soldier
is accepted without protest, and it is needless to say that
Colonel Robertson's discipline did not make him especially
popular with soldiers who had followed Ashby, and looked
upon the suggestion of needed discipline as a reflection upon
their fighting qualities.   So it became the popular sentiment
among the men that Robertson was more at drilling than he
was at fighting.

Nevertheless the brigade did some splendid fighting under
him in the campaign against Pope, which shortly followed,
and for which both the brigade and the commander received
high praise in official reports of that campaign.   It is well
known, however, that the brigade won fame for the commander and not the commander for the brigade, and that
Robertson, not being a capable commander in the field, was
soon after that, at the suggestion of General Stuart, relieved

of the command of the brigade and sent to South Carolina to organize the cavalry for which he was particularly fitted.

Munford, with the Second Virginia Cavalry, overtook Jackson at Ashland, and led his advance every day in the Seven Days' Battles around Richmond.

The Ashby brigade, including Chew's Battery, now under Colonel Robertson, being left for a time to observe the movements of the Federals in the Valley, moved east of the Shenandoah to near Harrisonburg, Fremont having retired to a short distance north of that place, and Shields occupying Luray.

Here a partial reorganization of the brigade was undertaken. The twenty-six companies that had composed the command of Ashby were still known as the "Seventh Regiment," and though numerically of brigade proportions, had been commanded by only two field officers, Genl. Turner Ashby and Maj. Oliver Funsten.

Although Ashby had been promoted to the rank of brigadier-general on May the 27th, the campaign had been too active under him to allow time for reorganization.

The overgrown Seventh Regiment was now reduced to the ten original companies. Ten other companies composed the Twelfth Regiment, and the remaining companies were formed into the Seventeenth Battalion.

An election of officers now took place. While the regimental officers now elected, were preferred by the men for gallant and skillful services under Ashby, and were most capable and well qualified for commanders, yet, owing either to General Jackson's not recommending them, or to the War Department's arbitrary overruling of the elections for reasons known only to the officials, they did not receive commissions.

The reorganization was completed a few days later between Conrad's Store and Swift Run Gap, when Col. William E. Jones, late of the First Virginia Cavalry, was appointed colonel of the Seventh Regiment, Capt. Richard Dulaney lieutenant-colonel, and Capt. Thomas Marshall major. Col. Asher W. Harman was appointed colonel of the Twelfth; Lieut. Richard Burks, late adjutant of the Second Virginia Cavalry, was appointed lieutenant-colonel, and Capt. Thomas B. Massie major. Capt. William Patrick was appointed major of the Seventeenth Battalion.

The Second Virginia Cavalry, under Colonel Munford, and the Sixth Virginia, under Colonel Flournoy, which had been under Genl. George H. Stuart of Maryland, had been at the request of the officers commanding them, and upon the recommendation of General Ewell, transferred and assigned to Ashby's command.[1]

The brigade, therefore, at this time consisted of the Second, Sixth, Seventh and Twelfth regiments and the Seventeenth Battalion, all Virginia cavalry, and Chew's Battery of horse artillery.

Col. William E. Jones of the First Virginia Cavalry, and Col. Beverly Robertson of the Fourth, each having failed of re-election to the command of those regiments, and both of them having been West Pointers, and having been assured of commands in the Confederate Army by the authorities at Richmond, were now assigned to this brigade, Jones as colonel of the Seventh, and Beverly Robertson to command of the brigade with rank of brigadier-general.

---

[1]Statement of General Munford in a letter to the reviser of this work.

The Second Virginia Cavalry, under Colonel Munford, as before stated, was temporarily detached to act with Jackson's division in front of Richmond.

The success of Lee on the Chickahominy, to which Jackson had so signally contributed, had the effect of withdrawing Shields, Fremont, and Banks from the Valley, and their armies marching eastward by way of Sperryville and Warrenton, were consolidated into the army of Genl. John D. Pope, a new army sent out to protect Washington, or to co-operate with McClellan in the attempt upon Richmond, as circumstances might require.

This army was then occupying positions on the upper branches of the Rappahannock River, and numbered 47,000 to 50,000 men of all arms.

With this army were the two cavalry divisions of Bayard and Buford, 6,000 strong, and led by those enterprising Federal cavalrymen.

Upon the withdrawal of the Federal armies from the Valley, Robertson's brigade was ordered to join Jackson near Richmond, which it did immediately, reaching there about July 10th.

Company B of the Twelfth Virginia, under Lieutenants Milton Rouss and George Baylor, having been left behind to operate in the lower Valley.

On the 13th of July Jackson, with Ewell's corps, was ordered to Gordonsville to dispute the advance of Pope, which on the 27th of July had been pushed as far as the Rapidan River, the upper fords of which were picketed by a portion of Robertson's cavalry.

Jackson was soon after reinforced by A. P. Hill's division.

The Robertson brigade, operating upon the front of this advance, was now strengthened by the return of the Second Virginia Cavalry under Colonel Munford.

For several days prior to the 2nd of August the Confederate pickets were driven in, but on the 2nd a reconnoissance in force was made, by the Federals proceeding from Raccoon Ford to Orange Court House. The reconnoitering force consisted of the Fifth New York Cavalry, Colonel De Forest commanding, and the First Vermont, under Col. Charles H. Thomkins, all under command of Genl. S. W. Crawford.

After driving in the Confederate pickets, the reserve, consisting of Company F of the Eleventh Virginia, Captain Dangerfield in command, was pushed to half a mile beyond Orange Court House.

Here the Seventh Virginia, under Col. William E. Jones, appeared upon the scene. Throwing out sharpshooters from McGruder's company, the enemy's advance guard was soon driven in, and the Seventh followed in a charge which turned back the head of the enemy's column and created much confusion in his main body.

The main street of Orange Court House was packed with the contending horsemen, the choice spirits of both sides pushing into the thick of the fight, the timid withdrawing.

In the meantime Major Marshall, with a squadron, made a flank attack by the railroad depot; but his own party was soon struck in the flank by a Federal company, that forced back his command and cut off his retreat. His pistols being empty, he tried to cut his way through, but was knocked senseless by a sabre stroke.

Colonel Jones had by this time come up to the head of the regiment, and shot the Federal trooper, who was about to kill Marshall, but so hard was the resistance that Marshall remained in the hands of the Federals. For while this was going on, another flanking party of Federals had attacked Jones' right and rear.

Lieutenants Neff and Mohler of Company K wheeled and charged this body, but were followed by about a dozen men only, and the enemy for the moment checked, returned to the charge and drove the rear companies up the plank road, wounding and capturing quite a number.

The main body of the Seventh, however, kept on their course, driving the enemy through the town; but soon again returned, having observed in the open field the great superiority of the enemy in numbers.

In this fight the Seventh had about 200 men present. The two Federal regiments must have had double that number.

"To Lieutenant Smith, commanding Company A; Captain McGruder, commanding Company B; Company C, commanded by Captain Myers at first, and, when he was severely wounded, by Lieutenant Myers; and to Company D, commanded by Lieutenant Brown," says Colonel Jones in his report, "my thanks are especially due, for noble bearing in the fight. Sergt. Clarence L. Broadus[2] of Company D is recommended for promotion for distinguished gallantry."

Colonel Jones acknowledged a loss of ten wounded and forty missing.

About an hour after the fight the Federals retreated, followed by the Seventh, which being reinforced by the

---

[2]This gallant soldier returned to his command after the loss of his arm, and continued in the service to the close of the war. He served the first year of the war in the Tenth Virginia Infantry, and in 1862 re-enlisted in Ashby's cavalry.—*From Jones' Official Report.*

Sixth Virginia, under Colonel Flournoy, pursued the Federals vigorously as far as Rapidan Station.

The action at Orange Court House was soon after followed by an advance of Jackson's army, which now consisted of the divisions of Ewell, A. P. Hill, and his own; that of A. P. Hill having recently arrived.

Having learned that only a portion of Pope's army was at Culpeper Court House, Jackson resolved to attack it before the arrival of the remainder, and on August 7th moved from Gordonsville for that purpose.

On the morning of August 8th, the Federal cavalry north of the Rapidan was driven back by ours under Brigadier-General Robertson.

On the evening of the 8th, the Seventeenth Battalion and a part of the Sixth Regiment marched towards Madison Court House.

The main force of the Federal cavalry retreated towards Culpeper Court House, making a feeble resistance. A part fell back towards Madison Court House, and were pursued by a portion of the Sixth, under Colonel Flournoy, and the Seventeenth Battalion, under Major Patrick. At several points they attempted to rally, but each time being vigorously charged they broke and finally ran, leaving about twenty wounded and prisoners in the hands of the Confederates.

For five miles the chase continued, the Seventeenth Battalion and the Sixth Regiment pursuing in the direction of Madison Court House.

On the 9th was fought the battle of Cedar Run, in which Robertson's cavalry took little part, the main body being stationed on Jackson's left, while Colonel Jones, with the Seventh, who had been sent to Madison Court House, returned towards evening and after dark passed to Jackson's right and front.

The battle of Cedar Run was still going on. Jackson was still pursuing Banks, eager to drive him beyond Culpeper Court House.

In the darkness, the Seventh charged a body of the Federal cavalry and forced them to take shelter under their infantry.

A prisoner captured in this charge gave the first information of Seigel having arrived to reinforce Banks. Upon this being told to Jackson the pursuit was discontinued.

The following day all the cavalry with Jackson was put under the command of Genl. J. E. B. Stuart.

Robertson's brigade, which was now added to Stuart's division, consisted of the Second Virginia, Col. T. T. Munford; the Sixth Virginia, Col. P. S. Flournoy; the Seventh Virginia, Col. W. E. Jones; the Twelfth Virginia, Col. A. W. Harman, and the Seventeenth Battalion, under Major Patrick.

On the 20th of August Stuart's command led the advance of Jackson's army in its movement against Pope.

The Second Virginia Cavalry, under Colonel Munford, was ordered to keep on the left of Jackson's army and keep pace with its movements.

The rest of Robertson's brigade, accompanied by Stuart, marched by way of Stephensburg, a village four miles east of Culpeper, and when nearing Brandy Station encountered a force of Federal cavalry.

The Seventh Virginia led the Confederate advance and soon engaged the Federals, who after a stubborn resistance were forced back beyond Brandy Station upon their support.

It was now evident that the enemy was in heavy force, and in fact they had five regiments on the field, the First New Jersey, the Second New York, the First Pennsylvania, the First Maine, and the First Rhode Island.

General Robertson, with the Sixth, Twelfth, and Seventeenth battalions, was sent to the left to sweep across the open country and flank the enemy's position.

At first, as Stuart advanced, the enemy fell back along the road towards Rappahannock Station, but about midway between Brandy Station and Rappahannock Station, he made a determined stand in solid columns of squadrons on the ridge, with skirmishers deployed.

With these the Seventh soon became engaged, and quickly followed with a charge. Immediately opposing the Seventh were the First New Jersey, the Second New York, and the First Pennsylvania.

Says the Federal general, Bayard, in his report, "As soon as the leading regiment of the enemy came up, they formed and quickly charged with loud shouts and wild yelling. The sudden charge and yells of the enemy seemed to strike panic in the men, so that they soon began running."

Robertson was now sent for in haste to support the Seventh. He had mistaken the road and borne too much to the left. The enemy, however, did not profit by the delay, and Robertson arrived in time to join in the battle. The remaining regiments were hurled in succession upon the enemy's main body, which fell back and took refuge under the protection of his batteries planted beyond the river.

"In the action at Brandy Station," says Stuart, "Colonel Jones, whose regiment so long bore the brunt of the fight, behaved with marked courage and determination." The enemy occupying woods and hedgerows with dismounted

men, armed with long-range carbines, were repeatedly dislodged by his bold onslaughts, while Flournoy and Harman
nobly supported the Seventh at the critical moment.

In this engagement General Robertson acknowledged a
loss of three killed and fourteen wounded. He captured
sixty-four prisoners, many of whom were wounded. The
Federal loss nowhere appears in the reports.

The armies of Lee and Pope now lay confronting each
other on the opposite banks of the Rappahannock.

On the morning of August 21st, with the apparent design
of opening a way for a general advance of the Confederates,
Stuart directed Col. T. L. Rosser, commanding the Fifth
Virginia Cavalry, to move with his command for Beverly
Ford, and to re-seize the opposite bank by a sudden attack.
This was successfully accomplished by Colonel Rosser, and
enough of the bank was held to make a crossing practicable
for the infantry.

In the meantime Robertson's brigade had crossed at a
ford above and prepared the way for an advance. For some
reason there was a change of plan, and Stuart's cavalry was
withdrawn to the south bank of the Rappahannock before
night.

As the positions of the Confederates on the south bank
were commanded by those occupied by the Federals who
guarded all the fords, it was determined to seek a more
favorable place to cross higher up the river and thus gain
the enemy's right. Accordingly, Lee's army on the 21st
began marching up the river, Jackson in front.

On the 23rd Jackson crossed Hazel River and proceeded
up the Rappahannock. The same evening a portion of his
troops crossed the Rappahannock, but owing to a heavy
rain they recrossed on a temporary bridge during the night.

In the meantime Stuart with his cavalry was engaged in harassing the enemy's rear. On the morning of the 22nd he crossed the Rappahannock at Waterloo Bridge and Hart's Ford, with all of his division except the Seventh and Third Virginia Cavalry and two pieces of artillery. He reached Warrenton in the afternoon and moved in the direction of Catlett's Station with the design of destroying the railroad bridge that crosses Cedar Creek at that point.

Had the object of the expedition been accomplished, Pope's line of communication would have been sundered, and the importance of success spurred Stuart to go forward, though a terrific thunderstorm drenched his troops and enveloped them with thick darkness. The downpour, too, threatened to make the streams impassable on his return.

Approaching Catlett's Station under cover of the stormy night, the Federal pickets were captured by the direction of Colonel Rosser, who commanded the advance, and his bold horsemen were soon in the midst of the enemy's encampments.

Pope's headquarters were near by, and they were guided to the spot by a captured negro. Pope himself was away, but many of his official household were there, and most of them with much valuable plunder were taken possession of. Among the captured articles was Pope's despatch book, revealing his plans and describing his embarrassments.

The destruction of the railroad bridge, the main object of the expedition, was not accomplished on account of the darkness and the heavy rain, but Stuart returned with much plunder and 300 prisoners.

Pope, now aided by the high waters, massing his army between Waterloo Bridge and Warrenton, seemed to defy his foes. But while Longstreet and Hill engaged his attention in front, Jackson began the celebrated flank movement which put him in Pope's rear.

Crossing the Rappahannock four miles above Hensons Mills on the 25th he reached Salem in the night. Next day, 26th, he passed through Thoroughfare Gap and, going through Gainesville, reached Bristoe Station on the railroad.

Stuart with his command was ordered to take part in Jackson's movement.

Early on the morning of the 26th he crossed the Rappahannock at Hensons Mills, and at Gainesville joined Jackson's column. To him and his command was entrusted the duty of guarding the two flanks. The main portion was kept on Jackson's right towards the enemy.

After crossing Broad Run, a few miles above Bristoe Station, the cavalry fronted towards the enemy, still in the direction of the Rappahannock, and covered Jackson's movement on the railroad bridge. When near it the Second Virginia, under Colonel Munford, made a bold dash and captured the station and most of the occupants.

From this point, by order of Jackson, Stuart, with the portion of Robertson's brigade not on outpost duty, proceeded to Manassas.

In the meantime, soon after the arrival of the Confederates at Bristoe Station, a train of cars passed, and escaping capture gave the alarm at all points north. The Federals, therefore, were fully prepared to give the Confederates a warm reception at Manassas, where there were immense quantities of army stores which were supposed to be securely stacked away. Jackson's tired and hungry men sorely needed these and Stuart was sent to take them,

Trimble's brigade of infantry being also ordered to support him.

The cavalry advanced until halted by the interior sentinels, and also being saluted by a fire of canister. On account of the darkness and ignorance of the ground, the cavalry waited until Trimble's command arrived, when the latter advanced and took the station.

The 27th was spent by the cavalry in chasing fugitives of the enemy's cavalry, and in capturing Pope's stragglers, that like rats leaving a sinking ship, were making their way towards a place of safety. One company—D of the Seventeenth Battalion, Robertson's brigade—near Manassas captured over 100 of them.

On the morning of the 28th the main body of Robertson's brigade rendezvoused near Sudley Church.

Jackson's forces were massed between Sudley Ford and the turnpike on Bull Run. Longstreet was not yet through Thoroughfare Gap, and the enemy was moving in between them to cut off Jackson.

On the 28th Stuart proceeded with portions of his two brigades towards Thoroughfare Gap, to establish communication with Longstreet. He reached the vicinity of Haymarket, capturing a detachment of the enemy on his way, but went no further, as Haymarket was occupied by a large force of the enemy, and he could see "Longstreet struggling through the gorge."[3] He sent a trusty messenger to Longstreet, and retired towards evening to rejoin Jackson, who was already engaged with the enemy.

The next morning, the 29th, he again set out intending. if possible, to reach Longstreet. Soon after leaving the

[3]From Stuart's Report.

Sudley Road, his command was fired into from woods on the roadside. It was now discovered that a Federal force was between Jackson and his baggage train.

Major Patrick,[1] commanding the Seventeenth Battalion (afterwards a part of the Eleventh Virginia Cavalry), was sent to take care of the baggage. Infantry also was sent to assist him, and some artillery.

Major Patrick was soon attacked by the enemy, but with a spirited charge drove them off. The loss to the Confederates was great, for in the charge Major Patrick fell mortally wounded. Says Stuart, "The sacrifice was noble, but the loss to us irreparable."

In the meantime Stuart, proceeding on his way, met the head of Longstreet's column between Haymarket and Gainesville, and informed Longstreet of Jackson's position. Here he took position with his command on Longstreet's right, and advanced directly upon Manassas, while Longstreet pressed down the turnpike to move into position on Jackson's right.

General Robertson with his brigade had the advance, and soon reported the enemy in front.

Rosser with the Fifth was soon engaged with the enemy on the left of the road, and Robertson on the right met the enemy moving towards Sudley. This was a critical

---

[1]Maj. Wm. Patrick, of the Seventeenth Battalion of Virginia Cavalry, was born near Waynesboro, Augusta County, Virginia, December 22, 1822. Was captain of the Augusta Troop when the State of Virginia seceded from the Union, and on that day started for Harper's Ferry.

This troop was then made Company E, of the First Virginia Cavalry, under Col. J. E. B. Stuart.

Captain Patrick was commissioned major in the summer of 1862, and assigned to command of the Seventeenth Battalion of Virginia Cavalry, which he commanded with ability until August 29, 1862, on

moment, for an army corps of Federals was in motion to strike Longstreet's flank.

In order to arrest the Federals, or at least to retard them, Stuart resorted to a ruse, and ordered a number of his men to drag brush along the road for some distance, that the clouds of dust rising, might create the impression upon the Federal commander, that Longstreet with large bodies of infantry was coming to his aid.

In the meantime three brigades of infantry were sent to reinforce Stuart, and the enemy soon retired in the direction of Manassas.

During the day Jackson had been fighting against greatly superior numbers, but succeeded in holding his ground until Longstreet arrived and took part in the battle, when the enemy was repulsed at all points.

Next morning, the 30th, Stuart's cavalry moved to the front and seized an important point of observation, from which the Federals could be seen massing their troops against Jackson's corps.

Intelligence of this was sent to Lee. About three P. M., after the Federals were repulsed, our whole right and left advanced. Robertson's brigade and the Fifth Virginia pushed forward on the extreme right.

---

which day he fell mortally wounded near Sudley Church. It was in the movement of Stonewall Jackson against Pope, known as the second Manassas campaign.

A Federal force had intervened between Jackson's main body and his baggage train. Major Patrick with his battalion, assisted by some infantry and artillery, was sent to protect the train. He was soon attacked by the Federals, but in a spirited charge, in which he drove back the enemy, he fell mortally wounded, dying on the 2nd of September.

Four batteries—Stribbling's, Rogers', Eshleman's, and Richardson's—moved along with the cavalry under the command of Col. T. L. Rosser. Soon they had an enfilading fire upon the enemy's lines which told with fearful effect.

In the meantime Robertson's brigade had reached the Lewis house on the ridge overlooking Bull Run. The Second Virginia, under Colonel Munford, was in front. A small body of Federal cavalry was seen.

Lieut.-Col. J. W. Watts of the Second, with one squadron charged and routed it, but before he had gone far discovered Buford's brigade of cavalry drawn up. The rest of the Second now coming up, the whole regiment was soon engaged with the enemy, meeting their charge with a countercharge.

Here a terrible hand-to-hand fight ensued, and the Federals with greatly superior numbers began to force back the Confederates, when the Seventh, under Capt. S. B. Myers; the Twelfth, under Col. A. W. Harman, and the Sixth, under Colonel Flournoy, coming up to the rescue, the Federals were soon forced from the field, and the Seventh and Twelfth continued the pursuit until the enemy were driven beyond the turnpike at Stone Bridge.

Says Stuart in his report, "Nothing could have equaled the splendor with which Robertson's regiments swept down upon a force greatly outnumbering them."

In this fight Colonel Brodhead of the First Michigan was mortally wounded by Lieut. Lewis Harman, adjutant of Twelfth Cavalry.

Three hundred prisoners with many horses, arms, and equipments were captured The loss in Robertson's brigade was five killed and forty wounded.

Pope was now in full retreat, and Jackson early the following morning, leaving Longstreet to bury the dead, followed in pursuit.

Stuart, with Fitz Lee and Robertson's brigades, preceded Jackson, harassing the enemy's rear.

Pope, falling back behind the defenses at Washington, was now let alone, and Lee turned the head of his column towards Maryland.

While Lee was crossing the Potomac, the Seventh and Twelfth regiments of Robertson's brigade, with the guns of Chew's Battery, were ordered to make a demonstration against the enemy and hold him in check.

The Federal pickets were encountered near Vienna, and resisting were driven in, suffering a loss of three killed. Quite a brisk skirmish now began between the opposing forces, which lasted until sundown, when Robertson's brigade withdrew.

On September 4th the brigade lost its commander. Genl. B. H. Robertson was ordered to the Department of North Carolina. "Where," said the general order, "his services are indispensably necessary for the organization and instruction of cavalry troops of North Carolina."

From this time until the latter part of October the brigade was commanded by Colonel Munford.

The command of Colonel Munford consisted of the Twelfth, now reduced to 120 men; the Second, numbering 200, and the Seventh Virginia Cavalry, under Major Myers.

The Seventeenth Battalion had been ordered on detached service, while the Sixth had been ordered to stay behind to collect arms and guard the captured property on the field of Manassas.

On the morning of September 8th Munford was ordered to Poolesville by Stuart, with instructions to expel the enemy from that place. His advance guard had hardly entered the town, when three regiments of Federals with four pieces of artillery appeared upon the scene, and driving out Munford's pickets pressed towards his main body and charged his most forward gun.

The Federals also charged the rifle piece supported by the Twelfth, when this regiment, gallantly led by Colonel Harman, pressed forward and drove them off, inflicting considerable damage, and suffering a loss of eight men killed and wounded.

Munford, however, seems to have been finally worsted in the fight, and fell back to the crossroads, where he could guard the approaches to Sugar Loaf Mountain. This point he held for three days, skirmishing with the enemy.

On the 11th, upon the advance of a Federal division under General Slocum, Munford retired to a point within three miles of Frederick City on the Buckeystown Road.

The advance now of McClellan's army forced back the Confederate line of cavalry pickets. Munford fell back to Burkittsville pursued all the way by Federal cavalry, who were intent upon capturing the trains guarded by him. The enemy were, however, kept away from these, though not without constant skirmishing.

The train having safely passed over Crampton's Gap, Munford there halted to dispute the Federal advance, placing three pieces of artillery in position. Having received orders from General Stuart to hold the Gap at all hazards, on the morning of the 14th, reinforced by two small infantry regiments, Munford posted his small force so as to make the best defense.

The infantry took position behind a stone wall at the base of the mountain, Chew's Battery and a section of the Portsmouth Battery on the mountainside. The cavalry, consisting of the Second and Twelfth Virginia, were dismounted and placed on the right and left flanks.

In a short time the enemy appeared and boldly attacked, hurling upon the position brigade after brigade of infantry until the whole of Slocum's division, assisted by a brigade of Heintzelman's, were engaged in the assault.

In the meantime two regiments of Mahone's brigade reinforced the Confederates, and the battle waxed hot and bloody.

For full three hours this little force of Confederates held the Gap against overwhelming numbers. Then General Cobb arrived with two more regiments to reinforce Munford and to assume command.

The ammunition of the Confederates, who had been so long engaged, was exhausted. Very soon the Federals pressing forward entered the Gap and drove the Confederates over the mountain.

The Federal loss in killed and wounded was over 700, while that of the Confederates was comparatively small; although on the retreat over the mountain many prisoners were captured. For after once the line of defense was abandoned the pursuit was hot and the retreat disorderly.

Colonel Munford, in his report to General Jackson of the operations of the brigade while under his command, says: "The cavalry fought here (at Crampton's Gap) with pistols against rifles. Captain Chew, as true as steel and ever

ready, deserves to be mentioned. Col. O. R. Funsten is a
noble man, and General Jones' brigade is second to none I
have ever yet seen in point of mettle."

In a private letter since the war, General Munford writes:
"We were ordered from Poolesville, Maryland, to Crampton's Gap, and were closely followed by Slocum's division
and Franklin's corps, 30,000 strong. Jackson had been sent
to capture Harper's Ferry. Chew's Battery was left with
me with a part of the brigade to hold that Gap. General
Stuart with Hampton's command went southward along the
mountain to co-operate with McLaws, whose division held
the Maryland heights. Genl. Howell Cobb of Georgia was
to support my command. At that time we were cavalry
with very few arms but sabres and pistols, and it was simply
absurd to expect cavalry to contend with infantry on a
mountainside. It was there that Chew's Battery delayed an
army several hours, supported by my command, which was
poorly supported by Cobb."[4]

The defense of Crampton's Gap for three hours, in all
human probability, not only enabled Jackson successfully to
invest Harper's Ferry and capture it with its garrison of
12,520 prisoners, 73 pieces of artillery, 13,000 small arms,
several hundred wagons, and great stores; but had Slocum
and Franklin succeeded in forcing the Gap early in the
afternoon of the 14th, they would have taken McLaws in
reverse with overwhelming numbers, and separated as he

---

[4]It is plain from General Munford's account, and he being in command, with orders to "hold the Gap at all hazards," was in best position to know—that the cavalry was at great disadvantage, and the
infantry having arrived too late to assist, it was the artillery under
Captain Chew that delayed the Federal Army three hours at Crampton's
Gap. An achievement without parallel in the annals of the war.

was from Jackson by the Potomac River, might have captured his force and raised the siege of Harper's Ferry.

The command had been given to Munford by Stuart to hold Crampton's Gap at all hazards. Had he indifferently executed that order, it is impossible to estimate how great and far-reaching a disaster might have befallen the Confederate arms.

The Seventh Regiment had on the 10th been ordered to report to General Jackson for operations against Harper's Ferry.

On the same day Jackson started from Frederick City, and on the 11th recrossed the Potomac en route to Harper's Ferry, and drove the Federals out of Martinsburg before him to swell the garrison at Harper's Ferry.

In this almost bloodless episode, which ended in the capture of the Federal garrison at Harper's Ferry, the Seventh, under Major Myers, accompanied Jackson, helping to mask the movement and otherwise furnishing aid.

The Seventeenth Battalion, under command of Maj. Thomas B. Massie, and a company of the Twelfth did not participate in the Maryland campaign until after the surrender of Harper's Ferry, September 15th, 1862.

On the 30th of September this battalion crossed the Blue Ridge at Snickers Gap, and spent several days scouting in the neighborhood of Winchester.

On the 7th of September Major Massie took his command on a reconnoissance towards Harper's Ferry, and when near Darksville met with a small force of Federals and charged and pursued them to the neighborhood of Martinsburg. In the charge many prisoners were captured, and Massie's command stringing out in pursuit, lost their proper position in the column.

On the return, when near Darksville, they were suddenly attacked by a Federal cavalry force. Forming his men as best he might in the streets of Darksville, he gave battle, and after a contest in which several of the Confederates were killed and wounded he was forced to retreat.

In this skirmish the Federals had a force of five companies of cavalry, four companies of infantry, and a section of artillery.

Colonel Voss, who was in command of the Federals, acknowledged a loss of thirteen wounded.

Shortly after this skirmish Major Massie and his command joined Jackson at Harper's Ferry, where they occupied a position on his flanks, picketing the fords of the Shenandoah and Potomac until the surrender of the place.

The immense plunder captured at Harper's Ferry would have furnished enjoyment to the victors for several days, but the pressure on Lee in Maryland left no time for a glorification.

On the 16th Jackson's whole army, with the exception of Hill's division, began to retrace their steps to the side of Lee, who was now threatened with an attack from McClellan's army.

Soon the opposing forces gathered and confronted each other near Sharpsburg in Maryland.

The brigade being posted on the right of Lee's line near the river, did not actively participate in the hard-fought battle of Sharpsburg, Antietam as it is commonly called, although engaging in several skirmishes.

Lee's army, though more than decimated by the unequal contest of the day before, still defiantly confronted a foe who, though conscious of superior numbers, did not again move to the attack.

During the night of the 18th Lee safely withdrew to the south bank of the Potomac. The cavalry was the last to cross, and Munford's command brought up the rear, making the passage in sight of the Federals and under cover of friendly guns on the south bank.

The brigade now took position on the Confederate right near Boteler's Ford. Near this ford also was stationed Lee's reserve artillery, supported by two infantry brigades, Armistead's and Lawton's.

On the evening of the 19th four regiments of Federals crossed at this point and, making a vigorous attack, drove off the Confederate infantry and captured four guns.

The disaster would have been greater had not Munford covered the retreat of the infantry and artillery with his cavalry.

Shortly after the 20th of September Lee's whole army returned and took position south of Martinsburg.

While the jaded infantry was enjoying a well-earned repose, the cavalry kept watch on the front, occasionally engaging in skirmishes with the enemy.

When the brigade under Robertson crossed the Blue Ridge to operate with Jackson in June near Richmond, Company B of the Twelfth Virginia Cavalry was left in the Valley, and the services of this company while thus detached, under command of Lieutenants Milton Rouss and George Baylor, won for it a name, which being well sustained by its subsequent conduct during the entire war, made it famous throughout the Army of Northern Virginia.

The operations of the company were chiefly in the lower Valley. Shields, Fremont, and Banks having gone east of the mountain to join Pope, the other Federals had withdrawn to points on, and near to the Baltimore and Ohio and the Winchester and Potomac railroads.

Brigadier-General White occupied Winchester with a considerable force of all arms. General Reddin was occupying Front Royal August 10th and some time prior, with a force of 800 infantry of the Third Delaware Regiment, 400 cavalry, and a battery of artillery.

Company B at that time had its camp near Harrisonburg. Lieutenant Rouss being absent on short leave, Lieut. George Baylor, next in command, with thirty men started on a scout in the Luray Valley, and made a dash into Front Royal, which for its rashness and success had few equals in the annals of the war. The account of it is best told as far as practicable in Lieutenant Baylor's own language found in his "Bull Run to Bull Run," page 45:

"On the 10th of August with thirty men I started on a scout to Luray, expecting to find a small force of the enemy in possession of the town; but on marching there found the enemy had moved east that morning, and a few stragglers were captured. The night was spent in Luray with our friends. * * * The next morning with twenty-five men I started on the road to Front Royal. We inquired along the road as to the enemy's position, but failed to elicit any further information than that it occupied Front Royal. About noon on the 11th we had reached the vicinity of that town, but had encountered no foe.

"About one-half mile south of the place, however, we came suddenly upon the enemy's cavalry picket-post, and a charge was immediately ordered. Recklessly we dashed into the town, capturing the cavalry picket reserve, and finding the town occupied by a large infantry force. Our men were soon scattered, pursuing fleeing Yankees in every direction.

"Noticing a company of infantry forming in front of the hotel, and about forty men in line, I called Henry Beall and Charley Crane to my assistance and we dashed in among them, and drawing my pistol on the officer in command, demanded a surrender. He turned to his men and ordered them to 'ground arms,' an order quickly obeyed. Securing the officer, I directed the men to march out by the Luray Road.

"Just then another officer appeared on the scene, and he too was made prisoner. General Reddin, who was in command of the force, made his escape on a cart horse. Our handful of men were soon overwhelmed with prisoners, and I was satisfied we must beat a hasty retreat.

"In looking up our boys and getting them together, I found John Terrill and Bob North in among the infantry tents, slashing holes in them with their sabres and ordering the occupants to come out.

"Our situation was critical indeed, and gathering up as many of the prisoners as could hastily be gotten together, our retreat was begun.

"We left Front Royal with about 300 prisoners, most of them infantrymen, and among them a major and two captains.

"When about a mile south of the town, the enemy's cavalry, about 300 strong, appeared in our rear. About fifteen horses had been captured from the enemy. On these prisoners were mounted, and with the residue on foot in charge of fifteen men, were started off at a rapid pace towards Luray, while with ten men I undertook to cover the retreat. The enemy was held in check for some time, but finally broke our little rear guard and succeeded in releasing the foot prisoners, but those on horseback were brought off safely.

"In a running fight of five miles, with countercharges we kept this body of cavalry sufficiently in check to permit the mounted prisoners and guards to keep at a safe distance from recapture.

"In one of the enemy's charges Private Baker of our company was captured, a countercharge was ordered and Baker was released. In this engagement George Timberlake was slightly wounded; Orderly Sergt. Seth Timberlake, known as the 'Fighting Sergeant,' had his horse killed, and my horse was wounded in the shoulder and neck, and though losing blood, bore me safely through the conflict.

"The enemy's loss was ten killed and wounded, and two officers and thirteen men prisoners. The officers were Captains Darrell and Baker of the Third Delaware Regiment."

After this event Company B rested in camp, which was still near Harrisonburg, and on August 26th started on another expedition under command of Lieut. Milton Rouss.

Leaving a sufficient picket for the post under command of a sergeant, Lieutenant Rouss with thirty men started down the Valley to observe the enemy and follow the lead of opportunity in demonstrations against him. Winchester was at that time occupied by the Federals under Brigadier-General White, with a brigade of infantry, a battery of artillery, and 290 cavalry.

The neighborhood of Winchester was the objective point of Rouss' expedition, and the point arrived at was midway between Summit Point and Wade's Depot, at each of which places the enemy had a force of eighty infantry and five cavalry. The distance between the two depots is four miles, hence in either direction Rouss' command of thirty men was only two miles from the enemy, with the garrison at Winchester directly between his present position and his camp at Harrisonburg, and a part of that garrison consisting of 290 freshly-mounted cavalry.

At four o'clock P. M. the Potomac Railroad was reached and in a few minutes the sound of the passenger engine was heard. A quick disposition was made of the force, and obstructions were at once placed on the track to bring the engine to a halt. When the train had reached within 100 yards of the obstruction the command was given to halt, but the frightened engineer took no heed of the command. A pistol fire was at once opened upon the moving train, which came to a standstill just in front of the obstruction.

The engineer was immediately taken in hand, and some of the men entering the cars made prisoners of the eight Federal soldiers on board.

The few citizens on board were permitted to proceed on foot towards Winchester. The agent of the Adams Express Company in an attempt to escape was badly wounded in the thigh.

The express car was full of wines, fruit, and other delicacies which the Confederate troopers enjoyed with fine appetites, drinking bumpers of champagne to the health of Jeff Davis, the Southern Confederacy, and to each of their sweethearts by name.

The United States mail was also secured, and about $4,000 in money that was intended for the Federal pay-master.

The engine was put under full steam and started towards Winchester, and the cars set on fire and pine laid on to facilitate the burning. The telegraph wire was cut and the line destroyed for 200 yards.

Sending back the prisoners by Lieutenant Roland with thirteen men, Rouss with Baylor and seventeen men started to capture a small cavalry force at Middleway, some six miles north, in Jefferson county. Upon arriving in sight of the pickets he charged them, capturing them, three in number, without firing a shot, and pressed on quickly into the town, where the reserve, fourteen in number, were captured before they had time to mount their horses.

Loaded down with Federal prisoners and plunder, Rouss thought it prudent to return to his encampment, in accomplishing which he camped for an hour about daylight within five miles of Winchester, having passed within three miles of that place, seeing the Federal camp-fires.

This bold enterprise caused much excitement among the Federals, and soon thereafter White hastily evacuated Winchester, leaving four thirty-two pounders, which he first spiked, and burned the carriages; and destroying 70,000 pounds of forage and 60,000 rations besides other stores, tools, etc.

Rouss soon after moved his camp down the Valley, harassing the enemy wherever practicable.

On the 6th of September the company took active part in the affair at Darksville, under Lieutenant-Colonel Massie, of which mention has already been made; he having with him Company I of the Twelfth and a squadron of the Eleventh Virginia Cavalry, at that time consisting of only six companies and known as the Seventeenth Battalion.

On the 7th Company B took position near Charles Town and remained there until the morning of the 13th, when it was attacked by four companies of the First New York Cavalry, about a mile west of the town, and after a sharp brush the enemy retired. In this encounter Lieutenant Rouss and Private Cary Selden were wounded.

This company remained on detached service in the Valley until the early part of the winter of 1863, when it was recalled to its place in the Twelfth Virginia Cavalry, the brigade at that time being under the command of Genl. William E. Jones.

For six weeks Lee's army, after the battle of Sharps-burg, remained quiet, recruiting its strength.

In the meantime Stuart engaged in one of those bold raids that added so much to his fame.

On the 10th of October Stuart with a command consisting of about 1,800 men, each of his brigades furnishing 600, crossed the Potomac a little above McCoy's Ford. By eight o'clock in the morning the Federals were aware of this movement, but before any resistance could be organized the bold Confederates swept northward, spreading consternation among the thrifty farmers of Pennsylvania.

On either flank squadrons scoured the country for fresh horses, and in spite of McClellan's army along the Potomac, the chattels of the good citizens of Pennsylvania were appro-priated for the benefit of the Confederacy.

The first day's march brought the column to Chambers-burg, where the night was passed in the midst of a drizzling rain.

The news of the raid had been telegraphed from point to point, and in every direction preparations were made by the Federals to intercept Stuart on his return.

It had proved easy enough to enter the enemy's country. The more difficult task of getting out of it now confronted him. Stuart, however, was equal to the emergency. He determined that the "longest way around was the shortest way home"; so contrary to all expectations he turned his face eastward instead of westward, proceeding nearly to Gettysburg. At Cashtown he turned southward; as soon as he crossed the Maryland line, the flankers gathering horses were called in and the column closed up.

By rapid marching he disappointed all the expectations of the foe. Avoiding his enemy at one point, at another he brushed him aside, reaching Emmitsburg about sundown on the 11th.

There were yet forty-five miles to the Potomac. All night long his command moved at a trot, the artillery keeping up by means of fresh horses, ever ready. By daylight on the Twelfth he entered Hyattstown, twelve miles yet from a place of safety.

When near Poolesville the Federal cavalry under General Pleasonton were seen, when a sudden charge upon them cleared the road, and marching towards White's Ford he there crossed safely with all his command. The detachment from Munford's command on this raid was under Col. W. E. Jones. It was the second to cross at White's Ford.

The results of this raid were manifold. Twelve hundred horses were taken from the farmers of Pennsylvania, not to speak of other spoils. Perhaps the most valuable result was that it called into activity many thousands of the Federals, and used up their cavalry in their attempts to find and intercept Stuart.

Like all of Stuart's raids, however, it taught the Federals the advantage of a well-organized and numerous cavalry force, and stimulated them to increase and better equip this arm of the service.

While Lee was resting his men, collecting stragglers, and drilling new levies in the lower Valley, the Federals were similarly engaged, and with much greater resources to draw from.

The authorities at Washington wanted McClellan to move nearer to Washington, across the Potomac, fearing, as they always did, a surprise by way of Manassas.

McClellan, believing that if he crossed below Harper's Ferry, Lee would again invade Maryland, at first hesitated, but afterwards yielded, having left the important points along the Potomac heavily garrisoned.

On the 26th of October the Federals began crossing the Potomac in force at Berlin.

On the 29th the Second and Fifth corps crossed at Harper's Ferry, and the whole Federal Army, by November the 2nd, were moving on both sides of the Blue Ridge southward, to get between Lee and Richmond. Before this, however, Harper's Ferry had been occupied by a considerable force of Federals, and their advance was watched, and frequently attacked by portions of our cavalry.

On the 16th of October, and for a short time before, Munford's command was occupied in picketing from Walper's Crossroads, on the Baltimore and Ohio Railroad, to Berry's Ferry.

The Twelfth Virginia Cavalry, under the command of Lieutenant-Colonel Burks, was on picket at Charles Town, and with them Capt. B. H. Smith, Third Company Richmond Howitzers, and Lieut. J. W. Carter of Chew's Battery.

Early in the morning of the 16th a division of Federal infantry and artillery drove in our pickets, and for four hours were held in check by the Confederate force mentioned.

Our loss was two killed and five or six wounded; that of the enemy much greater.

For gallantry in this engagement Colonel Munford commends Lieutenant Carter, Colonel Burks, Captain Smith, and Lieut. L. F. Jones.

The latter part of October, the Confederate Army, in response to McClellan's southern movement, began to leave the Valley and set out for Culpeper Court House.

Munford's brigade was detached from Stuart's division and ordered to bring up Jackson's rear.

The Federals having now made the Rappahannock their line and threatening to advance on Richmond, Lee kept Jackson in the Valley to menace their flank if they moved further south.

While matters were in this condition, on November the 8th, Col. W. E. Jones was made brigadier and assigned to the command of the brigade, now called the Second Brigade.

On November the 10th, 1862, it was ordered from army headquarters that Jones' (the Second Brigade) was to consist of the Seventh, Twelfth and Sixth regiments, the Seventeenth Battalion, and White's cavalry.

In a skirmish at Philamount, on the 9th of November, four men of White's Battalion—Mortimer W. Palmer, R. Henry Simpson, David J. Lee, and Robert A. Ritacor—charged and drove out of the town fifty Federals, capturing two negroes and three wagons from their train.

On the evening of November 9th, Geary with 2,500 infantry marched from Bolivar Heights, and driving the Confederate picket from Halltown, pursued them beyond Rippon. The picket was a portion of the Twelfth Virginia.

On the 28th of October White's cavalry was organized into a battalion, and its captain, E. V. White, was promoted to major.

Up to this time this command, consisting of only one company, had been engaged in detached service chiefly, in the counties of Loudon, Va., and Montgomery, Md., and had won quite a reputation for dash and efficiency under its gallant leader.

At this time Major White was recovering from a wound he had received. The battalion was stationed in Snickers Gap. A Federal force, the Eighth New York, under Colonel Davis, attempted to force its way through the Gap, but was driven back.

On November 3rd another attempt was made upon the Gap with a heavy force of cavalry, infantry, and artillery, which was again repulsed with the assistance of Hill's infantry. At this time the main portion of Lee's army was still between Winchester and Martinsburg.

In this engagement White's men were forced through the gap across Castleman's Ferry, the Federals advancing to the river bank.

In the meantime, a battery belonging to A. P. Hill's corps, came to the rescue, and delivering a heavy fire upon the Federals massed upon the east bank, killed a great many and drove them in confusion up the mountain.

The Federal force in this engagement, consisted of forty-six cavalry, 219 of the Fourteenth Massachusetts Infantry, and a part of two other regiments of regulars. Their loss is not exactly reported, but the Fourteenth Infantry lost thirty killed and wounded. Among the rest five officers.

A few days after this, White went through the Gap and harassing the rear of the Federal column, captured twenty wagons and 102 prisoners. This was followed by other raiding expeditions of White, on the trains and camps of the

Federals now moving southward towards Fredericksburg, in which more wagons and provisions were captured.

On the 28th of November, however, the Federals had their revenge. General Stahl with a considerable force of cavalry crossed the Shenandoah at Castleman's Ferry, and attacked the small company on picket there belonging to White's command. White's camp of sick and dismounted men was but two miles further from the river, the rest of his companies being stationed elsewhere. The Federals soon drove the company on picket towards Berryville and pressed them vigorously.

White, who was sick at a house near the road, joined the rear of his men before the camp was reached, and was soon wounded in the thigh. All attempts to rally the men at the camp proved fruitless, and the retreat was continued beyond Berryville, where the enemy was met by a portion of the Twelfth Cavalry under Major Massie.

A vigorous charge by the Twelfth gave a serious check, but the victorious Federals advanced on the turnpike as far as the Opequon.

Colonel Burks, who commanded the Twelfth, reports that Company F, under Lieutenant Randolph, turned out first, and was followed by Capt. E. Sipe, commanding Company H; Lieutenants Harman and Myers, commanding Companies K and C—in all about 100 men.

The Confederate loss was twenty-seven captured, four wounded and two wagons captured. The Federals acknowledge a loss of fifteen killed and wounded, but they claim to have captured forty Confederates and killed and wounded fifty.

On the 12th of November Maj. E. V. White was sent on a scout with his battalion east of the Blue Ridge, and was so successful as to win praise from both Stuart and Lee for his boldness and discretion.

Crossing at Snickers Gap he went to Hillsboro in Loudon county and captured a picket of twelve infantrymen. Pushing on towards Leesburg he came up with some Federal cavalry, which he charged and routed, capturing two and wounding three.

On the morning of the 14th he came upon the company of Loudoun Guerrillas commanded by Capt. Means. These he charged and drove, pursuing them for five miles, killing one, a lieutenant, and capturing two.

Hearing that there was a company of Federals at Poolesville, he made for that point with ninety-three men in his command. Here he learned that one-half of the Federal force was out of town and that the remainder was quartered in the town hall.

Dividing his forces he advanced, attacking the hall from different directions. The garrison fired upon them, killing one man; but White's men poured in upon them such a well-directed fire, killing and wounding ten, that the rest surrendered.

While marching upon Poolesville he had sent a detachment to watch the enemy at Harper's Ferry, which was lucky enough to capture and parole a picket of twenty-six, thus swelling the number of Federals captured on this raid to seventy-seven.

The brigade during the month of December shifted its headquarters from point to point, according to the availability of forage, but gradually moved southward until about Christmas, when it camped at New Market.

General Jones, when not on the march, was an indefatigable organizer. While constantly sending out detached companies to deliver attacks at distant points, he kept the rest of the command constantly drilling and subjected to a rigid discipline, which greatly increased its efficiency.

On the 1st of December, Company D of the Seventeenth Battalion, under Capt. E. H. McDonald, was sent on a reconnoissance to Moorefield. The primary object being to recruit the company in men and horses, most of the men having homes in Hampshire county.

Upon reaching Moorefield, and being informed that no enemy was in the neighborhood, the company scattered through the town, and while so disorganized was surprised by a force of 200 Federal cavalry, who captured Captain McDonald and several of his men.

On December the 11th, a portion of the Seventh Virginia, while on picket near Martinsburg, was attacked by a superior Federal force and driven to Darksville, where being reinforced, it in turn drove back the Federals. The latter claimed to have captured thirteen prisoners in this encounter.

December 29th, 1862, Genl. W. E. Jones was assigned, by order of General Lee, during the absence of Jackson from the Valley, to the command of the Valley District and of all the troops operating in that region not embraced in the Department of West Virginia.

Of the same date as above was a letter to Colonel Davidson at Staunton from Lee, telling him that he had ordered General Jones to gather all the Valley troops and drive the enemy beyond the Potomac.

This was done in consequence of information stating that Milroy, stationed at Petersburg, was heavily oppressing the people of Mineral county.

Also a letter to Jones of same date, directing him to drive the enemy out of the valley of the South Branch.

About the 24th of December, 1862, Jones, then stationed at New Market, hearing that Cluseret had entered the Valley at Strasburg and was moving on Winchester, followed him with one regiment and a battery to Kernstown, where a light skirmish occurred, and Jones withdrew to New Market.

On the 2nd of January, 1863, Jones, commanding a force composed of his brigade and Chew's Battery, together with the First Battalion, Maryland Cavalry; First Battalion, Maryland Infantry, and the Maryland Battery, marched on Moorefield and reached there on the morning of the 3rd, having marched rapidly in order to surprise and overcome the Federal force at Moorefield before it could be aided by the Federal force at Petersburg.

Having selected an inferior position for his artillery, the shells from his battery fell short, while those of the enemy reached him.

In the meantime the Federals from Petersburg came within striking distance and opened upon his rear. The batteries of this force also opened on him with effect, while his shots again failed to reach them.

The two wings of his command could not unite, but fortunately, those of the enemy were in a like condition.

Fearing that the enemy would receive reinforcements from New Creek, he determined to withdraw, which he did after holding his position two hours.

A picket of twenty Federals were captured near Moorefield in the morning by a part of the Seventh under Lieutenant Vandiver, and the Sixth and the Seventh, under Colonel Dulany, captured forty-six more at Petersburg.

Late at night the two wings of Jones' command united about ten miles above Moorefield. The following morning an attack was determined upon, but the enemy being reinforced Jones withdrew, having met with only partial success.

He had captured in all ninety-nine prisoners, having no loss but two men wounded.

In his report the following are spoken of with praise: Colonel Dulany, Lieut. C. H. Vandiver, Privates J. W. Kuykendall, and J. S. Hutton, of the Seventh Virginia Cavalry.

The attack upon Moorefield in midwinter though apparently fruitless, yet had the effect of alarming the Federals, who thought it the advance of a strong movement down the Valley upon Harper's Ferry. In consequence, Washburn on the 8th was ordered to fall back from Moorefield to Romney, twenty miles further north.

Four days later General Milroy, who was at Winchester, telegraphed for help against a foe that his own imagination had conjured up, and on the 17th he again telegraphed that Jones with 2,700 infantry was between him and Strasburg, but adds, "I have no fears for this place," and ends in asking for Washburn's two regiments, saying, "It is cruel to keep me here so helpless."

After his return from Moorefield General Jones was ordered by General Lee to organize a force in the Valley, including his own, Colonel Davidson's at Staunton, and Imboden's, and endeavor to curtail the operations of the enemy if he could not force him to retire. At this time there was a great outcry for this from the people of the lower Valley, on account of Milroy's assessments for the support of his army and of his brutal treatment of the non-combatants. Jones was, however, much restricted in his movements by the scarcity of forage, and midwinter having now arrived, he busied himself preparing for the spring campaign, drilling his men and recruiting his forces. He was always, however, wide-awake and did not fail to strike a blow when an opportunity presented itself.

Early in February the Thirty-fifth Battalion, under command of Lieut.-Col. E. V. White, was detached by General Jackson and sent to arrest certain parties living in Loudoun county, Virginia.

Milroy still remained at Winchester, strengthening his position and acting the petty tyrant towards the defenseless citizens of that section. He seemed to think that he had missionary as well as military duties to perform. He resorted to every kind of espionage to ascertain the opinion of the women, as well as the male non-combatants, who were at his mercy; and tried by threats and ill treatment of the staunchest Confederates to make proselytes to his political creed. This disgraceful conduct only served to intensify the loyalty of the people to the Southern cause.

General Jones, while in camp at New Market, devoted his time to fully organizing his command and perfecting them by daily drill in military exercises.

In January the Seventeenth Battalion, increased by the addition of new companies, was organized into a regiment and was thenceforward the Eleventh Regiment, of which

Major Funsten, promoted to a lieutenant-colonelcy, was put in command.

He entered upon the work of regimental organization with great zeal, and in a short time the new regiment was strong in numbers and full of an *esprit du corps,* the effect of which was seen at the first opportunity presented for its display.

On the morning of February 26th an event occurred which broke the monotony of winter quarters. It was occasioned by the adventurous enterprise of Capt. F. A. Bond of Brown's Battalion of Maryland Cavalry on picket near Strasburg.

Having learned that the Federal picket near Kernstown might be captured, without orders from General Jones, commanding in the Valley, he attacked the picket and capturing them, made off with his prisoners.

Apparently enraged at his audacity, about 500 Federal cavalry of the First New York and Thirteenth Pennsylvania regiments followed him in hot pursuit. From Kernstown to Strasburg, over thirteen miles of frozen turnpike, went pursuer and pursued.

When the head of the flying column reached the pickets of General Jones they too joined in the flight to some distance beyond Woodstock, still pursued by the wrathful Federals. Here they left the turnpike, and while some of the Federals pursued the flying pickets up the Back Road, which runs parallel with the turnpike, others attempted the capture of the wagon trains then in quest of forage in the neighborhood of Woodstock. They were, however, beaten off by Col. J. Herbert with a portion of the Maryland infantry encamped near by.

Hardly had they returned to the turnpike when there came in view the head of the Confederate column coming to punish in turn the Federal audacity. These troops had been ordered forward from New Market by General Jones at the first news of the Federal dash, and consisted of a portion of the Eleventh, under Colonel Funsten, numbering about 120 men. At the head of the column rode Funsten and Jones.

Says Colonel Funsten in his report to General Jones: "Led by you we dashed past their rear guard, who occupied an eminence near the road, and charged the rear of the column. So sudden and impetuous was the attack that every attempt, of which there were several, made by their officers to form a line and rally, was unavailing.

"We pressed them hotly, using both sabre and revolver with good effect, to Cedar Creek bridge, a distance of about twelve miles, where a part of them made a stand. I halted the front of the column preparatory to renewing the charge, my command being greatly reduced by the capture and guarding of prisoners, of whom the number already taken was greater than that with which I made the attack. The casualties in my regiment were two killed and two wounded. It is always a delicate point to discriminate among those who have done their duty faithfully, but I cannot forbear to mention Captains W. H. Harness, E. H. McDonald, and F. A. Dangerfield."

Not far in the rear of the Eleventh in this mad ride for vengeance thundered the old Seventh. After a hurried march of nineteen miles they came up with the Eleventh at Strasburg, Colonel Dulany in command, and having with him about 220 men.

Says Dulany in his report: "When we reached the high ground beyond Strasburg, we found the enemy had returned and again formed about 300 yards south of Cedar Creek. As we came in sight of each other they seemed to advance slowly towards us, but when we got within 200 yards, our sabres drawn, they wheeled and went at full speed towards the bridge, crossed and again formed to receive us. As only two men could cross the bridge abreast, they could easily have prevented our crossing with their long-range guns, since their position was very strong and higher than the bridge. Changing the direction of our column, we crossed the creek at the ford, some 200 yards below the bridge.

"As soon as a portion of my command had crossed, the enemy broke, not waiting for us to close with them."

The retreat now became a race, the best mounted Confederates taking the lead. He continues: "As we came up with the rear not a man that I saw offered to surrender until driven back by the sabres of our men, or shot. Some, finding we were overtaking them, slipped from their horses and sought refuge in the houses along the road; and many had thrown their pistols away when captured."

After capturing about seventy prisoners, many of them wounded, the Seventh halted about a mile and a half beyond Middletown, after a race of twenty-six miles.

General Jones in his report to Lee says that his men captured 200 prisoners, killing and wounding many more. Some of these were captured by Brown's Battalion which, close behind the Seventh, participated in the chase. For gallantry and wise action on this occasion, General Jones warmly recommended Colonel Funsten to Lee for the vacant colonelcy of the Eleventh Regiment. The suggestion, approved by Lee, was, however, disregarded by the Government, and not long afterwards Col. L. L. Lomax was made colonel of the Eleventh. Being a West Point graduate and a dashing officer, he soon won the confidence of his men.

The brilliant affair down the turnpike furnished food for entertainment for many days. It had occurred in mid-winter and served to vary the monotony of camp life and the drudgery of the daily drill.

CHAPTER IV

March, 1863

Jones' expedition into western Virginia—Weak men and horses left in camp—Inclement weather and swollen streams—Dangerous crossing of the Potomac at Petersburg—Heroic assistance of citizens—Rev. Richard Davis—Fight at Greenland Gap—McNeil's Rangers co-operate with Jones—Colonel Harman enters Oakland, destroys railroad bridge—Cranberry Summit—Mountaineers unfriendly and bushwhack our column—Capture of Morgantown—Bridgeport and Fairmont—Destruction of oil wells—A river on fire—Return to the Valley—Results of expedition—Cross the Blue Ridge to join "Jeb" Stuart—A grand review—Battle of Brandy Station.

The soldiers of the brigade were anxious for another opportunity to enjoy the frolic of a warlike chase, not dreaming that their commander was hatching a scheme that would give them their fill of marching and fighting.

This was the famous West Virginia expedition. For more than a month before it took place, General Jones was busy studying all the known ways of destroying iron bridges, tunnels, and trestling.

He was evolving a plan to do such destruction to the Baltimore and Ohio Railroad, exposed as it was on account of its tunnels, bridges, and trestling to damage from hostile parties, that for six months at least no troops might pass over it.

During the month of March he made many trips to Staunton, with the design of perfecting his preparations for the expedition.

He had communicated his plans to General Lee and gotten his full consent and approval. Forage was gathered from all quarters to get his horses in condition for the long and tedious march. Frequent inspections were held and the arms as well as horses carefully looked after.

The soldiers knew instinctively that something serious was impending, but what it really was they were far from surmising.

Having arranged with Genl. J. D. Imboden and his command, for a concert of action against the Baltimore and Ohio Railroad, Jones determined to move on the 21st of March.

On the day previous orders were issued to the regimental commanders to have issued eight days' rations and forty rounds of ammunition, and on the 21st to meet him at Brock's Gap.

The men and horses unfit for a hard campaign were left behind under Colonel Funsten, near Harrisonburg, while Maj. S. B. Myers[1] of the Seventh, an experienced and efficient outpost commander, was stationed near Strasburg with several well-mounted companies, one from each regiment of the brigade.

---

[1]Maj. Samuel B. Myers, of the Seventh Virginia Cavalry, a native of Pennsylvania, but having become thoroughly identified with all that pertained to the home of his adoption, few men of Southern birth and traditions made greater sacrifices for the cause of the South than he.

He was the owner and operator of Columbia Furnace in Shenandoah County, Va. Upon the withdrawal of Virginia from the Union, he at once raised a company of cavalry among the sturdy farmers and hearty mountaineers of the Shenandoah region, which was one of the first enlisted in the regiment of Col. Angus McDonald, and was known as Company C of the famous Seventh regiment, from which developed the Ashby Cavalry and Laurel Brigade. He later was promoted to major of the regiment, and after the wounding of Colonel Dulany, and the death of Lieut.-Col. Thos. Marshall he was usually in command of the regiment.

There was no braver, more sagacious nor enterprising officer in the service than Major Myers. He was severely wounded at Orange Court

On the 21st the column started. Besides his own brigade General Jones took with him Wicher's Battalion of mounted riflemen, Brown's Battalion of cavalry, and the Maryland Battalion of infantry under Colonel Herbert, and what artillery he had.

At the outset the weather was inclement, and the continual rains made the roads so muddy that the column was forced to move slowly.

Before the South Branch of the Potomac was reached it was swollen by the downpour, and all idea of crossing it at Moorefield was abandoned.

This disappointment secured the safety of the Federal force under Colonel Mulligan at Petersburg, which General Jones had hoped to intercept and capture.

The route now had to be changed, but from Moorefield the wagon train under convoy of Colonel Herbert, together with the artillery, was sent back with orders to return by way of Franklin and gather up the "surplus bacon" along the route, which order was successfully accomplished.

After making a detour from the projected route, the column, now relieved of baggage and artillery, reached Petersburg, where the river was found to be still high and

---

House and his horse was shot under him. The wonder is he was not killed in battle. He had many narrow escapes and several horses were killed under him. Among others his favorite white charger "Bill." He was stricken with a disease incident to the exposures of the war and died at his home, on the 25th of February, 1865. He was appreciated and beloved both by the soldiers of the Laurel Brigade and by the people throughout the Shenandoah Valley.

During the absence of the Brigade under General James in West Virginia, Major Myers was left in the Valley with three companies of cavalry. With these he planned and executed a successful ambuscade upon the Federals south of Strasburg, in which he killed, wounded and captured a large number.

dangerous to cross. Men who would be quick to charge a
battery if ordered, were appalled at the rushing, angry
waters. Besides the ford was exceedingly rough unless the
exact path was followed.

Men with weak horses were not forced to attempt the
ford, and a few here turned back. A number of citizens
of the neighborhood, loyal to the South, and who were
familiar with the crossing, having provided themselves with
long poles, boldly rode out into the river and took stations
at regular intervals along the ford, with their horses' heads
directly up stream. They constantly warned the troopers
to keep their horses' heads up stream, and when a horse
would start down would tap him on the neck with a pole,
and thus help to keep him in the ford.

There was no bantering nor frivolity among the men,
each one realizing the danger and the necessity of keeping
his horse in the ford. While there were only one or two
men actually drowned, there were many narrow escapes, a
notable one being that of Sergt.-Maj. James Figgat of
the Twelfth, whose horse falling, he was swept off, but
grasping the tail of a trooper's horse nearest him, was towed
across in safety.

The following is General Jones' official report of the
incident: "When but a part of the Sixth Virginia, the
leading regiment, had crossed one man and horse were
drowned and two others narrowly escaped. But for the
timely assistance of Messrs. Hattan, Cunningham, and
other citizens of Petersburg, and Private Aaron Welton,
our loss must have been serious. The bravery and hardi-
hood evinced by them on this occasion is worthy of the
highest praise. The conduct of the Rev. Mr. Davis, chap-
lain of the Sixth, was here conspicuously good. His

example, courage, and abiding faith in Providence won the admiration of all."

After leaving Petersburg the route lay through Greenland Gap. Contrary to information received, this pass was occupied by the enemy, who had constructed entrenchments around a log church. The position could have been turned, but the time consumed would have created delay enough to probably endanger the success of the general plan. Accordingly General Jones determined to take the position by assault.

Lieutenant-Colonel Marshall with a portion of the Seventh was ordered to charge the works supported by Col. R. H. Dulany with the rest of the Seventh.

The charge was gallantly made. The enemy, apprised of the attempt, were fully prepared and received the bold troopers with a well-directed volley that emptied several saddles. The Seventh, however, pressed forward and the Federals were forced to retreat into the log church and a house near by. With port-holes between the logs they could fire with a sense of security and with great accuracy against an enemy that had no artillery.

In the charge of the Seventh, Colonel Dulany was unhorsed with a severe wound in the arm, and lay within easy range of the Federal marksmen. The outlook was very unpromising, but General Jones was bent on taking the position.

Some of the Seventh had gotten past the church and were in the rear of it. The sharpshooters of the Seventh secured the woods and hillside on the left. The mounted riflemen of Lieut.-Col. V. A. Wicher's Battalion, under Captain Chapman, were dismounted and thrown to the right. With great boldness they penetrated close to the building and secured the stone works erected by the enemy. A flag was sent out demanding a surrender. Upon this being scorn-fully refused, preparations were made to storm the buildings and, if necessary, to burn or blow them up.

The dismounted men of Brown's and White's Bat-talions, under their respective leaders, advanced to the assault, while the Pioneer Corps, under Lieut. William G. Williamson, moved forward with torches and powder ready for blowing up the buildings.

In the charge White's men "crossed a rocky and rapid stream in the face of a galling fire from the enemy in the church, and an enfilading fire from a portion of those con-cealed in a building to the right of the church. They rushed bravely on until they arrived at the church, where, knocking out the chinking and firing through the holes, they soon drove the enemy from one side of the house.

"In the meantime the Pioneer Corps coming up, broke out the window, set fire to a bundle of straw and threw it in, thus firing the lower part of the building."[1]

Fortunately for the assailants, General Jones had delayed the assault until near dark. This saved the Confederates from a much heavier loss. In the charge only four of the assailing column were killed and eight or ten wounded. General Jones' entire loss was seven killed and twenty-two wounded. The enemy lost two killed and six or eight wounded and eighty prisoners. Four wagons and teams and one ambulance were captured.

The stubborn resistance of the Federals greatly enraged the Confederates, who had suffered much the greater loss. Some insisted that the prisoners should be killed, but Gen-

---

[1]Colonel White's Report.

eral Jones said: "They fought like brave men and did their duty. They shall receive honorable treatment."

The same evening a "Swamp Dragon," one of a robber gang that was justly charged with atrocious crimes, was brought before him. The captor requested that he might kill him. Said General Jones: "You should never have taken him alive, but since you have brought him to me, he shall be treated as a prisoner of war."

From Greenland Gap the column advanced towards the North Western Grade. "Upon reaching this Col. A. W. Harman was sent with the Twelfth Virginia, Brown's Battalion, and McNeil's Company of Partisan Rangers to burn the railroad bridge at Oakland, Maryland, and to march from there by way of Kingwood to Morgantown.

"A squadron of the Eleventh, under Capt. E. H. McDonald, was sent from the same point to Altamont, twelve miles east of Oakland, to burn some small bridges and then to follow and join Colonel Harman.

"The remainder of the force moved on Rowlesburg, arriving at Cheat River about two P. M., April 26th.

"Having captured the pickets of the enemy and learning that there was a garrison of only 300 men at Rowlesburg, Col. J. S. Green, commanding the Sixth Virginia, was ordered to charge the place, the Seventh, under Colonel Marshall, and the Eleventh, under Colonel Lomax, to form his support.

"Capt. O. L. Weems of the Eleventh, with eighty sharp-shooters of his regiment and a part of Wicher's Battalion, was sent across the hills from the bridge on the North Western Grade to attack the east end of the railroad bridge at Rowlesburg and to burn it at all hazards."[2]

---

[2] General Jones' Report.

The attempt on Rowlesburg failed, and General Jones deemed it best to move on, leaving the railroad bridge and trestlework unharmed.

He had now penetrated far into the enemy's country. Forage was scarce and food for his men hard to procure.

Rumors of advancing columns of the enemy from several directions reached him. The country people were unfriendly, and frequently in the mountain passes his marching column was fired into by bushwhackers.

General Imboden up to this time had failed to unite forces with him or even to communicate with him as to his location and movements.

Next day Jones moved on to Evansville, and late in the evening learned that Lieut. C. H. Vandiver and a party of eight men had captured the town of Independence and the home guard of twenty men. A force was immediately thrown into Independence and the bridge near by was effectually destroyed.

"At daylight Harman joined the brigade, bringing the first tidings of his and McDonald's success at Oakland and Altamont."[3]

Colonel Harman had moved with his usual celerity upon Oakland, capturing a company of fifty-seven Federals. After destroying the railroad bridge east of the town and the railroad and turnpike bridges over the Youghiogheny River, he moved on to Cranberry Summit, where he captured the guard of fifteen men and destroyed the railroad property.

In the meantime Captain McDonald with a squadron of the Eleventh had burned the bridges at Altamont, and following up Colonel Harman's line of march was endeavor-

[3]General Jones' Report.

ing to overtake him. Harman, however, with scrupulous care was burning all the bridges over which he crossed. Besides, his burning of bridges had roused the mountaineers, and the woods became alive with bushwhackers ready to waylay the now perplexed squadron of the Eleventh. After fording many deep streams and continuously marching, Captain McDonald succeeded in joining Harman.

April the 27th, the day of the capture of Oakland, being Sunday, and the hour about eleven o'clock A. M., the good people of the town had just turned out for church. The late Hon. William L. Wilson, sometime member of Congress from West Virginia, and Postmaster-General under President Cleveland, was a private in Company B of the Twelfth Virginia Regiment, which led the charge into the town. Wilson, than whom there was no braver nor more efficient soldier in the Southern army, and who was naturally of a jocular and cheery disposition, seeing a young man and young woman together apparently agitated at the sudden appearance of the Confederates, addressed some reassuring remarks to them.

"Don't you think the Rebels are better looking men than the Yankees?" said Wilson to the young woman.

"Not you, anyway, with that moustache the color of buttermilk!" replied the girl.

The laugh was on Wilson, who had been cultivating with some pride the then budding moustache which in after life contributed in no small degree to his pleasing and striking appearance.

The whole command reuniting on the 28th of April marched on Morgantown, and arriving there about noon crossed the suspension bridge to the west side of the Monongahela River. Here a halt was made of a few hours. At dark the column moved on Fairmont. Approaching the town from the west it was discovered that the hills commanding the road were occupied by the enemy. By turning to the right the position was flanked and the Confederates entered the town at a charge pell-mell with the flying Federals. The enemy retreated up the river by both the east and the west banks, uniting with the force of Federals stationed for a guard at the railroad bridge. The Confederates pursued vigorously, and after a brief conflict the Federals on the west bank, numbering 260, raised the white flag and surrendered.

The prisoners' arms were hardly stacked before a Federal reinforcement arrived on the scene, consisting of artillery and infantry. Their first salutation was a round volley of artillery and musketry which to many of the Confederates was the first indication of their presence.

Colonel Marshall at once moved his horses under shelter of a hill, and dismounting his men armed them with the captured muskets of the enemy.

The volleys of the Federals were now quickly returned, and "the reception of the newcomers was soon too warm for a long tarry."

On the opposite side of the river Colonel Harman, with the Twelfth and the skirmishers from the Eleventh, Brown's Battalion and White's Battalion, pushed the enemy vigorously. The Federal reinforcements on Harman's side were driven off, and he asked for reinforcements to enable him to capture the whole command. "But," says General Jones, "as the bridge was my main object, I preferred to exert my whole energy in its destruction, and to allow the troops who could do me no more harm to escape."[4]

_____
[4]Jones' Report.

Under the supervision of Lieutenant Williamson and Captain Henderson the work of destruction now began, and soon after dark the magnificent structure tumbled into the river. The bridge was of iron, three spans, each 300 feet.

In the charge on the town one piece of artillery was captured by Lieut. B. F. Conard and four men of Company A, White's Battalion. It was afterwards spiked and thrown into the river.

In this affair General Jones' loss was three wounded; that of the enemy, twelve killed and many wounded, besides 250 prisoners.

Leaving the wounded in the hands of friends, at dark the command moved on, still indulging in the hope that General Imboden would soon be found. Learning that Clarksburg was occupied by the enemy, the Monongahela was crossed and the Federal force at Bridgeport, five miles east of Clarksburg, was captured, the work being done by the Maryland cavalry under Maj. R. Brown.

As nothing better offered itself at this point, a bridge to the left of the town was destroyed and a captured train run into the stream.

The next day an early start was made towards Philippi, and along the march many horses and some cattle were picked up.

Upon reaching Philippi about noon, the led horses and cattle were sent off to Beverly, and the rest of the command moved towards Buckhannon, where there was constant expectation of falling in with Imboden's command.

On May the 2nd, a few miles from Buckhannon the first certain intelligence of him was received from one of his men on furlough, who met Jones' column in the road. From him it was learned that Imboden was at Buckhannon, at which place the two commands soon united.

A joint movement was now made upon Clarksburg. At Weston, after a rest of two days, the attempt upon Clarksburg was abandoned and the commands separated, General Imboden going southward, while General Jones went forward to destroy the Northwestern Railroad.

On the 6th of May Colonel Harman, with the Eleventh and Twelfth and Wicher's Battalion, moved on West Union, while with the rest of his command General Jones went to destroy the railroad at Cairo.

Colonel Harman found the garrison at West Union too strong to be dislodged, but feigning an attack with a part of his force, he diverted their attention, while with the remainder he succeeded in burning the bridges east and west of the town and capturing nineteen prisoners.

At Cairo General Jones gained an easy victory. The garrison of twenty-one men surrendered without firing a gun.

The fruits of the victory hardly paid for the trouble of gaining it, the cavalry, already well jaded, having marched eighty miles without unsaddling.

The command now moved on Oil Town, and the work done there made a lasting impression upon those engaged in it.

The oil wells were owned mainly by Southern men who had been driven from their homes and their property appropriated by the Federal Government or by Northern men.[5] This, it appears, was the chief reason for destroying the works. All the oil tanks, barrels, engines for pumping, engine-houses, wagons, etc., were burned.

---

[5]General Jones' Report.

"The boats filled with oil in bulk burst with a report almost equal to artillery and spread the burning fluid over the river."

Flowing over the surface of the meandering streams that led to the river the fiery wave rolled on with the current. Soon as far as the eye could reach the river was on fire, sending up dense columns of black smoke that by contrast increased the brightness of the conflagration.

General Jones had strict orders from General Lee to respect private property. He did all he could to have these orders obeyed by the troops and never overlooked a violation of them even when circumstances greatly palliated the act. It was hardly to be expected that men traveling through a hostile country, themselves and horses at times almost starved, would wait for permission from the proper authority to gratify their pressing wants. Stores were frequently plundered, although General Jones more than once punished those caught in the act; on one occasion belaboring with his sabre a soldier who had tied behind his saddle a bundle of hoop-skirts.

Two saw-mills were burned, one at Fairmont that was engaged in making gun-stocks for the Federal Government, and another at Cairo because it would have been used to saw material to repair the damages done to the railroad.

From Oil Town the command moved to Summerville, where General Imboden and his force were found, and the raiders now turned their faces homeward. The work of destruction had been done. Many cattle had been seized and nearly every trooper returned leading a captured horse.

In thirty days Jones' command had marched 700 miles, gathering by the way subsistence for man and horse. Some twenty-five or thirty of the enemy had been killed, three times that number wounded, and 700 prisoners captured.

It had burned sixteen railroad bridges and rendered useless one tunnel, thus for quite a time interrupting the use of the Baltimore and Ohio Railroad for the Federals; but what was most important, they had brought back for the use of the Confederacy 1,000 cattle and 1,200 horses.

The entire loss of the Confederates upon the raid was ten killed and forty-two wounded.

"Throughout this arduous march," says General Jones, "the men and officers have evinced a cheerful endurance worthy of tried veterans. They have shown skill in gleaning a precarious subsistence from a country desolated by two years of oppressive tyranny and brutal war that would have won the admiration of the most approved Cossack."[6]

General Lee, in his endorsement of General Jones' report, says: "The expedition under General Jones appears to have been conducted with commendable skill and vigor, and was productive of beneficial results. The injury inflicted on the enemy was serious, and he will doubtless be induced to keep troops to guard the railroad that otherwise might be employed against us. General Jones displayed sagacity and boldness in his plans and was well supported by the courage and fortitude of his officers and men."

On its return the last week in May, the brigade rested a few days in camp at Mt. Crawford, and in the first week in June crossed the Blue Ridge to join the cavalry corps of "Jeb" Stuart near Culpeper Court House.

---

[6]General Jones' Report.

On the 5th of June a grand review of all the cavalry of the Army of Northern Virginia was held in the plains between Brandy Station and Culpeper Court House.

Upon a commanding point from which could be seen the whole corps as it was marshaled for the display, Stuart watched their motions with admiring eye and waited for them to pass in review.

The soldierly pride of each body from company to brigade was stirred, and as they marched in squadron front past their commander even the horses seemed to know that they were on dress parade.

Each regiment appeared different from every other, and in turn evinced some peculiarity that evoked admiration from the lookers-on.

The Carolinians were easily distinguished. They rode with military primness and were mounted on steeds of delicately-shaped limbs with glistening eyes and full of fire and motion. At their head rode Wade Hampton, then in the full bloom of manhood and looking every inch the soldier he proved himself to be.

The Lower Virginians challenged attention by the graceful nonchalance of their riding, and the ease with which they moved along, yet having the steady front of veterans.

The Valley and Piedmont men, of which Jones' brigade was composed, were from the blue-grass section, and the strong, well-limbed horses gave to their squadrons an impression of massive and warlike strength. The riders like centaurs appeared almost one with their steeds. General Jones rode at their head, evidently proud of his command, but with disdainful air, for he hated the "pomp and circumstance of war."

Among scenes that made good riding conspicuous, and where there seemed to be some enjoyment of glory won in previous battles, not a few missed the lamented Ashby, the recollection of whose surpassing horsemanship brought back so vividly his short but glorious career.

Stuart's 8,000 horsemen first passed the grandstand at a walk, then rounding their circuit went by at a charge, while the guns of the artillery battalion on an opposite eminence lent to the scene the charms of mimic warfare.

When the "performances" were ended the men returned to camp, having gained that day much information in regard to the cavalry's strength, and were inspired with additional *esprit du corps.*

Many, however, grumbled at the useless waste of energy, especially that of the horses; and when it was announced a few days afterwards that there was to be another grand review on the 8th, the grumblers were even more numerous and outspoken. Complaints, however, ceased in a measure when it was learned that Genl. Robert E. Lee was to be present and witness the review.

On the appointed day the corps again assembled and marched in review. General Lee, always careful to husband the energies of his troops, would not allow the squadrons to charge nor the artillery to fire, and the ambitious equestrians had to content themselves with marching at a walk past the grandstand.

Lee had already begun moving his army northward to enter upon his Gettysburg campaign, and the cavalry was ordered to camp towards the Rappahannock and hold the fords of that river.

Jones' brigade had particular charge of the road that crossed at Beverly Ford. On the night of the 8th the Sixth Virginia held Jones' front, picketing Beverly Ford and camping near St. James' Church.

Nearby and somewhat in advance of them the battalion of horse artillery bivouacked; for orders had already been issued to march at an early hour the next day.

From this point the river was distant about two miles, and the road for half the distance was shut in by continuous forests until an eminence is reached that commands the country about Beverly Ford.

Jones' men lay down that night little dreaming that there would be fought on the morrow the greatest cavalry battle of the Civil War, or indeed of modern times, on the very ground where they had passed in the harmless review. There were some, however, who thought the Yankees would soon come over the river to inquire the meaning of all the reviews reported by their scouts.

In the meantime General Pleasonton, commanding the Federal cavalry, had determined upon making a reconnoissance in force across the Rappahannock, in order to press in Lee's outposts and unmask the position and movements of the main army. So, on the 8th of June, while the Confederates were engaged in their pageantry, the Federals were concentrating for an advance next day over the fords of the Rappahannock in the direction of Culpeper Court House.

Pleasonton's force consisted of three divisions of cavalry and two of infantry, with one reserve cavalry brigade in addition. One column, including the first cavalry division, the reserve cavalry brigade and one brigade of infantry, all

under the command of Genl. John Buford, crossed at
Beverly Ford. The remainder of the force under General
Gregg was sent across by Kelly's Ford, about four miles
below the railroad bridge, Pleasonton accompanying the
column under Buford.

As no fires were left in the Federal bivouac on the night
of the 8th, the Confederates on the south bank of the Rappahannock remained in profound ignorance of the designs
of the enemy. The rattle of small arms at the ford in the
early dawn conveyed the first information of the hostile
movement.

At the head of the advancing Federal column was the
Eighth New York Cavalry under the command of Col. B. F.
Davis. It was met at the ford by Company A of the Sixth
Virginia, under Captain Gibson, and gallantly resisted.
Yielding to numbers the company gradually fell back, being
favored in their retreat by ditches in the low grounds on
either side of the road, which, by preventing an attack
towards their flank and rear, confined the assault to the
limits of the narrow road.

In the meantime the Sixth Regiment was aroused. The
call to arms was quickly responded to, and in a short time
Maj. C. E. Flournoy, hastily getting together about 150
men, came rapidly to the rescue. Charging down the road
he struck with vigor the head of the Federal column and
forced it back for a short distance.

The fight was at close quarters, and for a short time was
fierce and bloody. In a few minutes the Sixth sustained a
loss of thirty men, that of the enemy being probably less.

Yielding to superior numbers, Major Flournoy slowly fell back, the enemy being loath to pursue, as appears from the following incident:

"Lieut. Owen Allen of Company D, who was in the charge above mentioned, was riding in the rear of Flournoy's retreating column. Seeing a Federal Officer in the road some seventy-five yards in front of his column, which was halted, Allen advanced upon him with his horse at a canter.

"The officer's attention was given to his own men, to whom he was waiving his sword as if to order them forward. Remembering that he had but one shot in his pistol, Allen reserved fire until within swords length of his foe. Perceiving his danger, Colonel Davis turned upon Allen with a cut of his sabre, which Allen avoided by throwing himself on the side of his horse, and at the same moment fired and Colonel Davis fell. He met a soldier's fate, and at the hands of one as brave and daring as himself.

"Sergeant Stone of Company H, Sixth Regiment, and Private G. Larue of Company D now came forward to the assistance of Lieutenant Allen. Others of the enemy advanced at the same moment, when Sergeant Stone was killed almost instantly, and Allen and Larue, finding themselves alone in the presence of a large force, made a hasty retreat to their own lines."[7]

In the meantime the Seventh, under Lieut.-Col. Thomas Marshall, had already reached the field and struck the enemy on the left of the Sixth.

General Jones was with them and had brought the brigade off in such a hurry that many of the men rode bareback into the fight.

Indeed there was no time for dallying. Not far from the enemy, and far in advance of any support, was the battalion

[7]McClellan's "Campaigns of Stuart," page 265.

of horse artillery, which the bold dash of the Confederates alone saved from capture.

As the Seventh approached the enemy on the left of the Sixth, which was charging down the road, it came under the fire of the enemy's sharpshooters protected by woods. Continuing to advance it dispersed the sharpshooters, and penetrating the forest some distance encountered a large body of Federals.

After a brief encounter, in which two men of the Seventh were killed, Marshall was ordered to fall back. Retiring slowly, he, with dismounted men, retarded the Federal advance.

Two guns of Hart's Battery were now in position in the road and had opened on the enemy. When the Seventh retired these guns were without support, but the gallant artillery covered their own retreat, keeping the enemy at bay with canister.

The Federals had now been retarded long enough to allow the wagons to move to the rear, and the artillery to be put in position near St. James' Church.

General Jones formed his line in connection with the artillery, bringing up to their support the Eleventh and Twelfth regiments and the Thirty-fifth Battalion.

The Seventh had in the fighting gotten far off to the left, and for the rest of the day participated with W. F. Lee's brigade in its repulse of the enemy.

The Sixth veered to the right, and united with Hampton, who had now come up and formed on Jones' right.

There was now a slight breathing spell on Jones' front, which faced an open field, beyond which was a thick woods, from which Federal sharpshooters delivered a scattering fire, but their heavy columns did not continue to advance. Genl. W. F. Lee was pressing their right flank, while Hampton had partially enveloped their left.

Jones was now ordered to move forward and press their center. With the Twelfth in front, under Col. A. W. Harman; the Thirty-fifth Battalion, under Lieut.-Col. E. V. White; and the Eleventh, under Colonel Lomax, on the left, Jones advanced. The edge of the woods held by the enemy smoked with the rifles of hidden sharpshooters as the grey squadrons crossed the open grounds in front of the woods. Just as Harman reached the forest, a murderous volley was poured into his ranks, and Buford's troopers came charging up the road right upon them.

The head of the Twelfth was shattered, and out into the fields rushed the Federals. The bulk of the Twelfth was still fighting, and the Eleventh and White's battalion rushed into the mêlée.

There was now charging and countercharging. Squadrons cut in two and, again reuniting, turned upon the daring foe. Grey and blue were intermingled; men were captured and recaptured, and for a brief space the issue was doubtful.

In the midst of the tumult of battle the Sixth Pennsylvania and the Sixth United States Regulars made a most daring charge. Breaking through the fighting squadrons in the open field, they made straight for the Confederate guns at the church. Shrapnel and canister greeted them, but they rode on undismayed, and dashing up to the very muzzles went past the guns.

Immediately they were attacked on both flanks by Jones' and Hampton's squadrons and driven back; and though they suffered heavy loss, they returned as they came, with ranks well closed up.

Again there was a breathing spell, and nothing but the dropping fire of the skirmishers on General Lee's front broke the stillness that succeeded the storm. No bluecoats were even in sight. Perhaps they had gone back to the ford and the battle was over. The surgeons were looking after the wounded, and the soldiers were telling of their hairbreadth escapes and boasting of victory.

But a sound of cannon was heard far to the rear. The reports ceased in number and seemed to be getting nearer. Presently a courier on a foaming horse galloped up to General Jones with orders from General Stuart to lead his brigade with all speed to Fleetwood Hill, a mile and more to the rear of the position he then occupied.

Fleetwood Hill was the commanding position of the field contended for.

Gregg with a full division of cavalry and artillery in proportion had crossed the Rappahannock at Kelly's Ford, and having evaded Robinson's command, was moving rapidly in the rear of Stuart's position in the direction of Brandy Station, and was in cannon shot of Fleetwood Hill, which was then occupied only by one gun of Chew's Battery, a howitzer commanded by Lieut. John W. Carter. This gun being only supplied with a few rounds of damaged ammunition, could do no execution, but made a brave show of defending the position, and the boldness of Carter created the impression upon Gregg that he was well supported. Hence he delayed to make an immediate attack upon the position with his cavalry, but opened a cannonade upon it with three rifle guns.

Moments were now precious, and the best description of the situation is given by Maj. H. B. McClellan, chief of staff of Stuart's cavalry corps, in his "Life and Campaigns of Stuart," page 271, here quoted.

"The nearest point from which a regiment could be sent was Jones' position, one and a half miles distant from Fleetwood. The Twelfth Virginia, Col. A. W. Harman, and the Thirty-fifth Battalion, Lieut.-Col. E. V. White, were immediately withdrawn from his line and ordered to meet this new danger. The emergency was so pressing that Colonel Harman had no time to form his regiment in squadrons. He reached the top of the hill as Carter was retiring his gun, having fired his very last cartridge.

"Not fifty yards below Col. Percy Wyndham was advancing the First New Jersey Cavalry in magnificent order, in column of squadrons, with flags and guidons flying.

"A hard gallop had enabled only the leading files of the Twelfth Virginia to reach the top of the hill, the rest of the regiment stretching out behind in column of fours. It was a trying position both to the pride and the courage of this regiment, to be put into action in such manner, that a successful charge seemed hopeless. But with the true spirit of a forlorn hope Colonel Harman and the few men about him dashed at the advancing Federals. * * * And now the first contest for the possession of Fleetwood Hill was on, and so stubbornly was this fought on either side, and for so long a time, that all of Jones' regiments and all of Hampton's participated in the charges and countercharges which swept across its face."

So far McClellan.

It was Company B of the Twelfth, Lieut. Milton Rouss in command, and only fifteen to twenty men, who first reached the crest of the hill and charged and received the counter-charge of Wyndham and the First New Jersey.

Sergt. George Lewis and Privates Upshur Manning and Warner McKown of Company B were killed and four others of the company wounded in this encounter.

In referring to this charge, McClellan in a footnote, page 272, says:

"The result of this charge was always a matter of mortification to this gallant regiment and its leader. It is but just that I should say even at this day, that the whole responsibility rested with me and not with Colonel Harman. The Colonel was not aware of the extreme urgency of the case, and his regiment was only advancing at a trot. Seeing this I rode down the hill to meet him and ordered the gallop, and put him into the fight in the disorderly manner narrated. I have, however, always believed that the circumstances justified the sacrifice of this regiment; for had Colonel Wyndham obtained undisputed possession of the summit, with time to make arrangements for holding it, the subsequent fighting would probably have had a different result."

For a moment only the enemy was checked, though portions of the Twelfth came gallantly to the aid of their leader. Forced back by the onward sweep of Wyndham's squadrons, the head of the Twelfth was shattered, but fought in the general mêlée with the supports that came up.

It was now White's turn. The long gallop had disarranged his column, but he paused for a moment to make a hasty formation before assailing the foe. While Harman's assault had failed, it had not been fruitless, for it broke the solidity of the Federal front. Wyndham having his regiment in squadron formation, charged *en masse* to meet the assault of Harman's unorganized handful. The enemy's array was no longer compact. His squadrons in the tumult of battle were separated.

White, seizing his opportunity, hurled three of his companies under Major Ferneyhough against the foe on his right, and the other two companies he led against a body of troops on his left.

A part of Hampton's brigade now participated in the contest for the possession of the hill, and there was charging and countercharging, squadrons broken and again reformed, the gallant spirits on both sides refusing to yield.

White, having driven off the troops on his left, returned to find the hill again in possession of the Federals.

Meantime Harman, who had not been idle a moment, having reformed his regiment, united with White in another desperate effort to take the hill. The bluecoats were hard to move, but their steady valor yielded to the impetuous rush of the Confederates.

Harman, chafing under his recent repulse, raged like a lion in the combat that ensued. Dashing at the leader of the Federal horse, he engaged him in a personal encounter and was severely wounded.

The brave hearts of the Twelfth and White's Battalion pressed forward, dealing vigorous blows, and the enemy, yielding to the fierce assault, finally gave way and abandoned the hill.

During the contest for the position the Federals had been greatly aided by a battery posted at the foot of the hill lying eastward. It became necessary now to drive away or capture this battery. White was ordered to charge it. Hastily reforming his men, and reinforced by a company of the Sixth Virginia, he rode at the guns.

Across an open plain for 300 yards, exposed to a murderous fire, the bold horsemen galloped. The cavalry supports

of the battery delivered steady volleys, while the brave can-
noneers poured grape and canister into the ranks of their
assailants. As nearer they came the more rapid and deadly
were the discharges.

Could they live under such a fire? The smoke partly
obscured the issue, but through the rifts were seen the charging horsemen bearing down upon the foe. Once more the
cannons blazed forth, and now, mid flame and smoke,
White and his men were seen among the guns. Some fought
hand to hand with the brave artillerists, while others dashed
at the cavalry supports. These soon gave way and broke in
full retreat. But the gunners were unconquered and refused
to yield, using their small arms against the cavalrymen.

White, sending a portion of his men after the broken
cavalry supports, with about twenty troopers turned back
and galloped to the guns, around which was raging a hand-
to-hand conflict.

"There was no demand for a surrender or offer to do so
until nearly all the men, with many of their horses, were
either killed or wounded."[8]

The capture of the guns was not yet accomplished, for
help for the gallant artillerists was near at hand. Bodies of
Federal horse bore down upon White and almost surrounded
him. The dearly won prize was wrenched from his grasp,
and he was forced to cut his way out through the ranks of
the bluecoats to avoid losing heavily.

Once more the guns were in the hands of the Federals,
but most of those who had manned them lay dead or dying
near by. Around the now silent guns stood a body of Federal horse. To the right and left the battle was still raging.

---

[8]White's Report.

General Jones, who, as we have seen, remained near St. James' Church with only the Eleventh and his artillery, had been ordered to take part with his troops in the fight at Fleetwood Hill. He reached the field just as White had been driven away from the guns of Captain Martin's battery.

The Eleventh, under Col. L. Lomax,[9] was now ordered to charge. As with well-closed columns it swept across the ridge, a galling fire of small arms greeted it, for the other section of Captain Martin's battery near the Miller house was still intact.

The fighting of Hampton's regiment had almost by this time cleared the hill east of Stuart's headquarters, and they were still engaged when the Eleventh reached the scene of strife.

With steady gallop the Eleventh went forward, passing through the guns that White had been compelled to surrender, taking them and many of the cavalry prisoners.[10]

Now dividing his force, Lomax sent "Capt. E. H. McDonald with a squadron after the fugitives east of the railroad, while with the remainder of his regiment he assailed three regiments of cavalry awaiting him near the depot, which force he completely routed."[11]

The fighting around the station and along the railroad east of it was stubborn, and it was not until after repeated charges of the men of the Eleventh that the Federals gave way.

----

[9]Genl. L. L. Lomax, colonel of the Eleventh Virginia Cavalry, Laurel Brigade; frequently by seniority in command of the brigade. A dashing and successful officer, promoted to brigadier-general, and later to major-general, commanding a division of Cavalry Corps, Army of Northern Virginia.

[10]Lomax's Report.

[11]Jones' Report.

Gregg was now totally discomfited and withdrew his troops, going off, however, at "his own gait" to make connection with Buford at Beverly Ford.

Mention here should be made of a charge of the Sixth that occurred about the same time White was charging the right section of Captain Martin's battery. The Sixth, under Major Flournoy, joined Hampton in his attack upon Gregg's right. Being ordered by Hampton to move quickly in the direction of Brandy Station, while on his way he received orders from General Stuart to cut off 300 Federals who were near the Miller house.[12]

These he soon routed, but was suddenly attacked in the flank and forced to retire towards the Miller house. Here a Federal battery was discovered, which opened furiously upon the retreating Confederates.

The gallant Sixth, now almost surrounded, charged the battery, rode up to the muzzles of the guns and captured them.

Here also the artillerists bravely defended the pieces with their revolvers, and speedily aided by a heavy force of Federal cavalry, drove off the men of the Sixth.[13]

The Eleventh now went towards Stevensburg to guard against another attack from that direction, while the Twelfth, Sixth, and Seventh regiments were from this time on held in reserve, alternately supporting the artillery at Miller's house and reinforcing Genl. W. F. Lee on our extreme left.[14]

When Jones and Hampton withdrew their brigades to meet Gregg's attack at the Fleetwood house Buford, who

---

[12]Flournoy's Report.
[13]Flournoy's Report.
[14]Jones' Report.

had marched from Beverly Ford, had apparently nothing
in his front to prevent his advancing and attacking Jones
and Hampton in their rear.

Just at that time, fortunately for Stuart, Genl. W. F. Lee
was threatening Buford's right flank, and thus prevented a
movement which might have proved disastrous to the Confederate arms.   Indeed from the time that Gregg made his
appearance beyond Fleetwood Hill and fired his first cannon
shots at what he supposed was a Confederate force near
Stuart's headquarters, to the time when he was driven from
Fleetwood Hill, not much over thirty minutes had elapsed,
although Jones and Hampton were more than a mile away
when the ominous roar of Gregg's guns first attracted their
attention.

Buford, therefore, had not much time in which to make
his arrangements for an advance, menaced as he was by
Genl. W. F. Lee, and before anything could be done Gregg
was beaten and retiring towards the Rappahannock.

Stuart now formed a new line, and in the evening there
was heavy fighting between Buford's and W. F. Lee's
troops, Jones' brigade, except a part of the Seventh, being
held in reserve.

In this battle the Confederates lost 523 officers and
enlisted men, while the loss of the Federals was 936.   The
Confederates captured 486 prisoners, three pieces of artillery, and six regimental and company flags.   There were
on the field or near it, twenty-one Confederate regiments
opposed to thirty-four Federal regiments.

The fighting was mainly done by fifteen regiments, five of
which belonged to Jones' brigade.

Of the total Confederate loss in killed, wounded, and missing—523, the loss in Jones' brigade was 130 killed and wounded, the number missing not known.

Says General Jones in his report: "My brigade bore the brunt of the action. We ended the fight with more horses and more and better small arms than we had in the beginning. We took two regimental colors, many guidons, and a battery of three pieces. We took many prisoners, probably 250, as one regiment, the Eleventh, reports 122."[15]

---

[15]For the splendid fighting done by the commands of Hampton, W. F. Lee, Fitz Lee, and the horse artillery only incidentally mentioned in this narrative, the reader is refered to "The Campaigns of Stuart's Cavalry," by Maj. H. B. McClellan. While credit is also given to the Federals for the gallant charges of their cavalry and the stubborn bravery of their artillerists.

CHAPTER V

June, 1863

A short rest—The Army of Northern Virginia moves northward—
Jones' brigade guards the line of the Rappahannock—Federal cavalry in search of Lee make for the passes of the Blue Ridge—Aldie
and Middleburg—Fight at Upperville—Stuart makes famous raid in
rear of Federal Army—Jones' and Robertson's brigades left to
defend passes of the Blue Ridge—Operations of White's Battalion
—In Maryland—Sixth Virginia meets Sixth United States Regulars near Fairfield and defeats the latter—Joy of victory turned to
sadness by news of Lee's failure at Cemetery Ridge—Jones and
Robertson hold the passes of Jack Mountain—Jones saves Ewell's
wagon train—Buford and Kilpatrick thwarted—Fighting between
Hagerstown and Williamsport—Gallant charge of the Eleventh
Virginia Cavalry — Funkstown and Boonesboro — Willamsport
relieved and Lee's wagon train saved—The Seventh Virginia retali-
ates upon Sixth Regulars—Artillery practice upon a flying target
—Lee recrosses the Potomac—The brigade ordered south of the
Potomac to cover Lee's communications with Winchester—The
Twelfth, under Colonel Harman, on detached service near Har-
per's Ferry—Capture of Federal picket reserves—Colonel Harman
falls into the hands of the enemy—Brigade encamps near Charles
Town and engages in reconnoitering and skirmishes—Lee retires
up the Valley and crossing the mountains resumes the line of the
Rappahannock.

A short but well-earned rest was enjoyed by Jones' men
after the battle of Brandy Station.

The movement of Lee's infantry northward soon necessitated great activity on the part of the cavalry.

Ewell was already engaged in the successful movement
that ended in the capture of Milroy at Winchester. Longstreet followed, crossing the Blue Ridge through Ashby's
and Snickers Gaps.

A. P. Hill's corps brought up the rear, and while it was passing northward, Hampton's and Jones' brigades guarded the line of the Rappahannock.

On the 17th of June Fitz Lee's brigade, under Col. T. T. Munford, was attacked near Aldie by General Gregg's division of cavalry.

After a most gallant resistance Munford, in obedience to orders from Stuart, retired towards Middleburg. The enemy had been so severely punished that he did not follow.[1]

Aldie is in a gap in the Bull Run Mountains, and is directly east of Ashby's Gap in the Blue Ridge. A turnpike connects the two points, passing through Upperville and Middleburg. The next mountain pass in the Blue Ridge north of Ashby's is Snickers Gap, from which also a road runs to Aldie, making with the turnpike from Ashby's nearly an isosceles triangle, having the twelve miles of the Blue Ridge between the gaps mentioned for its base. The space between is a rich and well-cultivated section of the beautiful Piedmont country of Virginia, with county roads intersecting it. It is well watered by the mountain streams which, with the rolling and sometimes broken plains and numerous stone fences, render it ill adapted for cavalry movements.

After the retirement of Col. T. T. Munford from Aldie Stuart, with his headquarters on the road from Middleburg to Aldie, stationed his cavalry at different points to command the passes of the Blue Ridge.

He was threatened by a large cavalry force under General Pleasonton, supported by General Barnes' division of infantry of three brigades.

---

[1]Munford's Report.

On the 19th of June General Gregg moved out from Aldie
and attacked Stuart, strongly posted a few miles west of
Middleburg on the Upperville turnpike. After a stubborn
fight Stuart fell back about half a mile and took a new position, from which the Federals did not attempt to drive him
that day. In the evening Jones' brigade arrived and was
posted on the road to Union, covering that place, which is
north of the turnpike and about five miles from Upperville.

The next day Jones was reinforced by General Chambliss'
brigade. On the morning of the 21st Gregg, now reinforced
by Buford's division of cavalry and one brigade of infantry,
1,500 strong, advanced on the Union and Middleburg roads,
Buford attacking Jones and Chambliss

Gregg's movement, it seems, was a mere feint to divert
Stuart until Buford could brush away Jones and Chambliss
and assail the Confederate left flank.

Jones and Chambliss, however, proved no small obstacle,
and Buford, despite his superior numbers, made slow
progress. There was sharp fighting along the whole cavalry
front, Gregg no longer making a feint, but pushing forward
and dealing vigorous blows.

Stuart, feeling unable to cope with a foe so greatly
superior in numbers, fell back slowly before Gregg, and
ordered Jones and Chambliss to abandon the Union Road
and retire gradually towards Upperville.

Their contemplated line of retreat was seriously inter-
fered with by Buford, who, pressing forward and inclining
towards Stuart's left flank, forced Jones and Chambliss to
deviate towards the mountain.

The artillery of both brigades was put in the road and the
cavalry on the flanks, Chambliss to the left and Jones to

the right. In front bearing towards Upperville was a hill which they aimed to reach and thence give battle to the enemy. In this they were anticipated by Buford, who, being on the inside of the circle around the circumference of which the Confederates were marching, reached the hill first and blocked their way. Although the enemy was strongly posted with a stone fence in front, the Confederates immediately assaulted the position.

From behind a stone fence the Federal dismounted squadrons with their carbines delivered successive volleys, to which the Confederates with their pistols made but an ineffective response.

Another stone fence along the road prevented Jones' artillery from getting immediately into position. However, a part of this fence was soon pulled down and Captain Chew, quickly placing his guns into position, opened a galling fire on the foe at close range. His well-aimed shots, crashing into the heads of the Federal regiments, provoked a charge upon his battery. On came the bluecoats in fine style, massed in column and flanked with battle lines of carbineers, who showered bullets among the gunners and into the ranks of their supporting squadrons. The leaden hail fell thick and fast, rattling on the smoking pieces and wounding some of the artillerists.

Says Colonel Chew, referring to the part performed by his battery in this engagement: "When we reached the hill opposite the position of the enemy a squadron of our cavalry, I think under Captain Hatcher, had let down the fence and charged in the direction of Upperville. Our cavalry was forming on the west side of the road in considerable confusion. We put the guns on the east side of the road, but finding this position would not be supported, I had a gap let down in the fence on the west side of the road, and put my guns into position so as to command the gap and the fields in front.

"The enemy frequently charged up to the stone fence, but it was easy to make the gap so hot with canister that they would not venture across. Our cavalry had formed in the field behind us, and after remaining there for some time commenced to move off towards the Upperville turnpike. The guns were served with deadly effect, and kept the enemy completely in check until we had an opportunity to retire."

The effect of Chew's guns was apparent. Not less than forty-five horses by actual count had been shot down in one place, at the opening in the fence referred to. The number of killed and wounded Federals is not known, but if in proportion to the number of horses the loss must have been heavy. The cavalry made several ineffectual attempts to protect the battery, which all the time seemed in imminent peril, and which retired from the field under the protection of its own discharges.

Never was the brigade taken at greater disadvantage than in this engagement. Buford had arrived first at a point intersecting Jones' line of march, and assailed him on the left of his marching column in a road parallel with the eastern foothills of the Blue Ridge. The road, as already stated, was between stone fences, which made it impossible for Jones to get his regiments into any sort of formation, and the stone fences beyond in the fields occupied by the enemy furnished protection for his sharpshooters, who fired with deadly effect into the almost helpless Confederate masses.

The Twelfth, under Colonel Massie, was ordered to pass through a gap in the fence and check the advance of the enemy, but such a heavy fire was concentrated upon the opening that the head of the regiment was shattered and thrown into confusion. Captain O'Ferrall, commanding Company I of the Twelfth, was here desperately wounded.[2] Several were killed here and quite a number wounded.

At this juncture the Eleventh, under Colonel Funsten, was ordered to charge, and a portion of the Seventh, led by Colonel Marshall, charged up to the stone fence to the left of Chew's Battery. This combined attack in a measure retarded the Federal advance, but it was the well-served artillery that repulsed the enemy.

Chambliss and Jones now together advanced upon the retiring foe and made connection with Stuart's forces, then falling back towards Ashby's Gap.

In reference to this engagement General Buford says in his report: "The enemy brought four twelve-pounder guns into position, and made some excellent practice on the head of my regiments as they came up. The gunners were driven from their guns, which would have fallen into our hands but for two impassable stone fences. The enemy then came up in magnificent style from the direction of Snickersville, and for a time threatened me with overwhelming numbers."

In this fight Jones, who had three regiments on the field, White's being on detached service, lost in the Seventh, five killed and sixteen wounded; in the Twelfth, two killed and eleven wounded; in the Eleventh, seven killed and twenty-four wounded.

---

[2] Capt. O'Ferrall survived the war, was elected to Congress and later became Governor of Virginia.

The next day the Federals withdrew from Upperville, and Stuart's headquarters were re-established at Rectortown.

On the 24th Stuart, taking with him all of his cavalry except Robertson's and Jones' brigades, started on his raid in the rear of the Federal Army. Jones and Robertson "were left in observation of the enemy on the usual front, with full instructions as to the following up the enemy in case of withdrawal, and joining our main army."[3]

The reason assigned by Major McClellan in his "Campaigns of Stuart's Cavalry" for Stuart's leaving Jones' brigade behind, is that it was the largest in the division, and because Stuart regarded Jones as "the best outpost officer" in his command.

On the 29th of June Jones' brigade left Snickersville and united with that of General Robertson at Berryville. The Twelfth Virginia Cavalry had already been sent on picket duty near Harper's Ferry.

June the 30th a part of this regiment, under Lieutenants Lewis Harman and George Baylor, surprised and captured a Federal cavalry picket reserve in Bolivar, killing one and capturing twenty-one prisoners, among whom were two officers.

White's Battalion, which had been detached a few days after the fight at Brandy Station, accompanied Ewell's column against Winchester. When about to cross the Blue Ridge, Ewell permitted White to make a raid on Point of Rocks. When near the place White sent Company B, under Lieutenant Crown, to the north side of the town to cut off the retreat of the Federals. Here Lieutenant Crown came

---

[3]Stuart's Report.

up with Cole's Battalion and routed it, capturing thirty-seven prisoners.

In the meantime White had routed Means' command in the town and captured about twenty prisoners, and when Crown returned was engaged in setting fire to two railroad trains that had just arrived.

After gathering up the spoils of war, White with his battalion returned to Loudon and there remained until ordered to join Ewell in Maryland.

About the 30th of July Jones' brigade, in company with Robertson's, set out for Maryland. The Twelfth Regiment was left near Charles Town to picket towards Harper's Ferry.

The Sixth, Seventh and Eleventh regiments crossed the Potomac at Williamsport and, going by way of Chambersburg, reached Cashtown July 3rd.

Towards evening General Jones, by order of General Lee, moved his command towards Fairfield to take position in the rear of Lee's line of battle. About two miles from Fairfield the Sixth United States Cavalry was met enroute to capture the cavalry division wagon train which, but for the timely arrival of Jones, would have fallen into their hands.

The two columns met face to face in a lane having on both sides a stout post and rail fence. The country was open but cut up into small fields fenced in a similar manner. Neither party could form any estimate of the force opposed to it, and circumstances forced immediate action. Major Stair, in command of the Federals, upon discovering the Confederates, deployed mounted men on his flank, who with their carbines could pour a destructive fire into a column advancing down the lane.

The Seventh Regiment being in front, General Jones at once ordered Lieut.-Col. Thomas Marshall to charge the enemy. The command was quickly obeyed, and with its usual dash the Seventh moved towards the foe. But the head of the column soon encountered a terrible fire from the flanking squadrons, those on the right partly concealed and covered by an orchard.

Shattered and broken the head of the charging column faltered, the men behind it halted, and soon the whole regiment returned in spite of the strenuous efforts of some of the officers to force it forward.

The failure of the Seventh, General Jones' old and favorite regiment, was clearly due to the fire from the mounted men on the flanks, who, being unmolested, shot with deadly effect into the charging column.

General Jones was greatly disappointed and mortified. Riding up to the Sixth Virginia, who were in the rear over a rising ground out of sight of the repulse of the Seventh, he said, "Shall one —— regiment of Yankees whip my whole brigade?"

"Let *us* try them!" cried the men of the Sixth.

The order was at once given to charge. Forming rapidly and with eagerness to be in front, the Sixth moved off with a steady gallop, with the gallant Colonel Flournoy at the head of the column. Some of the Seventh moved abreast of the column in the field, and to some extent disturbed the mounted bluecoats on the flanks[4]

With drawn sabres the grey troopers bore down upon the foe, now flushed with victory and waiting with confidence the onset.

----

[4]Colonel Marshall's Report.

The Clarke Cavalry, under Captain Richards, was in front, and many of the Seventh, smarting under their recent defeat, joined in the charge.

Again the fire from the mounted men on the flanks told with deadly effect upon the ranks of the assailants. Under it Adjutant Allen and others fell at the head of the charging force. But the Sixth never slackened pace, and its steady advance soon caused dismay among the Federals.

The leading files of blue began to hesitate and half turn. Officers were seen pressing through the column to the front, making efforts to keep the men steady.

Major Stair, commanding the Sixth United States Regulars, bravely struggled to stem the tide, as his troops, shrinking from the rush of the Confederates, turned to flee. For a moment there was some resistance, as the head of the grey column plunged into that of the blue.

The gallant Major Stair fell desperately wounded, with his skull crushed by a sabre cut from Lieutenant Duncan. Capt. G. C. Gram, second in command, was also wounded and captured.

The Federals now broke into a wild rout, the men of the Sixth riding among them and slaying or capturing at will.

For a mile the pursuit was kept up, until the village of Fairfield was reached.

In this fight the Sixth United States Regulars seemed almost annihilated. Their total loss was 242; six men killed, five officers and twenty-three men wounded, and five officers and 203 men captured or missing.

The Seventh Virginia lost three killed and twenty-one wounded. The Sixth Virginia lost three killed and seventeen wounded.

During the fight at Fairfield Lee was engaged in an attempt to take Cemetery Hill. The roar of the artillery supporting Pickett in his desperate charge was still reverberating as the Confederates galloped down the lane towards Fairfield.

After the battle in the evening twilight, as the men talked over their success, the joy of victory was dashed with sadness, when it was learned that Lee had failed to take Cemetery Hill. There were whisperings of retreat during the night. Next day, the 4th of July, Lee's whole army began its march back to the Potomac. Jones' brigade and Robertson's were ordered to hold the passes of Jack Mountain and keep back Federal raiders from the wagon train.

In the evening it was reported that the enemy was advancing in force on the Emmitsburg and Waynesboro roads.

General Jones, fearing that Ewell's train, then on its way to Williamsport, would be attacked, asked leave to go with his command to protect it. He was allowed the Sixth and Seventh regiments, and Chew's battery, but the Seventh was afterwards ordered back and the Fourth North Carolina, under Colonel Fernbee, took its place.

It rained incessantly all night; the road was soon badly cut up; the ruts got deeper and deeper. At many points where mountain streams crossed the road the weaker teams would stall and block the way. Through the mud and darkness the artillery floundered along. Wagons with broken axles abandoned by their drivers had to be passed, and sometimes broken-down ambulances filled with wounded were encountered.

It being wholly impracticable to push ahead the artillery, or even the cavalry, General Jones went forward with his staff.

Arriving at the junction of the Emmitsburg road with the one upon which the train was moving towards Williamsport, he found there Capt. G. M. Emack's Company of Maryland, with one gun, opposed to a whole division of Federal cavalry with a full battery.

"He had already been driven back within a few hundred yards of the junction of the roads. Not half of the long train had passed.

"This little band of heroes was encouraged with the hope of speedy reinforcements, reminded of the importance of their trust, and exhorted to fight to the bitter end rather than yield. All my couriers and all others with firearms were ordered to the front, directed to lie on the ground, and be sparing with ammunition. The last charge of grape was expended and the piece sent to the rear.

"For more than two hours less than fifty men kept many thousands in check, and the wagons continued to pass along while the balls were whistling in their midst."[5]

At last the Federals with a cavalry charge swept away resistance and got possession of the road.

General Jones in the darkness was separated from all his command and made his way through the woods to Williamsport. Here he found everything in confusion, and began to reorganize the stragglers for the defense of Lee's army train.

The enemy was momentarily expected. But soon a force of Confederate cavalry and infantry arrived and General Imboden took command.

---

[5]Jones' Report.

General Jones now made his way back through the enemy's lines to his brigade on the night of the 5th. In the morning he rejoined his brigade at Leitersburg, and returned with it by way of Smithtown and Cavetown and the old Frederick Road, so as to participate in the attacks on General Kilpatrick at Hagerstown.

General Kilpatrick, who had pushed Jones and Emack aside at Monterey Gap, captured over 300 prisoners and forty wagons.

On the 6th he withdrew to Boonesboro. Here it was arranged between Kilpatrick and Buford that the latter should attack Lee's trains at Williamsport, while Kilpatrick kept Stuart back in the direction of Hagerstown.

Stuart, divining their intentions, attacked the Federals at Hagerstown, and after a stubborn resistance drove them before him.

But according to the plan prearranged, Kilpatrick retired towards Williamsport with his artillery, having a heavy line of skirmishers on both sides of the road. The fields adjoining were crossed frequently by post and rail fences and afforded shelter for the skirmishers.

Already the sound of cannon was heard in the direction of Williamsport, and it was evident that unless aid was furnished quickly the trains at Williamsport would fall into Federal hands.

Stuart at once determined to press the enemy. Chambliss' brigade of North Carolinians charged, "the Ninth and Thirteenth Virginia participating with marked gallantry. Robertson's two regiments and Jenkins' brigade kept to the left of the road, moving in a parallel direction with Chambliss.

"The column on the flank was now hurried up to attack the enemy in the flank, but the obstacles, such as post and rail fences, delayed its progress so long that the enemy had time to rally along a crest of rocks and fences, from which he opened with artillery, raking the road."[6]

Jenkins' brigade was ordered to advance, dismounted, and dislodge the enemy. Over the broken and difficult ground Jenkins' men moved forward, driving the foe. Mounted cavalry pressed the retreating ranks of blue, but Kilpatrick brought up fresh squadrons and hurled them upon the lines of the Confederates. Their onset was met by a counter-charge conducted by Col. James B. Gordon, commanding a fragment of the Fifth North Carolina Cavalry. Before his impetuous rush the blue lines fell back in some disorder.

The Eleventh Virginia, under Colonel Lomax, was now ordered to charge, for a simple repulse was not sufficient.

The guns of Buford, assailing General Imboden, who was defending Lee's trains at Williamsport, admonished Stuart that partial success would mean defeat, and that nothing but a victory that swept Kilpatrick from his path would save the trains at Williamsport. Kilpatrick, knowing this, aimed above all to gain time and had cunningly placed his guns and squadrons so as to retard the advance of the Confederates.

When the Eleventh was ordered to charge, two regiments of Federals were drawn up in line across the turnpike and the field to the left, their artillery on the brow of the hill raking the turnpike; their right protected by a stone wall with only one gap in it by which to enter the field.

---

[6] Stuart's Report.

The Eleventh was moved parallel with the turnpike until within about 500 yards of the enemy's position, when it turned into the turnpike under a heavy fire from the enemy's battery.

It then moved slowly until within 200 yards of the enemy, when the command to charge was given.[7]

Right down the straight turnpike, swept by the Federal guns, with drawn sabres rode the Eleventh under the gallant leadership of Colonel Lomax.

Bullets from the blue line in front; bombs, grape and canister from the Federal battery tore through their ranks. No line of sharpshooters, no supporting squadrons with their volleys disturbed the Federal gunners. They shot with deliberation and with telling effect.

Under the terrible fire men and horses fell headlong. Hands that grasped the flashing steel relaxed their hold, and brave hearts that erstwhile swelled with expectation of victory, felt the bitterness of death. Each step forward multiplied the danger, as with increased rapidity the flaming guns sent forth their missiles of destruction. But nothing could stop the impetuous rush of the grey troopers, as with lifted sabres and battle shouts they plunged through the smoke towards the foe.

The blue masses in the turnpike did not abide the onset, but turned and fled, leaving many prisoners in the hands of the Confederates.

Colonel Lomax, discovering two squadrons in the field still in line and moving towards the stone fence, which would afford them good protection from a charge and from the fire of his men, reformed his regiment and moved back

---

[7]Lomax's Report.

on the turnpike to the gap. Here again, as at Upperville, the enemy concentrated his fire upon the gap, while many of the Federals, to save their artillery, bravely rushed to the breach as the Eleventh poured through. Near the opening the fight waxed hot and bloody, but once in the field the Confederates pressed forward, driving the enemy before them.

The Federals now hastily retreated, going by the Downsville Road. The siege of Williamsport was raised and Lee's trains were saved.

In this fight the Eleventh captured 100 prisoners and fifty horses, killing and wounding many of the enemy.

The next day the Seventh had an opportunity to repay the Sixth United States Regulars for what it had suffered at their hands at Fairfield, and the debt was paid with interest.

On the road leading to Funkstown the two regiments met, Lieutenant Marshall in command of the Seventh. As before, the Seventh was the first to make the attack, and this was done with so much energy that the regulars broke and fled, pursued for nearly five miles by the Seventh.

Says Colonel Marshall: "Our column pressed upon them with great rapidity, killing and wounding a number and taking some sixty prisoners."

The sweets of victory were not unalloyed. In the pursuit the thirst for vengeance carried the head of the column too far. The regiment was stretched for some distance along the road and in disorder.

The Federals at last rallied, and seeing the small numbers of their pursuers, turned upon them; and now the Seventh, after repeated efforts to rally, retired hastily, losing nine prisoners and having two men wounded.

Lieut. Nicholas Nolan, who commanded the regulars in this fight, admits a loss of fifty-nine killed, wounded and missing, of whom ten were killed.

Near Boonesboro Stuart made a bold demonstration of his cavalry, threatening an advance upon the enemy, in order to cover Lee's retrograde movement. Jones' brigade being in front, encountered the enemy on the Boonesboro Road at Beaver Creek bridge, and pressed them back to the verge of the village.[8] In this contest, the fighting being mainly on foot, Fitz Lee's and Hampton's brigades participated in a very handsome manner.

The Federals were forced back from the village to the mountain pass, from which point, with artillery posted on the heights, they prevented Stuart from entering the town.

There was now a spirited and deafening combat between the artillery of the opposing commands, on ridges facing one another, while in the valley between skirmish lines of dismounted men fought with their long-range guns.

Having accomplished his object of putting the enemy upon the defensive, towards evening Stuart withdrew. "The enemy observing this from his mountain perch, tried to profit by it with a vigorous movement on our heels, but was foiled. As the last regiment was passing the bridge over Beaver Creek, a squadron of the enemy more bold than the others galloped forward as if to charge. Steadily a portion of the First North Carolina Cavalry awaited their arrival within striking distance, but before reaching their vicinity the enemy veered off across the fields.

"Here a Blakely gun of Chew's Battery advantageously posted marked their movement, and although the squadron

---

[8]Stuart's Report.

moved at a gallop, never did sportsman bring down flying birds with more unerring aim than the aim of the Blakely firing upon that moving squadron. In vain did it turn to the right and to the left. Each shot seemed drawn to the flying target with fatal accuracy until the enemy, driven by the shots of the Blakely and followed by the derisive shouts of our cavalry, escaped at full speed over the plain."[9]

Stuart new fell back slowly, his men encamping the night of the 8th near Funkstown. On the 10th and 11th Jones retired by the Cavetown Road. On the 13th Stuart withdrew all his cavalry from Lee's front and massed it on the left of the main body of the army, in expectation of a general advance of the Federal force. During this movement the Eleventh Virginia, under Colonel Lomax, while retiring through Hagerstown was charged by the enemy's cavalry from two streets. These assaults were quickly repulsed by the sharpshooters of the regiment, having suffered a loss of three wounded in the skirmish.

On the 13th of July Jones' brigade was sent across the Potomac to cover Lee's communications with Winchester.

It now appearing that the enemy, instead of attacking, was entrenching himself in our front, General Lee determined to cross the Potomac.

Accordingly, during the night of the 13th the Army of Northern Virginia returned to the south side of the river. Stuart's cavalry, with the exception of Jones' brigade, stayed in the infantry trenches during the night, and crossed the next morning.

When General Jones with the rest of the brigade was in Pennsylvania, the Twelfth Regiment, under Col. A. W.

[9]Stuart's Report.

Harman, remained in the neighborhood of Harper's Ferry, operating against the enemy as occasion offered.

During the night of the 30th Lieutenants Lewis Harman and George Baylor with forty men attacked the enemy's picket-post near Harper's Ferry and captured one lieutenant and nineteen men.

By July the 2nd the Federals had abandoned Harper's Ferry and the Maryland Heights, but after the battle of Gettysburg, on the 7th, they returned to the Maryland Heights, and on the 14th reoccupied Harper's Ferry.

Col. A. W. Harman, who had just returned from home, having recovered from the wound received at Fleetwood, went with a squadron on a reconnoissance to Bolivar Heights.

Taking a squad of six men he went somewhat in advance and to the left of the road. Suddenly the enemy appeared in force and charged.

Colonel Harman's horse fell, stunning him. He and Lieutenant Eastham and two men from Company B who were with him were captured. The rest of the squadron, under Capt. George J. Grandstaff and Lieut. George Baylor, who were in the road, bravely met the charge of the enemy and drove him back in confusion, taking twenty-five prisoners.[10]

On the left of the line, guarded by the Twelfth, Maj. J. L. Knott was as usual very active. When the enemy advanced towards Shepherdstown he attacked them and captured thirty-three prisoners.

On the 16th Jones' brigade went into camp near Charles Town. Within the next week there were a few small skirmishes, but nothing worthy of note occurred.

---

[10]Col. T. B. Massie's Report.

At this time the Shenandoah from recent rains was much swollen, and the Federals took advantage of it to cross the Potomac and march along the east side of the Blue Ridge, taking possession of the gaps in the mountain as if to get between Lee and Richmond.

Jones' brigade was ordered to picket the lower Shenandoah as long as necessary for the safety of Lee's right flank, and then to follow the army.

Lee now moved up the Valley, and crossing the Blue Ridge, by the 1st of September had resumed the line of the Rappahannock.

By the middle of September the main army had withdrawn behind the Rapidan.

CAPT. WILLIAM N. McDONALD

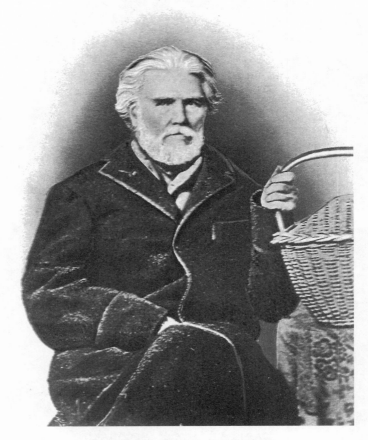

COL. ANGUS W. McDONALD

GENL. TURNER ASHBY

DR. NELSON G. WEST

REV. JAMES BATTLE AVIRETT
and JOHN (Black Hawk) COOK OF GENERAL ASHBY'S
HEADQUARTERS MESS

ASHBY'S CHARGE AT MIDDLETOWN

MAJ. WILLIAM PATRICK

GENL. THOMAS T. MUNFORD

BRIG.-GENL. WILLIAM E. JONES

MAJ. EDWARD H. McDONALD

OLIVER RIDGWAY FUNSTEN

MAJ. SAMUEL B. MYERS

COL. RICHARD H. DULANY

COL. E. V. WHITE

COL. ASHER W. HARMAN

LIEUT. B. C. WASHINGTON

LIEUT.-COL. THOMAS E. MASSIE

THOMAS L. ROSSER

MAJ. JOHN W. EMMETT

GENL. J. E. B. STUART

MAJ. HOLMES CONRAD

GENL. WADE HAMPTON

ROSSER'S DEFEAT OF CUSTER AT TREVILIAN'S STATION, VA.

LIEUT. PHILIP B. WINSTON

MAJ. F. M. MYERS

CAPT. J. W. CARTER

LIEUT.-COL. THOMAS MARSHALL

CAPTURE OF
MAJOR-GENERALS CROOK AND KELLY

COL. M. D. BALL

BRIG.-GENL. JAMES DEARING

CAPT. HUGH H. McGUIRE

MAJ. JOHN LOCHER KNOTT

MAJ. JAMES THOMPSON

MAJ. FOXHALL A. DANGERFIELD

CHAPTER VI

September, 1863

Brigade returns to watch the fords of the Rappahannock—Differences between General Stuart and General Jones—The latter court-martialed and removed to another field of operations—Personality of Jones and attachment of his troopers—Admiration and loyalty of the men soon won by "Jeb" Stuart—Federals under Meade advance towards Culpeper Court House—Hard and continuous cavalry fighting against Buford and Kilpatrick, in which the brigade now under command of General Lomax takes prominent part —Capt. Samuel B. Coyner of the Seventh Virginia Cavalry killed — Enemy surround and capture one of Thompson's guns of Chew's Battery—A front and rear fight at Jack's Shop—Successful charge against infantry by Company B of the Twelfth Virginia— Second battle at Brandy Station—Fight at Fauquier Sulphur Springs—Notable exploit at the Rappahannock bridge—Stuart in a tight place at Auburn—Bold dash and escape of his command.

The Gettysburg campaign was over, and the army, after an active service of three months, was back once more in the section of country from which it had started northward. There was time now for retrospect. The campaign was reviewed by the troops with various conclusions.

The failure of Lee's magnificent army to take the heights of Cemetery Ridge and win a decisive victory north of the Potomac disheartened some.

"Never again," they said, "would Lee invade the North. Henceforth the battles must be fought on Confederate soil, and the Southland alone be ravaged by the hand of war."

If such gloomy forecast appeared to many well founded, they were on this account more resolved to fight harder for success. With them the most distressing feature of the repulse at Gettysburg was the disappointment of Lee. That his army was not regarded as a beaten one was shown by the refusal of the enemy to attack it at Hagerstown.

It might be that experience had taught the wisdom of a defensive policy, whatever might happen, they were as ready as ever to follow Lee as far north as he might wish to lead them, even to the banks of the Hudson.

During this short period of rest the time was occupied in recruiting the strength and numbers of the cavalry, and in reorganizing it into brigades and divisions. The whole force was now divided into two divisions, commanded respectively by Generals Wade Hampton and Fitz Lee; Jones' brigade becoming a part of Hampton's division.

It was during this period, too, that the brigade was deprived of its much loved commander, Genl. William E. Jones. His removal was due to an unfortunate personal difference between himself and his superior officer, Genl. J. E. B. Stuart. About the 1st of September General Stuart ordered him under arrest and preferred charges against him for using disrespectful language to his superior officer.

The result of the court-martial was that General Jones was removed from the command of his brigade and assigned to duty in southwestern Virginia. It was generally understood that the court based its action upon a recognition of the fact that the good of the service necessitated the removal of Jones from under the authority of General Stuart, the incompatibility of their dispositions being apparent. Though the action of the court was unquestionably dictated by a proper regard for the public good and the maintenance of superior authority, yet from force of circumstances it was liable to misconstruction. For some time after, the impression prevailed among the rank and file of the brigade, that their commander had been sacrificed to the animosity of General Stuart.

A succession of stirring events, however, with the sense of comrade-ship in danger, Stuart's uniform kindness to Jones' old troopers, his quick personal recognition of the men, even the humblest private, coupled with his personal bravery and dashing leadership, soon won for him the admiration and affection of the men. Loyalty to the Southern cause, however, would have attracted them to any commander who would lead them to victory.

General Jones' connection with the brigade had much to do with the compactness of its organization. His great talent in this respect had been wisely exercised in increasing its efficiency. He looked after everything, and his close attention to details had effected many needed reforms. At first he was regarded as a martinet, but afterwards, when better understood, he was greatly respected and loved by rank and file.

Totally unlike Ashby, except in his modesty, which almost amounted to bashfulness, with neither superb horsemanship nor martial presence to impress the imagination of his soldiers, yet when the hour for action came the brigade felt itself always strong and ready to do its full part, and confident in the courage and ability of its leader. His personal appearance was not suggestive of the dashing brigadier, much less did it aspire to the pomp and circumstance of office. The faded slouch hat was decorated with no nodding plume, but while it served to conceal the baldness of his head it partly shaded a strong and noble brow. His features were plain and the expression determined yet kindly. His eyes of steady blue glistened with intelligence, and at times his countenance glowed with a rather cynical humor.   He was entirely self-adjusted in all his notions and opinions, and his remarks were almost always original and striking.

In the confusion of ideas brought about by the war, he was not tempted to forget the standard of truth and honesty he had set up for his own guidance.   And never was needle truer to the pole, than he, to what he conceived to be his duty.   His affection for his troops was deep and strong. He refused to fare better than they, and on the march, when necessary to bivouac in the rain he would not sleep himself under shelter, though a house might be within a few steps of him, but with his oilcloth around him would lie down in the rain or snow among his troopers.   His contempt for all kinds of display perhaps made him go too far in the other extreme, especially in the matter of dress.   The insignia of his rank, if worn at all, was usually concealed by his coat collar, and he was frequently taken by his own men for a private in the ranks.

Once, on his West Virginia raid, when the troops were crossing the Gauley River, a soldier who was afoot was anxious to find some way to get over dry-shod..   He asked another soldier to assist him.   The latter, pointing to General Jones, who was sitting in a skiff near the shore, said, "Maybe that old fellow there will row you across."

Going up to General Jones he said, "Old man, I will give you a dollar to take me over the river."

"All right," said the General, "jump in."   And he rowed him over, greatly enjoying the joke.

It was during the session of the court-martial before which General Jones was arraigned, that the Confederates were forced to abandon Culpeper Court House, by a general advance of the Federal Army across the Rappahannock.

About midnight September 12th, 1863, Stuart received information that General Meade would on the following day make a forward movement.

Steps were taken to start the baggage trains on the way to the Rapidan as soon as practicable, and every necessary precaution was taken to delay the enemy's advance.

At the first streak of dawn the Federals drove in the Confederate pickets at the river, and crossing in heavy force about a mile south of the Rappahannock bridge, formed in line of battle. Three divisions of cavalry, followed closely by Warren's corps of infantry, constituted the advance column. They were met at first by Jones' brigade only, commanded by Col. L. L. Lomax. White's Battalion had not yet returned from detached service, and on that day Lomax's command consisted only of the Eleventh, Seventh, Twelfth, and Sixth Virginia Cavalry.

As the odds against him were clearly overwhelming, Lomax only attempted to retard the enemy as much as his force would permit. No detailed account of the fight is given, as there were no official reports of it from Confederate sources. The Federal reports, however, warrant the inference that their advance was hotly contested.

The First Brigade, under Col. H. E. Davies, led the advance. The Confederate outposts were pressed back, as the Federals moved forward, confident in their strength. Upon approaching the railroad there were signs of serious resistance. The enemy was charged by the Seventh Virginia, under Colonel Marshall, and driven back some distance in confusion, but reinforcements pouring to the front, soon the blue lines again advanced.

The grey troopers were not idle. Colonel Lomax had posted his squadrons at points of advantage, and as soon as

the enemy's column moved forward, it was met and driven
back with a sabre charge. Chew's Battery did effective
work, taking positions close to the enemy and sending bombs
with unerring aim into his ranks. The enemy, in spite of
overwhelming numbers, did not have it all his own way, and
Lomax's purpose to delay him for a time was successfully
accomplished.

Retiring from the vicinity of the station, with heavy lines
of skirmishers supported by mounted squadrons, and Chew's
Battery from different points maintaining a constant fire,
Lomax halted on a range of hills northeast of Culpeper
Court House. Here, according to Federal accounts, Lomax
made a gallant stand with four regiments against the two
divisions of Federal cavalry under Buford and Kilpatrick.

Says General Kilpatrick in his report: "The enemy here
made a determined resistance with a battery of artillery and
a large force of cavalry."

The "large force" consisted of no more than the Eleventh,
Twelfth, Seventh and Sixth Virginia Cavalry. With these
four regiments Lomax held his ground for quite a time
against the overwhelming odds. Not until the Federals,
swinging around their left threatened the Confederate rear
and right, did Lomax abandon his position.

On the hills south of the Court House another stand was
made. Lomax was here joined by W. H. F. Lee's brigade
under Col. R. L. T. Beall, and the two brigades for several
hours resisted all attempts to drive them from this position.
Charge after charge, gallantly made by the Federals, was
met with countercharge by the men in grey and repulsed,
while the scattered columns of the Federals were torn with
shells from Chew's guns.

Says General Kilpatrick in his report: "I rode over and led the Fifth again into the woods. Here we met with General Custer, who was heavily engaged, and did all that men could do to advance. We were, however, overpowered by numbers, and the Second New York was flanked, and its extreme right driven in. At this juncture the affair looked badly and I feared the command would be driven back, but I brought up the First West Virginia Cavalry, the last regiment at my command, which had only the day before been supplied with Spencer rifles. Hitherto they had not taken any active part in the engagements, and on my call sprang from their horses and, led by Colonel Richmond, rushed into the woods."

It will thus be seen from Federal accounts how hotly the ground was contested. Being "overpowered by numbers," is the usual Federal excuse for the failure of an advance movement.

When it is remembered that the two brigades of Lomax and Lee were confronted by two divisions of Federal cavalry, the numerous repulses of the Federals must be attributed rather to the valor and skill of the Confederates than to their superiority in numbers.

It was in one of these hand-to-hand conflicts that the gallant Capt. Samuel B. Coyner, commanding Company D of the Seventh Virginia, was killed.

When it became evident that the small Confederate force could no longer hold the position against Buford's and Kilpatrick's divisions, Stuart, who had taken command, began to withdraw his troops. One gun of Chew's Battery stationed on a hill north of Culpeper Court House, being very near the enemy in a commanding position, had greatly punished the Federals. More than once, mounted and on foot, ineffectual attempts had been made to capture it. But as Lomax withdrew a Federal regiment, concealed by a railroad cut, passed beyond the gun and turning came up in its rear. The squadron supporting the gun, discovering the Federal regiment making for their rear, gave way without resistance, leaving the gun helpless. Captain Chew, discovering the situation and seeing the impossibility of saving the gun, started with Lieutenant Thompson to make their own escape. Noticing that the officer leading the charging regiment was far in advance of his command, they bore down upon him, exchanging several shots as they approached. A well-aimed shot from Thompson's pistol unseated the gallant Federal, and seizing the reins of the riderless horse, Thompson led him off as he and Chew in a gallop made good their escape.

Stuart, having held his position long enough to secure the safety of his trains, fell back towards the Rapidan at his own gait.

On September the 22nd Stuart had an engagement with the enemy at Jack's Shop in Madison county, that threatened at one time to end in a serious disaster. Of this affair no reports can be found from Confederate sources, while the Federal commander, Genl. John Buford, contents himself with speaking of it as a great Federal success.

It appears that General Buford, with one division of Federal cavalry, started from Madison Court House September the 22nd on a reconnoissance down the Gordonsville turnpike, expecting to connect with another division under General Kilpatrick, in the vicinity of Jack's Shop, not far from Liberty Mills.[1]

Stuart, hearing of Buford's coming, went out from Liberty Mills with a portion of Hampton's division and encountered him near Jack Shop.   Stuart, hurling regiment after regiment upon the strong columns of the enemy without making much impression.   In the midst of this struggle, Kilpatrick's division, with Davies' brigade in front, struck the turnpike just in the rear of Stuart's column.[2]

There was a rush of riders in hot haste informing Stuart of his danger, and the sound of small arms in their rear, soon made the Confederates understand the gravity of the situation.   Between the two Federal divisions Stuart was now hemmed in, and naught but a cool head and steady valor could extricate him.

Colonel Davies had come unexpectedly upon Stuart, and the surprise was mutual.   But to the Confederates, who were aware of Buford's hostile presence in their front, it looked as if a trap had been cunningly laid for bagging Stuart and his whole army.

Stuart, however, was equal to the occasion.   Placing the guns of Chew's Battery in an open field, at a point from which could be had a range and view to front and rear, the battery opened in both directions at the same time.   The bullets from the sharpshooters of Buford and Kilpatrick now interlapped among the Confederate ranks.   The perilous situation of the Confederates was understood by every soldier, but inspired by the coolness and gallant bearing of Stuart, as he quickly made his dispositions, every man resolved to do his best.

---

[1]From General Buford's Report.
[2]Davies' Report.

The task of breaking through Kilpatrick and reopening the way to Liberty Mills was chiefly assigned to Jones' brigade, then commanded by Colonel Funsten. A part of this command was dismounted and advanced upon the woods, while the mounted men charged where openings would permit. On the left was the Seventh, under Lieutenant-Colonel Marshall; on the right the Eleventh, under Major Ball.

The Twelfth, under Colonel Massie, occupying the center, advanced upon the woods close to the edge of which was a rail fence separating it from the open field. Openings in the fence were quickly made in the face of a heavy fire from the enemy's mounted and dismounted men in the woods. The nature of the ground was such that organization could not be preserved, and soon the men and officers of the different regiments, were mingled almost *en masse,* and rallied around the person of General Stuart, who urged and led them into action.

It was fortunate that Stuart met the rear attack of Kilpatrick with such promptness and vigor, for had there been delay sufficient for Kilpatrick to throw his whole force across Stuart's line of retreat, with Buford's strong division pressing his front line, it is hardly possible that Stuart could have escaped from the net set for him without loss of his artillery and a good part of his command.

The fighting in this engagement was close and fierce with both sabre and pistol, and there were some notable instances of personal adventure and heroism, rewarded afterwards by General Stuart, with official mention and recommendation for promotion.

Having swept Kilpatrick from his path and put him to flight, Stuart withdrew from the engagement with Buford;

followed by him, however, almost to Liberty Mills, where he crossed the Rapidan, being there reinforced by Wilcox's division of Confederate infantry.

The losses in this fight while considerable on both sides, considering the short time they were engaged, are not mentioned in either the Confederate or Federal reports except that Colonel Davies reports that Major McIrvin of Kilpatrick's staff, Captain Hasty of the Second New York, and sixty-nine prisoners fell in the hands of the Confederates.[3]

The severest loss to the Confederates in this engagement was in the death of that splendid soldier, Capt. John H. Magruder, of Company B, Seventh Regiment, who fell in the assault on Kilpatrick's column.

Thaddeus Baney of Company B, Twelfth Virginia, and Lieut. John Green of the brigade staff, were also among the killed.

After the affair at Jack's Shop, for two weeks there was comparative quiet along the cavalry front. Many of the men were furloughed to go home and procure fresh horses, while the rest gave themselves up to making the most of their freedom from active service.

The orchards of Madison county groaned under loads of precious fruit, the pastures were fine and the people kind and hospitable.

On the 10th of October all were again in the saddle near Madison Court House, Colonel Funsten of the Eleventh commanding the brigade.

---

[3]Major McIrvin was captured by Private B. C. Washington of Company B, Twelfth Virginia Cavalry, in a hand-to-hand fight, in which Washington disarmed McIrvin by a cut across his sabre hand. Washington was promoted to a second lieutenancy for his services at Jack's Shop.

General Lee had begun his flank movement on Meade's army, and was engaged in what is known as the Bristoe campaign.

As the success of the movement depended upon its secrecy, the cavalry were expected to screen the march of Lee's infantry. Funsten's command was in front of the column that moved towards Woodville on the Sperryville turnpike. It moved for the most part over blind roads or through the fields, twisting and turning under the shelter of woods and hillocks to avoid observation from the Federal signal-posts on the peaks of the neighboring mountains.

On the morning of the 11th the command had reached and was marching along the road that leads from Sperryville to Culpeper. Here it was joined by Stuart, who detached the Eleventh, under Lieutenant-Colonel Ball, and sent it towards Rixeyville on the Warrenton Road. Early in the day the Federal pickets were driven in. Their infantry camps showed that they had just been deserted in great haste, and the column moved forward at a trot.

When within a few miles of Culpeper Court House a regiment of infantry was seen emerging from the skirt of a woods into an open field and moving in the direction of Culpeper Court House.

Company B of the Twelfth Virginia, under command of Lieut. George Baylor, was in the advance, being that day detached and under the immediate direction of General Stuart for any service he might require.

As soon as General Stuart saw the Federal regiment, having no other force at hand he directed Baylor to charge it immediately. The enemy had reached the open ground and, forming quickly in line, delivered an irregular volley in the face of the troopers at close range, which, however, overshot them, doing but little execution. Having no time to reload and the horsemen bearing down upon them, they fled precipitately, having cast away their knapsacks and some of them their guns. But for an almost impassable ravine, which they had crossed before delivering their fire, a large number of them would have been captured. There were several killed and wounded and a few prisoners taken by such horsemen as crossed the ravine here and there.

Col. John Esten Cooke, then aide-de-camp to General Stuart, an eye-witness of the charge, says:

"Never have I seen him (Stuart) more excited. He was plainly on fire with the idea of capturing the whole party. The staff scattered to summon the cavalry, and soon a company came at full gallop. It was the Jefferson Company, under that brave officer Capt. George Baylor.

" 'Charge and cut them down!' shouted Stuart, his drawn sword flashing as he forced his horse over fallen trees and the debris of a great deserted camp. A fine spectacle followed. As the Federal infantry double-quicked up a slope Baylor charged. As his men darted upon them they suddenly halted, came to a front face as though they were the parts of some glittering machine. The muzzles spouted flame and the cavalry received the fire at thirty yards. It seemed to check them, but it did not. They had come to an impassable ditch. In another moment the infantry broke, every man for himself, and making a detour the cavalry pursued and captured large numbers."

General Stuart's official report of the incident is as follows:

"In our rapid pursuit of the enemy we found we had passed an infantry regiment of the enemy which had been on the outpost and was now marching parallel to our column on our right in the direction of Culpeper Court House. Every effort was made to close up the column, then elongated by pursuit, so as to catch this regiment, but apprehending it would escape, the only cavalry I could lay my hands on was ordered to charge the regiment as soon as it debouched into the open ground. This was gallantly responded to by a company of the Twelfth Virginia under Lieutenant Baylor, and but for an impassable ditch these brave men would have ridden over the enemy and cut them down with the sabre. They charged within twenty or thirty yards of the column and fired a volley into it, but were forced, from the nature of the ground, to retire, which was done without the loss of a man or horse, although the enemy's fire was delivered almost in their faces. The enemy did not further contest the field. They broke and ran, dropping guns, knapsacks and blankets, several of their number being captured."

Funsten, whose command now consisted only of the Twelfth and Seventh Virginia, gave the front to General Gordon's North Carolina brigade, and the whole column moved forward at a gallop towards Culpeper Court House.

As the leading files emerged from a dense woods upon a slope in sight and within a half mile of the Court House, they were saluted with well-directed volleys from a battery placed on an eminence near the town.

A squadron of Federal cavalry now made its appearance and was driven through the town by a gallant charge of Colonel Ferribee's regiment, Gordon's brigade. But it was soon discovered that Kilpatrick's whole division, 4,000 strong, was massed east of the Court House in a good position.

Stuart having only five regiments available, amounting in all to about 1,500 men, concluded not to attack the enemy at this point.   Turning the head of his column to the left, with Funsten's two regiments leading, the Twelfth in front, he marched rapidly towards Brandy Station and soon got into a road nearly parallel with the one leading from the Court House to the same point.   Before reaching this place it was apparent, from great clouds of dust on the right, that heavy masses of the enemy were moving in the same direction.

Soon, upon passing a belt of timber, the two columns came in full view of each other.

About a half mile to the right, on higher ground and on a line nearly parallel to Stuart's course, appeared the serried masses of Kilpatrick's column.   He, divining Stuart's purpose, was going at a rapid gait, giving him in fact a race for the hill at Brandy.   The point each was riding towards was nearly three miles off, and each step brought the forces a little nearer each other.   As they moved along at a trot, grey and blue sent up shouts of mutual defiance, brandishing their sabres menacingly, and occasionally solitary horsemen rode out from either column and exchanged shots.

It was a novel situation and a remarkable sight to behold. The compact masses of Kilpatrick, stretching back as far as the eye could reach, came on in all the panoply of war.   The sun shone brightly in a cloudless sky, and its beams glancing from the myriad glittering sabres presented a scene of martial splendor.

The manifest disparity of the opposing forces was by no means encouraging.   In his five regiments Stuart could not have numbered more than 1,400 men.   Kilpatrick acknowledges an effective strength of 4,000.

To the common soldier, as the endless stretch of the blue masses was surveyed, the odds seemed overwhelming, but Stuart was leading and they were content to follow.

Upon approaching the inevitable point of contact, Stuart kept rising in his stirrups as if looking for something on the other side of the Federal column, the head of which was now far in advance of his.

At last, when near the Botts' house, the smoke of a bursting shell was distinctly seen above the ranks of the enemy.

"That's Fitz!" cried Stuart, and immediately ordered a charge.

The Twelfth was in the advance and, under Col. Thomas E. Massie, led the charge. But the retreating column they were charging seemed to dissolve, and there was exposed to view a battle line of dismounted men confronting them. It was the First West Virginia Regiment, armed with Spencer repeating rifles. From this double line of carbineers flamed continuous volleys that carried death in the ranks of the Twelfth, but the files came pressing on with shouts. Right bravely the West Virginia men stood to their work. They could see what fortunately the men of the Twelfth could not see, blue squadrons assailing the column, charging on the right flank. Nothing, however, could stop the onset of the Twelfth, and before it got within sabre's length the First West Virginia broke in headlong flight, hotly chased by the grey troopers for half a mile.

In the meantime the Federals were not idle. Observing the charge of the Twelfth, Colonel Davis led two regiments against the two North Carolina regiments supporting the Twelfth Virginia. Taken in flank the troops were thrown into disorder and broken. The pursuing Federals were met by the Seventh Virginia and driven off, the contest drifting all this time towards the neighborhood of Brandy Station.

While thus engaged there was much confusion. Many of the bombs from Genl. Fitz Lee's batteries fell in the ranks of the Confederates.

Hearing the shouts of the Twelfth, and seeing the rush of the bluecoats towards the body of men he was attacking, he mistook the movement for a Federal reinforcement and was checked rather than encouraged by it.[4]

The Federals, still pushing on, soon gained the hill, and planting their batteries raked the approaches to it with shell and shrapnel.

Stuart, now uniting with Fitz Lee, vigorously assailed the Federal position. The fighting here was chiefly done by Lomax's and Chambliss' brigades.

"Our dismounted men were several times surrounded by the enemy's cavalry, but were each time rescued by gallant charges of their mounted comrades."[5]

Driven from the woods around Brandy Station the enemy took position with infantry and artillery supports on Fleetwood Hill.

Deeming it unwise to assail him here, Stuart forced him to retire by ordering Fitz Lee by a flank movement to threaten his rear.

He then withdrew, much harassed by our cavalry, and crossed the Rappahannock about sundown.

The losses sustained by the Twelfth, which had three companies detached, and the Seventh, amounted to thirty-three

[4]Stuart's Report.
[5]Stuart's Report.

killed and wounded. They captured in this fight 200 hundred prisoners.[6]

Referring to the first charge upon the Federal column, which was led by himself, Captain Baylor, in his "Bull Run to Bull Run," page 166, says:

"On the afternoon of October the 11th, we reached the Barbour house, overlooking Brandy Station, and found Kilpatrick's division of cavalry moving back from Culpeper in the direction of the station. It was a magnificent spectacle. Our artillery was not in reach and few of our cavalry up.

"But General Stuart, being apprised that Fitz Lee had arrived on the opposite flank of the enemy at Brandy Station, ordered the Twelfth, under Colonel Massie, to charge the column and cut off Kilpatrick's retreat. Company B was in front of the regiment, and down the slope it went and reached a point near the station, where it was discovered that the enemy had enveloped us, and it became a race on our part to escape capture. We were so intermingled with the enemy that they could not use their guns and pistols without endangering their own men. Lieutenant Washington and myself were near together on the retreat, and jumping a ditch his horse fell and pinioned him to the ground. As my horse cleared the ditch safely, Washington called for help, but with visions of Forts McHenry and Delaware before me and a host of pursuers behind, I was constrained to leave him to his fate. I escaped and he was taken prisoner, but did not remain long in the enemy's hand, as he appeared next morning in camp, minus horse and arms, having made a miraculous escape during the night."

General Stuart, in his report, says:

"The Twelfth Virginia Cavalry, Lieutenant-Colonel Massie commanding, was at the head of the column, and having been

---

[6]Stuart's Report.

ordered to charge did so in the most gallant manner, cutting off 1,200 or 1,500 of the enemy, all of whom would have been killed or captured had not the headlong rapidity of the pursuit, added to the difficult character of the ground, so greatly extended the column as to impair for the moment the efficiency of its action. The loss to the enemy in killed, wounded and missing was considerable, the two regiments of Colonel Funsten's command alone having taken 200."

General Kilpatrick, in his report says: "Many gallant charges were made by the division, and many equally gallant charges by the enemy repulsed. The division fell slowly back, one brigade after another, in good order, and finally crossed the Rappahannock and went into camp about eight P. M."

The next morning, October 12th, Colonel Funsten was ordered to march to Rixeyville and move in front of Generel Ewell's column. About two miles from Jeffersonton Ewell was met with, and here the Eleventh Regiment, under Lieutenant-Colonel Ball, which had been detached for two days, rejoined the brigade.

In and around Jeffersonton, strongly posted behind hills, fences, and a stone wall that enclosed a churchyard, were two regiments of Federal cavalry. The Eleventh, dismounted, had already made a vigorous assault upon the position, but had been repulsed with considerable loss.

Colonel Funsten now sent Colonel Marshall with the Seventh to assail the left and rear of the enemy, he himself going with the Twelfth, Lieutenant-Colonel Massie commanding, towards their right and rear.

About a half mile from Fauquier Springs, in the pines, Colonel Funsten suddenly came face to face with another Federal regiment of Gregg's division. The Twelfth, being ordered to charge, quickly responded with pistol and sabre upon the opposing column. Though somewhat surprised, the Federals made a short and stubborn fight, and then retreated towards the river.

In the meantime Colonel Ball with the Eleventh, having failed in his assault on foot upon the Federal position at Jeffersonton, now, with his regiment mounted, made a vigorous charge upon his right flank, and succeeded in driving back the cavalry supporting the enemy's sharpshooters. The latter were cut off, but were in part saved from capture by fresh troops coming to their assistance. Ball fell back for a moment, but reforming again, with repeated charges forced the Federals down the road to the point where Funsten was. This Federal force, now uniting with the one in Funsten's front, pressed bravely forward. The Twelfth again charged, aided by a portion of the Eleventh, and a bloody and doubtful contest now raged with disorder on both sides, through the piney thickets and heavy timber, and over occasional spots of cleared but rocky ground.

The shouts of officers and men calling their commands to "stand fast" and "come on," and the cries and oaths of the combatants at close quarters, mingled with the rattle of small arms, intensified this war scene.

Here Lieutenant Poague of the Eleventh, who in many a previous battle had shown extraordinary gallantry, after performing prodigies of valor, fell mortally wounded.

The Federals were gradually forced back. Though often rallying and advancing with stubborn courage, at last broken and in full retreat they recrossed the river, leaving many of their dead and wounded and 200 prisoners in the hands of the Confederates.

The Federal version of this affair is given in part by General Gregg in his official report. He says: "They charged impetuously in front and on both flanks with infantry and cavalry, and we were driven into the woods, where for half an hour the fight raged furiously. At this juncture information was brought that the enemy had possession of the road in my rear, and that we were surrounded. This information having found its way to the men, created some confusion, and it became impossible to reform the command, and I was compelled to retire in some confusion, fighting, however, every foot of the ground. It was here that Major Young, Fourth Pennsylvania Cavalry, and Lieutenants Cutler and Martin of my staff were wounded."

Sending now the Seventh and Eleventh Virginia to cross the river higher up, Stuart made arrangements to force a passage at Warrenton Springs.

The Rappahannock at this point is narrow and deep, and across it was a bridge hardly more than a gangway of planks. On the east or north bank, the land rises gradually for a half mile into a ridge, which at that time was heavily wooded. Between the crest of this ridge and the Springs Hotel, the ground was open, except, that about half way from the river to the top of the hill, was a body of timber running west of and reaching to the Warrenton Road. On the ridge General Gregg, the officer in command of the Federal force, had planted a battery, placing one gun near the river. The northern bank of the river above and below the bridge, was lined with sharpshooters, most of them in rifle-pits.

Under Stuart's personal supervision the Twelfth Regiment was ordered to charge the bridge and dislodge the enemy on the other side. Company B of the Twelfth Virginia, under Capt. George Baylor, was to make the dash, the rest of the regiment to follow in supporting distance. Behind the Twelfth and on a wooded eminence, eight guns of General Long's artillery were prepared to support the assault, though this fact was unknown to most of the cavalrymen.

At the command to charge Baylor's company, compactly formed, with sabres drawn, moved promptly forward from cover of a wooded knoll, first at a trot and soon quickening into a gallop, Colonel Massie closely following with the rest of the regiment. Immediately the guns from the Federal battery and those of Long opened with a deafening roar. So loud for a few minutes were the discharges of artillery, that the shells bursting over the charging squadrons were hardly noticed, and the smoking carbines of the sharpshooters, who lined the opposite bank of the river and delivered steady volleys, were almost inaudible.

Straight for the bridge rode the men of the Twelfth. Upon reaching it at full speed, the front ranks of the advance company being more than midway upon it, it was discovered that the plank flooring at the farther end had been taken up, which made it impassable. Notwithstanding this check, under the steady fire of the enemy, they withdrew quickly from the bridge, and dashing into the river through a disused ford below, were so quickly among and over the rifle-pits that the astonished Federals were driven out and captured in large numbers.

An account of this charge led by Captain Baylor is given in his "Bull Run to Bull Run," as follows:

"Pressing on to the river at Warrenton Springs we found the enemy had posted his artillery on an eminence beyond the

stream, and placed dismounted men in rifle-pits near the banks
of the river to contest our advance. Dismounted men were
thrown forward on our side supported by a small force of our
infantry.

"The horse artillery not having come up, General Long of
Ewell's corps opened fire with eight guns on the enemy's batteries and supporting squadrons. At this juncture General
Stuart ordered me to charge with Company B across the river,
and drive the enemy from their rifle-pits.

"I had been for some time a spectator of the futile efforts of
the infantry and dismounted men to effect a crossing, and to
accomplish this with a cavalry dash struck me as impracticable.
But a soldier's duty is to obey, do or die, assured that a bold
front is half the battle. * * * Generals Robert E. Lee,
Ewell, Stuart, and others were in full view watching the movement. It was the occasion of our lives.

"The order was given, and down the road the company
dashed amid a shower of bullets, and reached the bridge over
the river to find the flooring torn up. Here we were forced to
halt, turn about, and strike for a ford below. This movement
was effected without faltering, and soon the river was crossed,
and the rifle-pits, with a large number of prisoners in our possession. The rest of the regiment now coming to our aid, the
prisoners were secured and turned over to the infantry."

General Stuart, in his official report, speaking of the incident, says:

"This little band of the Twelfth Virginia Cavalry was
worthy of special praise as it was made under circumstances of
great embarrassment. Charging first up to the pier of the
bridge, it was discovered that it had been taken up, thus expos-
ing them to a dangerous fire from the enemy on the opposite
side. Nothing daunted in purpose, however, they turned about
and took the road to the ford below, which they plunged into
in the face of the enemy's fire without halt or hesitation."

Maj. H. B. McClellan, assistant adjutant-general of the cavalry corps and Stuart's chief of staff, who was present, thus describes the charge in his "Campaigns of Stuart and His Cavalry," page 386:

"Now the Twelfth Virginia was ordered to charge the bridge. Lieutenant Baylor's company still had the front. Darkness was settling down upon the field. Along a narrow causeway Baylor lead his men in a column of fours.

"In the face of a sharp fire from the rifle-pits, he reached the very abutment of the bridge before he discovered that the planks had been removed and that a crossing was impossible. He must retrace his steps and try the ford. There was no hesitation nor confusion. 'By fours right about wheel. Forward!' And in a moment he had descended from the causeway and his column was plunging through the narrow ford, where hardly four could ride abreast. It was a gallant sight, and called for wild huzzas from the Confederate infantry, many of whom were spectators of the scene. Up the hill went Baylor, and in a few moments the rifle-pits were cleared of the enemy and the approaches of the bridge were under our control."

At the close of the Bristoe campaign, as it was called, this company was the recipient of a unique compliment from the commander-in-chief of the Army of Northern Virginia. It was an order from General Lee through General Stuart, that a furlough of ten days be given to Company B of the Twelfth Virginia Cavalry as a recognition of their gallant conduct.

Gregg now slowly withdrew, followed by Funsten, whose command bivouacked that night near Warrenton.

"In the operations of this day the Twelfth Regiment captured between 275 and 300 prisoners, and the Eleventh 150, with their horses, arms and equipments. The casualties in these regiments amounted to three officers killed and wounded."[7] Of the number captured by the Twelfth, forty-seven were taken on the road while moving from the Springs to Warrenton. They had been on picket at points above the Springs, and while falling back came up in the rear of the Twelfth, which they mistook in the darkness for a Federal regiment, and so fell into the hands of the Confederates.

On the 13th of October Stuart made a reconnoissance towards Catlett's Station, going by a road that led through the village of Auburn to this point. Sending General Lomax in advance with his brigade, he followed with Funsten's and Gordon's brigades, taking also seven pieces of artillery and some ordnance wagons.

General Lomax, upon reaching Auburn, learned that a large body of Federal infantry were at Warrenton Junction, distant from Auburn about four miles. He at once sent word to Stuart, and halted his command.

About four o'clock P. M. Stuart arrived at Auburn. Leaving Lomax there to guard his rear, he pushed on with Funsten's and Gordon's brigades towards Catlett's Station. When within two miles of the station he saw large bodies of Federals marching along the railroad eastward. Halting under cover of a piece of woods, he was quietly watching the movement when a messenger rode up post-haste and informed him that the Federals were in possession of Auburn, having driven off Lomax. In point of fact a whole corps of the enemy was falling back on a road that led eastward through Auburn, and Stuart became aware that he was hemmed in between the moving columns of

---

[7]Funsten's Report.

Meade's vast army.   Hastily retracing his steps he approached Auburn, seeking some way of escape.   Finding
the road blocked by the Federals and apprehensive of attack
in case he should be discovered, Stuart at once moved his
command out of the road he was traveling off to the right
into a narrow valley between two wooded hills, and halted
in close column waiting for developments. Soon night set
in and the hungry and tired troops, now fully aware of the
situation, with eyes and ears busy, waited and wondered
what fate had in store for them.

The enemy was marching within speaking distance of
them, and as they plodded along, stopping now and then
to build fires that made their column distinctly visible, they
seemed a flowing stream of armed men.

Stuart's reason for staying so close to the highway was
that he hoped to find an opportunity for breaking through.
But hours passed and the Federal stream was continuous.
All night long the procession of artillery and infantry
moved on.

While thus watching it was of supreme importance to
conceal his presence from the enemy.   Every kind of noise
was forbidden.   The men spoke in whispers.   Sabres were
not allowed to rattle against canteens, and guards were stationed to enforce profound silence.   Even the horses seemed
to realize the necessity of being quiet, though now and then
a hungry mule of the ordnance teams would protest with
rising voice against the unpleasantness of the situation,
which sound, if heard by the Federals, was no doubt taken
to come from their own column.

The long and dreary night was nearly spent, but to crush
out every hope, just at the first grey streak of dawn ap-

peared, right close in front a body of Federal infantry halted, stacked arms, and went to making coffee. There was no alternative now but to prepare for battle.

During the night Stuart had sent six messengers to inform General Lee of his position. All six succeeded in the attempt by one o'clock at night. These messengers were six privates, who volunteered for this dangerous service, which required that they should go in and through the Federal column. Their names are Robert W. Good, First Virginia Cavalry; Ashton, Chester, and Sharley of Mc-Gregor's Horse Artillery; and Privates Crocket Eddins and Richard Baylor of Company B, Twelfth Virginia Cavalry. Had they been caught in the attempt they would probably have been shot as spies.

Believing that Lee was aware of his perilous situation, as day approached Stuart listened anxiously for the sound of firearms in the direction of Warrenton; making, however, arrangements if no aid came, by a bold stroke to take care of himself.

The stars were already fading from the sky when, hearing the welcome sound of musketry on the other side of the Federal column, Stuart opened fire on the enemy. His seven guns, under Major Beckham, had been posted so as to be barely concealed by the rising crest of an intervening hill. At the word of command they were quickly advanced, and with simultaneous roar poured canister at close range into the Federal masses in the road. The Federals, amazed at the sudden and close assault, were at first panic-stricken and ran helter-skelter in every direction, but rallied by the officers, soon fell into line. With bold front they now advanced and assaulted the position of Stuart's guns, taking advantage of the slope of the hill to get close to the guns before they charged.

Gordon's brigade remained in the saddle, while Funsten's command was dismounted and posted to support the artillery.

Confident in numbers the Federals pressed forward, but soon recoiled before the cannon fire and the volley of Funsten's dismounted men.

Renewing the attempt with increased numbers they now approached on the left flank, but a gallant charge made by the First North Carolina Cavalry, under Colonel Ruffin, drove them back in confusion. The brave Colonel Ruffin was killed in this charge.

In the meantime the firing on the other side of the road had ceased, and taking advantage of the check afforded by the bold dash of Ruffin's regiment, Stuart pushed forward and crossed the road with all his command without losing "a wheel." He now retired towards Warrenton, Funsten's brigade bringing up the rear, and striking the route the enemy had lately marched captured many stragglers.

On the morning of the 15th Stuart pursued the retreating Federal cavalry, which fell back upon infantry supports.

At Bull Run a stand was made, but, dismounting his men, Stuart attacked *en masse* with great spirit and soon drove the foe across the Bull Run. Hearing that a wagon train had not yet crossed, Stuart attempted to capture it. Finding the road upon which it moved was covered by a heavy force of Federal cavalry, he ordered Gordon to attack it in front while he detoured with Funsten's brigade towards their right flank

After a very circuitous route he reached at dark a point only a short distance from the ground where Gordon had been engaging the enemy. The road passed through a dense thicket of pines and was barricaded.

The Twelfth Regiment being in front, Colonel Massie commanding, was ordered to charge the barricades. This was gallantly done, and the enemy was driven from his strong position to precipitate flight.

CHAPTER VII

October, 1863

A new commander—Sketch of Thomas L. Rosser—The Buckland races
—Camp at Flint Hill—At Hamilton's Crossing—Night surprise of
a Federal camp—Dash upon Meade's wagon trains in the Wilderness—Back to Hamilton's Crossing—Hard fight at Parker's Store
—Watching Meade—Raid around Meade's army—Night attack
upon Sangster's Station and death of Captain Cartmell—Brigade
heads for the Valley and crosses the Shenandoah—Joins the force
of Early at Mt. Jackson—A Merry Christmas in the Valley.

While halted at Manassas the brigade received a new
commander, General Thomas L. Rosser. To the greater
part of the command he was then comparatively a stranger,
although known to many through report as a daring and
successful soldier.

The campaign was now nearly closed, and little was done
before the men returned to their old camp at Flint Hill, but
that little disclosed a mettle and dash in the new chief that
reminded the men of the days of Ashby.

While not possessing those peculiar qualities of Ashby,
which both attracted the admiration of his men and won
and cemented their individual affections, Rosser in personal
appearance, by education and experience, and by a reputation for courage and dash already acquired, appealed to
their soldierly instincts. Tall, broad-shouldered and mus-
cular, with black hair and moustache, dark brown eyes,
strong jaw, and a countenance denoting self-confidence, a
good horseman and always superbly mounted, the men of

the brigade recognized in their new commander the typical soldier, and transferred their loyalty to him.

When the Southern States seceded and established the Confederacy, Rosser was a cadet at the West Point United States Military Academy from Louisiana, being in April, 1861, a member of the graduating class. The demand for officers to command the United States troops caused the Government to issue an order declaring his class graduated by April the 13th, and the members of that class were ordered to Washington.

Rosser at once determined to resign, and on the 13th of April he and several other Southern men of his class, who afterwards became distinguished soldiers in the Confederate Army, resigned, left West Point and started southward.

Meeting with various interruptions, which caused them to take unusual and circuitous routes to the new "Land of Dixie," they at length reached Montgomery, Alabama, and offered their services to the Confederate Government. Their services were immediately accepted and they received commissions. Rosser was made a first lieutenant of Artillery and ordered to Wilmington, North Carolina, on recruiting service. Eager to be in the field he requested permission to attach himself to the staff of General Holmes, and shortly afterwards reached Richmond, where in time he was elected captain in the Washington Artillery. He participated in the first battle of Manassas, but only reaching the field towards the close of the fight, he joined in pursuit of the enemy.

After that battle, he was assigned to Stuart's command, and first served on outpost duty at Munson's Hill. Going to the assistance of General Robertson at Mechanicsville, he participated in that action with unusual boldness and vigor, and being much exposed in pressing the enemy, he was badly wounded. President Davis was present, witnessed the fight, and promoted Rosser, on the field, for gallantry, and he received the commission of lieutenant-colonel of artillery on June 10th, 1862.

On the 20th of the same month he was made colonel of cavalry and took command of the Fifth Virginia Cavalry.

The Fifth Virginia was but poorly armed when Rosser took command, but soon supplied itself at the expense of the enemy in the fight at Catlett's Station, in which it took conspicuous part.

Here also an incident occurred that came near costing Rosser his life. Some Federal infantry had been captured, and while the fight was going on Rosser was asked, "What shall we do with the prisoners?" To which he carelessly and, not meaning it, replied, "Kill them." One of the prisoners heard the reply and, taking him in earnest, told the others. Immediately they revolted and began to fight for their lives with stones, fence rails, and whatever came to hand. One prisoner, who still had his bayonet in the scabbard, drawing it threw himself furiously upon Rosser, wounding him in the arm and stabbing his horse. It was not until the mistake was explained and the prisoners assured of protection that they were pacified.

It was here (Catlett's Station) that Major Von Bourke, a Prussian soldier, aide-de-camp to General Stuart, climbed a telegraph pole and cut the wire with his sabre. The fact of his gigantic size and bulk is what is remarkable about the incident.

During the following week, including the Second Manassas campaign, Rosser was assigned to duties that required both unusual skill and audacity.

On the 30th Rosser was ordered, in conjunction with a part of the Ashby brigade and some artillery, to annoy the flank of the Federal infantry.

"This was done with splendid effect, Colonel Rosser, a fine artillerist as well as a bold cavalier, having immediate direction of the batteries."[1] In this action Rosser commanded all the artillery in Stuart's command, comprising Eshleman's and Richardson's batteries of the Washington artillery, and Stribbling's and Rogers' batteries. With these he directed an enfilading fire upon the Federal flank, and as they fell back he pressed his advantage with so much eagerness that his batteries were at one time half a mile in advance of the Confederate line. The enemy, seeing their exposed position, attempted by a desperate charge to capture Rogers' battery, which was the most advanced. The battery, however, defended itself by reserving fire until the enemy was within fifty paces, and then discharging deadly volleys of canister into his ranks.

From Manassas, Rosser with his regiment accompanied Fitz Lee into Maryland, and participated in the Maryland campaign of 1862.

Here, as well as elsewhere, Rosser with the Fifth Virginia, and generally accompanied by a section of guns, had serious work to do.

On the 13th of September the Federals pressed eagerly forward into Boonesboro Gap, in the South Mountain, for the purpose of raising the siege of Harper's Ferry.

---

[1]Stuart's Report.

Says Gen. D. H. Hill, who was defending the Gap: "There were two mountain roads practicable for artillery on the right of the main turnpike. The defense of the farther one had cost Garland his life. It was now entrusted to Col. Thomas L. Rosser of the cavalry, who had reported to me and who had artillery and dismounted sharpshooters. Rosser, Anderson and Ripley held their ground, and the Yankees failed to gain their rear."

After Lee withdrew from Pennsylvania and the Army of Northern Virginia again resumed its positions along the Rappahannock, Stuart engaged in his Dumfries raid,— December the 28th. In this Rosser took a leading part.

Says Stuart, speaking of the passage of the Occoquan: "General Fitz Lee discovered that the northern bank of the stream was occupied by the enemy's dismounted sharp-shooters in force. Without waiting to exchange shots they were gallantly charged by files, the Fifth Virginia, under Colonel Rosser, leading across a narrow, rocky and difficult ford. They crossed the stream and captured or dispersed the whole party."

Says Fitz Lee in his report: "The charge across the narrow, rocky ford of the Occoquan by file, in spite of the enemy's sharpshooters on the other side, was one of the most admirable performances of cavalry I have ever witnessed, and great praise is due to Colonel Rosser in this connection."

With this well-earned reputation General Rosser took command of the brigade, a body of soldiers whose reputation under Ashby, Munford, and Jones was not second to that of their new commander.

When the head of Stuart's column had nearly reached Bull Run, the further bank of which was held by the enemy, Rosser was ordered to seize McLean's ford. A body of the enemy's infantry was holding it, being strongly posted on some high ground beyond, and supported by artillery.

With his men dismounted and deployed as skirmishers, Rosser advanced under a heavy fire and took possession of both sides of the ford.

The enemy on the high ground remained in position and kept up such a galling fusillade that the Confederates were forced to shelter themselves under the banks of the creek, from behind which they replied to the fire of the enemy.

Night was now drawing near, and although Rosser was ordered by Stuart to fall back, he wanted to retreat under the cover of darkness.

The enemy was on the alert, and it was hazardous to leave the friendly shelter of the bank. At a preconcerted signal the men raised a yell as if about to charge, and then retreated rapidly. The ruse was discovered by the Federals, who at once pursued.

The horses of the brigade had been brought near the creek, and in mounting under fire some confusion occurred. But in crossing the run the Federals also were thrown into some disorder, and Rosser taking advantage of this, with a portion of his men held them in check, until aided by Stuart in successfully withdrawing.

Lee was already falling back, while Meade remained near Bull Run; but the cavalry under Stuart which followed Lee was pressed by the Federal horse.

Early on the 19th Hampton's division, to which Rosser's brigade then belonged, was engaged in preventing Kilpatrick's division from crossing Broad Run at Buckland, on the Warrenton turnpike.

At the same time Fitz Lee was retiring with his division on a line parallel to the Orange and Alexandria Railroad. At the suggestion of Fitz Lee, Stuart, who was in command of Hampton's division, withdrew before Kilpatrick for the purpose of enticing him to follow upon the turnpike, so that Fitz Lee could fall upon his rear.

Kilpatrick fell into the ruse, but with his usual caution left Custer's brigade to hold the ford, while he with the rest of his division followed Stuart within three miles of Warrenton. Here the sound of Lee's guns reached Stuart, and he turned upon the Federals. After some resistance they broke and fled down the turnpike, hotly pursued five miles.

Custer held the ford at Buckland against Fitz Lee, until most of Kilpatrick's men escaped through the woods, and then withdrew with his artillery.

The Federal loss was about 250 prisoners and a few wagons and ambulances. The pluck of Custer and the fast riding of Kilpatrick had prevented a much more serious disaster.

This incident has always been known by the cavalry as the "Buckland Races," it being more of a chase than a fight.

General Stuart, in his official report of it, says: "The force opposed to us on this occasion consisted of ten regiments of cavalry and six pieces of artillery commanded by General Kilpatrick, and I am gratified in declaring the rout of the enemy at Buckland, the most signal and complete that any cavalry has suffered during the war. It is remarkable that Kilpatrick's division seemed to disappear from the field for more than a month, that time being necessary no doubt to collect the panic-stricken fugitives."

After their experience at Buckland, the Federal cavalry followed the Confederates in their withdrawal at a respectful distance, and the old positions on the Rappahannock and Rapidan were resumed.

At Flint Hill, in Rappahannock county, the brigade took a short rest, which was much needed and much enjoyed. Provender was abundant, the orchards full of delicious fruit, and the rich autumnal grasses supplied an abundance of milk and butter which the hospitable farmers of the county dispensed to the soldiers. The merry-makings were numerous but soon over. In a short time the command was ordered to break camp, and return again to Hamilton's crossing, about eight miles above Fredericksburg. Here for several weeks it was engaged in picketing the fords from Germania to Fredericksburg.

On the 7th of November the Federal army forced a passage across the Rappahannock at Kelly's Ford and the railroad bridge, and resumed its old position near Culpeper Court House.

General Lee now retired beyond the Rapidan, and prepared to go into winter quarters.

On the 17th of November, Hampton ordered Rosser with his brigade to Chancellorsville. Before sundown Rosser was on hand with his troops, who were joyous at the prospect of some relief from the monotony of drill and picket.

After a few hours' rest, they set out in the night and marched towards Stephensburg, where a Federal regiment was stationed. Near daybreak they found the enemy and charged his camp. The darkness and the sudden attack made victory easy. The Federals fled and scattered, leaving about sixty prisoners, many horses and the camp equipage in the hands of the Confederates. Hampton's loss was one man killed and two wounded. After loading the captured wagons, he retired with deliberation, and recrossed the river unmolested.

The brigade now again returned to Hamilton's Crossing and resumed the monotonous duty of picketing the fords, though somewhat consoled by their share in the recent spoils of war.

Scarcely had they gotten comfortably fixed in quarters, when the news of a general advance of the Federals recalled them to the saddle.

To the surprise of the Confederates, Meade had on the 26th crossed the fateful river, and the next day with his whole army was marching up the Plank Road towards Orange Court House.

Rosser, upon the first report of his scouts, moved his brigade to Todd's Tavern as a good point of observation, and sought opportunity to annoy the enemy's marching column. He did not have long to wait, for on the 27th he learned that the Federals were moving up the Plank Road, and that they had neglected to picket the Brock Road, that crossed Meade's line of march, and led to Todd's Tavern. The tract, through which Meade was marching, was what is known as the "Wilderness." It was an almost uninhabited expanse of country, rendered so by the extreme poverty of the soil, and was covered with stunted trees and an almost impenetrable growth of underbrush.

On the morning of the 27th, with ranks closed up as much as the narrow road permitted, Rosser moved with caution towards the Plank Road.

Soon the rattle of the Federal wagon trains was heard, and upon a nearer approach, the confused hum of a marching army.

The advance guard now rode silently forward, the very horses seeming to step softly, and at a given signal from Rosser dashed into the Plank Road, followed by the main body. In an instant the wagon first passing was turned into the Brock Road. Those behind it were made to follow, and soon more than a dozen came thundering along with mules under whip and sabre down the narrow road towards Todd's Tavern.

In the meantime the hubbub at the crossing, and the sight of the charging Confederates, stampeded the teams that had gotten by, while those coming on, were abandoned by their drivers or wheeled around in an attempt to escape capture. Some were upset, others colliding with the rear ones became hopelessly entangled. The shouts of the terror-stricken teamsters, the frantic efforts of the mules to free themselves, mingling with the noise of the combat, made a scene of indescribable confusion.

In a few minutes the contest was over. From both directions the Federal infantry advanced to save their trains, which were being snatched from the very midst of the army. Exposed to a fire from opposite quarters, the Confederates beat a hasty retreat, and disappeared in the Wilderness. Not a few wagons had been broken or destroyed on the

Plank Road, the mules being cut loose and brought out. Of those driven off towards Todd's Tavern, some were burned for fear of recapture, after being rifled of their valuable contents by the troopers. But the net result of the enterprise was a goodly number of mules and wagons and twenty prisoners captured, with the loss of only one man.

Rosser, after securing his prisoners, moved along a road parallel to the Plank Road, bivouacking that night, in spite of a drizzling rain, almost in sight of the enemy's camp-fires. The next day he rejoined the main body of the cavalry.

On the following day Stuart, with Hampton's division, made a reconnoissance around the enemy's left, having Rosser's brigade in front.

The road through the dense forest was muddy, narrow, and rough, and the column in marching was often broken into single files.

Running across the line of march, was an abandoned railroad bed which was nearly parallel with the Plank Road, and distant from it a few hundred yards. Just beyond it, at Parker's Store, was stationed a Federal camp, and in the roadbed was a Federal picket. The advance guard, Company A of the Seventh, under Captain Hatcher, upon discovering the Federal picket, charged and pursued it, the brigade following closely, with the Seventh Regiment in front. Soon the camp of the enemy near the road on the right came in view, and Rosser ordered a charge, himself leading it. But Hatcher had pressed in hot pursuit of the picket, and the rest of the Seventh, except a few of the front files, was some distance behind, and the entire brigade was strung out in the narrow road on which it was advancing, fully a mile in length. So the action was commenced without formation, the men engaging in the fight as they came upon the firing line. The enemy poured a volley into these few and for a brief space kept them at bay. But the column soon closed up and the camp was charged and taken with many prisoners.

The woods was full of tempting articles of plunder, among which were savory breakfasts which had been hastily abandoned. The cold and hungry Confederates yielded to the temptation, and many broke ranks to gather the spoils of victory. In the meantime the enemy, heavily reinforced with a heavy line of skirmishers on the flanks, made a vigorous effort to recover the field. For full two hours a fierce struggle raged, each side refusing to yield. The action was chiefly between dismounted men, the dense forest growth preventing in large degree the advantageous movement of mounted squadrons. In the road, however, there was frequent charging of mounted men with varying fortune.

At last, with portions of all the regiments of the brigade, a charge was made down the Plank Road that proved resistless. The Federals, though pressed with sabre and pistol, stood manfully a while, then turned and fled, pursued with fury by the Confederates. For several miles the pursuit continued, the Federals losing heavily in killed, wounded, and prisoners.

The line of dismounted men disappeared before Rosser's front after the rout of the Federal horse. Remaining for a short time in possession of the field, Rosser at length withdrew with his captures.[2]

The next day at dawn all were in the saddle, confident that Meade would attack Lee's lines; but they were disappointed. Meade had come to Mine Run to go into winter quarters, and it did not seem likely that after crossing the Rappahannock he would fear to cross Mine Run. Another night of anxious expectation followed, such as generally precedes a great battle. At dawn, however, the reveille of the enemy was not to be heard, and it was soon learned that Meade had made off during the night.

After following Meade to the banks of the Rappahannock, the brigade retraced its steps and on the 5th of December resumed its old position at Hamilton's Crossing. The vicinity of the camp was almost an uninhabited waste. So bare had it been swept by the waves of war, that a few persimmons was all that rewarded the most industrious flanker. Forage was scanty, rations meagre, and the troops exposed in shelter tents, yearned for the full barns and plenteous tables of the Valley. Not a few took solace in the "starvation parties" given by the hospitable citizens of Fredericksburg, where the charms of wit and beauty banished remembrance of their discomforts in camp; but the most lived in hope that some lucky chance would remove them to the banks of the Shenandoah. Sooner than they thought the hope was realized.

On the evening of December the 16th, the brigade set out on what is known as the Sangster Station raid, an expedition attended not only with some hard fighting but with

---

[2]The casualties among the men of "The Laurel" in this fight were considerable. Among the killed was Richard Baylor of Company B, Twelfth Virginia Cavalry, a private distinguished for his gallantry.

a great deal of suffering, the horrors of which made a lasting impression upon every soldier who participated in it. General Lee having heard that one or two regiments of Federal cavalry were moving up the Shenandoah Valley from Winchester towards Staunton, directed Rosser to cross the Shenandoah in the rear of this force and prevent its escape. Accordingly on the 16th of December Rosser with his command marched to Fredericksburg, where he waited until low tide, and then crossed the Rappahannock about twilight. The fording was deep and some of the men had to swim their horses.

For the first three or four miles the road led through the old camping-ground of Burnside's army. The prospect, indistinct in the gloaming, recalled the fate of that mighty multitude, and the deserted cabins, many of whose last inmates lay buried near, were silent witnesses of the horrors of war. The road now led through a barren waste. It was rough and narrow, but the troopers were homeward bound, and for a few hours before drowsiness set in, moved on right merrily.

Soon the camp-fires of Meade's army were seen on their left, and they could not for a moment forget that they were within the enemy's line. About midnight the column halted and rested until morning, when the march was resumed. Rain now set in, at first a drizzle and then a downpour, drenching the men, swelling the streams, and making the roads sloppy and muddy. Rosser, being apprehensive, lest some of the streams ahead of him would rise so high as to impede his march, now moved faster.

All day long through the continuous rain, the men, wet to the skin, pushed on through mud and mire. Three days' rations had been cooked before starting, but these were now nearly consumed, and the improvident ones had quite exhausted their haversacks.

The Seventh Regiment was in front, followed successively by the Twelfth, Eleventh, and White's Battalion. Towards night the order came to close up at a trot. Night had already set in when the Occoquan was reached. It was found to be rising rapidly, but a passable ford was found at Wolf Run Shoals.

Up to this time Rosser, in his anxiety to cross the railroad without delay, and to hurry on to the Shenandoah before the rain had swollen it past fording, procured a guide who could take him through the country along byroads, so as to avoid the enemy's outposts.

The darkness and rain now made him change his plan, and he moved more rapidly, following the road that led to Sangster's Station, where he knew the enemy had a force guarding the railroad bridge.

Upon nearing this point, he came to the bank of a small stream which was rising rapidly, and evidently very deep. Loud bursts of thunder now accompanied the rain, and the bright flashes of lightning lifted for a moment the thick veil of darkness from surrounding objects. Beyond the angry-looking stream, right across the path of his advance, was a stockade fort, whose garrison had already discovered him.

A challenge and a shot from the sentinel on duty, reminded him that there was no time to examine the ford.

The Seventh Regiment, commanded by Col. R. H. Dulany, was ordered to cross and attack. The First Squadron, under Captain Hatcher, Company A, gallantly responded, and plunging across the stream dashed at the stockade.

Up and around it they went, crossing the railroad, the heavy force in the breastworks preventing their return. The rest of the Seventh, blinded by the darkness, passed down the stream without crossing it.

The Eleventh Regiment, commanded by Lieut-Col. M. Beal, was now ordered to charge. Rosser's stirring appeal to the men was answered with a loud cheer. Forming in close column, they moved steadily across the roaring creek, guided by the lightning flashes and the bursts of flame that came from the foe's receiving volleys.

"Although by this time, the enemy was thoroughly aroused, and was pouring sheet after sheet of fire into the head of Beal's column, the gallant old regiment went cheering through water, and in a moment was up the hill on the other side—and the stockade was ours."[3]

The brave Captain Cartmell of Company B was at the head of the First Squadron, and was instantly killed. Several others were wounded, some mortally, though most of the garrison, under cover of darkness, escaped.

Among the captures was a silver bugle and the flag of the one Hundred and Sixty-fourth New York, a part of which regiment had occupied the fort. The bugle was presented to Hatcher's squadron, and the flag, through Colonel Beal and the Eleventh, to the Virginia Military Institute. Afterwards, in 1883, when peace and mutual goodwill had returned, the flag, which was very beautiful, was presented, through the corps of cadets, to the Mayor of New York, and by him returned to its old regiment.

---

[3]Rosser.

After attending to his wounded and dead, Rosser moved on through the rain and darkness towards Upperville. Men and horses were well nigh exhausted, but the enemy was now certainly in the saddle in hot pursuit, and no rest could be taken.

All night the drenching rain continued. Towards morning it began to turn cold, and the falling drops, turning to sleet, increased the tortures of drowsiness and extreme fatigue. The horses, jaded and hungry, staggered through the mud, now stiffened with cold, while the men with garments frozen, bodies benumbed, and faculties almost palsied with distress, half unconscious, kept their places in the laboring column.

At sunrise Upperville was reached, and a halt was made to have breakfast and to feed the horses. Here some of the men had to be lifted from their horses, being stiff with cold and their clothing frozen to the saddles.

After an hour's respite the weary march was resumed. The rain had now ceased, and the clouds lifting, the welcome sight of the Blue Ridge cheered the hearts of the half-frozen troopers.

In a few hours they had crossed through Ashby's Gap and were once more upon the banks of the Shenandoah. The swollen, angry river barred their passage, and across its turbid waters lay the promised land, which, in spite of the terrible march, they had come too late to enter.

Rosser knew that the enemy was close upon his heels, and was apprehensive lest taking advantage of the swollen condition of the river, he would also endeavor to intercept him at Front Royal or Luray.

He had no choice but to move up the right bank until he found a practicable crossing. Again the weary column moved forward, picking its way over the rough and narrow road that winds along between the river and the mountain, now in worse condition by reason of the recent torrents.

At last when Front Royal was reached there was a halt, and the men went into camp for the first time in forty-eight hours, having marched in thirty-six hours more than ninety miles.

Next morning Rosser pushed on, and arrived at Luray a few hours before a division of Federals had passed through Thorton's Gap in his rear.

The river was still very high, but a crossing was effected with some difficulty at Conrad's Store, and on the 20th of December the brigade reached the army of General Early in the Valley.

It was now learned that the raiding party which Rosser had started out to capture, had returned to Winchester, and the brigade was permitted to go into camp and take a rest.

After such a tiresome march, the week's holiday which followed was much enjoyed. The horses were shod, and their strength recruited on the abundant forage of the Valley.

It was Christmas time too, and in spite of the ruin wrought by war, thanks to careful housewives, many good things remained. The half-starved troopers made the best of their opportunity, and gladly banishing thoughts of "grim-visaged war," yielded themselves to the cheerful festivities of Christmas time. If turkeys were hard to get, the savory sausage of the forehanded farmers was accepted as a fair substitute, and the apple, peach, and pumpkin pies, rye coffee, and sorghum molasses, galore, made one think that plenty, if not peace, had again returned to the land.

CHAPTER VIII

January, 1864

Rosser with Fitz Lee—They make midwinter raid to capture cattle for
Lee's army—March down the Patterson Creek Valley—Capture a
Federal wagon train—Move towards New Creek—Return to Early
in the Valley—Fitz Lee with his division returns to the Army of
Northern Virginia—Early and Rosser make the Petersburg raid
—Returning, the Laurel Brigade camps at Weyer's Cave—Rest and
hilarity—Across the Blue Ridge to catch Kilpatrick—Return to
Valley—The camp in Rockbridge county—Recruiting—Grant
moves his multitudes—A call from Lee—The Laurel joins Lee in
the Wilderness—The 5th and 6th of May—Join Hampton at
Shady Grove—Yellow Tavern—Death of Stuart.

The cavalry being not only the eyes and ears of the army,
but also foragers for it, it was not in the nature of things
that Fitz Lee's force, being now augmented by the arrival
of Rosser's brigade, could long remain idle in camp. An
expedition west of the mountains was ordered by Early to
secure cattle for the use of Lee's army, and at the same time
to capture detached bodies of the enemy and do such
damage to his communications on the Baltimore and Ohio
Railroad as might be found practicable.

The expedition under General Fitz Lee started in the latter days of December. The citizens of the Moorefield and
South Branch valleys were loyal, with few exceptions, to
the Confederacy, and most of them zealous in its cause,
and had consequently suffered, both in their persons and
substance, from the frequent predatory visits of the Federals.

When it was known that the expedition was made for the purpose of procuring beef for Lee's army, it was not long before droves of well-fed steers were on their way to "Dixie."

Upon arriving at Moorefield, Fitz Lee learned that a Federal force, eight or nine hundred strong, was at Petersburg and strongly fortified behind entrenchments and abattis. For the want of artillery and because much of the small-arms ammunition had been ruined in the storm, he decided not to attack Petersburg, but to move upon the enemy's line of communication on the Baltimore and Ohio Railroad.

On the morning of January the 2nd, he marched down the South Branch, and began to cross the Branch Mountain at Mills Gap. Rosser's brigade led the advance, with the Eleventh Virginia in front, followed by the Seventh.

Upon nearing the top of the mountain, the road was found to be blockaded with fallen trees, and a way had to be opened by axemen. While engaged in this, scouts reported that a Federal wagon train, moving in the direction of New Creek, was approaching the point where the road on which Rosser was marching forked with the Petersburg and New Creek road.

Rosser at once hurried up his foremost regiments, and the men at many places leaped their horses over the fallen trees in their eagerness to get to the front.

After passing the top of the gap and rounding a curve in the road, they came in sight of the train, which was moving slowly and in careless security, attended by a small guard of soldiers. There were about forty wagons, six mules to each, loaded, as was afterwards found, with ammunition, hides, and sutlers' stores.

Rosser ordered the Eleventh, commanded by Maj. E. H. McDonald, to charge the train, and the Seventh, commanded by Colonel Dulany, to follow closely in support. The column emerged from cover of the woods, and with loud shouts galloped down the mountainside. The train quickened its snail-like pace into a run, and then rushed along at a furious speed. In their eagerness to escape, the faster teams tried to pass the slower ones, and then followed upsets and collisions, mules entangled, kicking to free themselves from harness, and great confusion. It seemed at first an easy capture, the guard in sight making off to the woods. But as the train halted, about seventy-five infantrymen leaped out of the wagons, and running up the hillside beyond the road, began to fire upon the nearest horsemen. They were soon charged by a small portion of the Eleventh, under Major McDonald, and most of them compelled to surrender. Among the captured sutlers' stores were canned goods of every description, which were much enjoyed by the victors.

Fitz Lee now moved down Patterson's Creek with foragers on the flanks gathering cattle and sheep. At Burlington more sutlers' stores were captured, and a blockhouse abandoned by the enemy was destroyed.

After a short delay at Burlington the column moved on to Ridgeville and pitched camp. This place was six miles from New Creek, against which Fitz Lee intended to advance the following day. But a severe snowstorm set in during the night, and next morning Fitz Lee withdrew and returned to the Valley, going by way of Romney and

Brock's Gap to Harrisonburg. He took back with him 400 cattle and 110 prisoners.

Very soon after his return Fitz Lee with his command rejoined the Army of Northern Virginia. Rosser's brigade, however, remained with Early, then in command of the Valley district.

After a short rest the brigade participated in another cattle expedition across the mountain that proved quite successful, and the fruitful results of which were due in a great measure to Rosser's skillful handling of his command.

On January 28th, 1864, General Early, with Rosser's brigade, Thomas' brigade of infantry, all the effective men of Gilmore's and McNeil's Partisan Rangers, and four pieces of McClannahan's Battery, moved from New Market to Moorefield.

On the 29th Rosser, with the cavalry and artillery, accompanied by Early, reached Moorefield somewhat in advance of the infantry. Scouts having reported that a large train was on its way from New Creek to Petersburg, Rosser was ordered to cross over the Branch Mountain and capture it.

Accordingly, on the morning of the 30th, he marched from Moorefield, having besides his own brigade one or two pieces of McClannahan's Battery.

Moving by way of the Moorefield and Alleghany turnpike, when nearing the top of the mountain, he found the road to be blocked with fallen trees, and the gap held by a regiment of Federal infantry. Rosser, dismounting the Twelfth Regiment, made a vigorous attack, and soon forced his way through, driving the enemy before him, who retired in the direction of Medley to meet the train which was then coming up towards Petersburg.

Upon discovering Rosser's approach the Federals parked their train of ninety-five wagons at Medley, and prepared to defend it. The guard consisted of about 800 infantry and a small body of cavalry, which seemed amply sufficient to keep off an inferior number of Confederate cavalrymen. Rosser at once determined to attack, though having all told not more than 400 men. The Twelfth Regiment, under Colonel Massie, was ordered to go around and fall upon the enemy's rear, and the other regiments, partly dismounted, were advanced upon his front and flank.

The attempt was a bold one. The Federals were in a defensive position, superior in numbers, and at that time dismounted cavalrymen were hardly considered a match for disciplined infantry.

Encouraged, however, by the confidence of their leader and stimulated by the sight of the rich prize, the Confederates moved forward with spirit to the assault. The Federals stood firm and repulsed the first onset, inflicting some loss. Rosser determined to attack again, as by this time a piece of artillery had reached the field, which he ordered to immediately open upon them, and the sight of its bursting shells spreading panic among the teamsters, was exhilarating to the Confederates.

After one or two salutes from his gun, Rosser renewed the attack. The dismounted men advanced on the enemy's left, while the cavalry, led by Major Meyers, charged in front. The Federals broke and fled in disorder, leaving all their wagons and forty-two prisoners in the hands of the victors. With the retreating Federals the teamsters carried off mules belonging to nearly forty wagons, which escape was owing greatly to the fact, as stated by General Rosser, that the Twelfth Regiment, from some misunderstanding, had failed to get in position in the rear before the retreat began. The wagons were loaded with bacon, sugar, coffee, and other army supplies, and proved to be a very valuable capture.

In the engagement Rosser lost in killed and wounded twenty-five men. The enemy's loss was greater. Their dead and wounded were left on the field, but the number is not reported.

On the morning of the 1st of February Rosser, now reinforced by Thomas' brigade of infantry, moved against Petersburg. Upon arriving there, it was found that the Federal force was gone, having abandoned in their haste a considerable quantity of ammunition and commissary stores.

From Petersburg Rosser, in obedience to orders from Early, moved down Patterson's Creek to collect cattle, and do what damage he could to the Federal communications on the line of the Baltimore and Ohio Railroad.

After sending Colonel Marshall with the Seventh Regiment to hold the gap at Mechanicsburg against General Averill, who was expected from Martinsburg, Rosser marched down Patterson's Creek to its mouth, sending parties out to bring in cattle and sheep. Upon reaching the line of the Baltimore and Ohio Railroad at the mouth of the creek, he captured one guard there, and destroyed the railroad bridges over the Potomac, Patterson's Creek, and the canal. With his prisoners and cattle, he now retraced his steps, moving cautiously to avoid Averill, who, he learned, had forced the gap at Mechanicsburg and gotten in his rear.

By taking by-roads at different points, Rosser succeeded in eluding Averill, who, mistaking his purpose, or fearing to come up with him, adroitly kept out of his way while pretending to pursue him.

Rosser with all his prisoners, about 1,200 cattle, and other captures reached Moorefield unmolested by the enemy.

Captain John McNeil also arrived, bringing from beyond the Alleghany 300 cattle.

General Averill, disappointed on all sides, now approached Moorefield and menaced it. Early recalled Thomas' brigade, which had started for the Valley, and ordered Rosser to withdraw through Moorefield as if in retreat. He thought to draw Averill into the clutches of his infantry, but the wily Federal, whose caution now served him a good turn, refused the bait and halted. Early, after waiting a few hours, set out for the Valley, taking with him fifty of the captured wagons, 1,500 cattle, and 500 sheep.

Stuart's appreciation of what was done by Rosser and his command on this expedition, is shown in the following endorsement of Rosser's report: "The bold and successful enterprise herein reported furnishes additional proof of General Rosser's merit as a commander, and adds fresh laurels to that veteran brigade, so signalized for valor already."

Upon its return to the Valley the brigade went into camp near Weyer's Cave. Many of the sutlers' stores found in the captured wagon train, had been appropriated by the soldiers, and for several days the new camp was the scene of festive mirth. Brandied cherries, pickled oysters, boned turkey, and other delicious canned edibles, formed a part of the menu, while Boston gingerbread and Goshen cheese were served *ad libitum*.

The weather was bright and cool. There were daily visits to Weyer's Cave, not a few picnics, and an occasional horse-race. The luxuries disappeared rapidly, and when the sugar and coffee had been exhausted, the troopers began to yearn for another raid.

The opportunity soon came. On the evening of the 29th of February the command was again in saddle, and started across the Blue Ridge.

Kilpatrick and Dahlgren were then making their notorious raid on Richmond. Rosser marched rapidly to take part in the pursuit. At the outset the weather was fine, and many of the men not dreaming of a long march, left their overcoats in camp. By night the clouds thickened, the moon and the stars were hid, and a drizzling rain began to fall. By and by a stiff northeaster blew, and before midnight it began to sleet. The falling drops freezing as soon as they touched horse or man, enveloped each in a sheet of ice. The moon from behind the clouds furnished enough light to make objects visible, and the appearance of the moving horsemen was weird and ghostlike. Hat, coat, equipments, hair, and beard covered with ice, furnished a complete disguise. The horses, too, were masked in glistening white, and shivering with cold the men moved on in profound silence, nothing being heard but the steady tramp of the column.

After an all-night ride Charlottesville was reached. There a short rest was taken, and thence by forced marches the command proceeded, sometimes marching all night, until they went into camp within six miles of Richmond. Kilpatrick was, however, not overtaken, though so closely were his heels dogged, that frequently in the night, the country people insisted that Rosser's men were a part of the enemy. After marching and countermarching for two weeks in vain pursuit of the doubling Federals, a rest of two days was taken at Gordonsville, which was greatly enjoyed in spite of the scarcity of food and forage.

March the 16th the brigade started back to the Valley, making short marches until by the 31st it was settled in comfortable quarters near Lexington, Virginia. Though the section of country in which the new camp was pitched was rich and as yet untouched by the devastating hand of the enemy, its abundant supplies had been much exhausted to feed Lee's half-starved veterans. The army ration was reduced to a quarter of a pound of meat and one pound of meal a day. The soldiers submitted, though they reserved the right to grumble, and seldom failed when opportunity offered, to supplement the deficiency at the tables of the hospitable farmers in the vicinity. Although food was scarce the air and water were fine, and among a people full of patriotic zeal, ardor for the cause was rekindled.

Indeed it was a period of happiness for many, who far away from scenes of war, with reviews and dress parades, enjoyed its pomp and circumstance, while giving full range to the enjoyment of the charms of peace.

It was a season, too, of growth for the brigade. New recruits were added, fresh horses brought in, and the old ones rested, if not fattened.

With the approach of spring, came rumors of the moving of Grant's vast multitude. Lee had appealed to the mothers of Virginia to send all the laggards to the field, to help him in the desperate struggle he felt was approaching. In response to this, recruits poured in, and the brigade got its share of what was called the "new issue." Many of the sick and wounded had recovered and rejoined their regiments, so that the brigade was now much stronger both in quantity and quality of material than it had been since its active campaigns.

When the flowers of April foretokened, alas, the return of war and a leave-taking from the new-found friends, there was no hanging back now, as formerly, at the prospect of quitting the Valley. The trumpet call of Lee had stirred the depths of the Confederate heart. Like the slogan of the Highlands, "Lee needs help!" was the word passed from house to house, and from mountain and plain came the sons of Virginia in response.

The Valley men were behind none in their eagerness to take part in the decisive struggle; and when on a bright May morning the column descended the slopes of the Blue Ridge and turned towards the banks of the Rappahannock, there was a look of firm resolve in the faces of the gallant troopers, which said that they would do their best for Lee and their country.

May the 4th, 1864, Grant crossed the Rapidan and the Wilderness campaign began.

After breaking camp at Wolf Town, Madison county, May the 4th, Rosser's brigade moved up and joined Lee's army, passing the infantry in breastworks at Mine Run and encamping on Lee's right.

From all appearances the morrow promised to be a busy day.

That night a prisoner captured by some of the Eleventh Regiment was brought into Rosser's camp. Many questions were put to him by some of the soldiers, as to what was thought of Grant, the new commander of the Army of the Potomac. His answers indicated that there was great confidence in Grant's luck and energy.

"Where is your pontoon train?" said one. To the surprise of all he responded, "Grant has no pontoon train."

"How, then, are you going to get back over the river?" asked another.

"Grant says," answered the Federal quietly, "that all of his men who go back over the river can cross on a log."

This, with other trifling incidents that soldiers eagerly seized upon, showed that the Federal army under its new leader, confiding in numbers and Grant's luck, meant serious work.

Next day, the 5th, the sun rose hot and lurid. The heat of the night had been oppressive and the men poorly refreshed by broken slumbers, were called early into the saddle.

The command moved down the Catharpin Road, which led to Todd's Tavern. A short distance west of the river Po, a strong force of the enemy was encountered. On both sides of the road it was heavily wooded, and the fight began between dismounted men on the flanks. At first these lines were strengthened, and for some time the battle was of an infantry character. It continued to increase in intensity, the enemy using his artillery with considerable effect. Soon the enemy began to yield to the impetuosity of the attack. But a Federal battery on a hill sorely annoyed Rosser, who now became impatient to get to close quarters. There was no charging practicable except by fours in the road, and that which was in front and to be overcome was an unknown quantity. Had Rosser been aware that a Federal division, Wilson's, was confronting him, he might have been more cautious. Under the circumstances, there seemed nothing else to do but go forward, and the whole brigade was ordered to advance by fours. The Twelfth was in front under Col. Thomas Massie; next came the Seventh, followed by the Eleventh, with White's Battalion bringing up the rear.

The Twelfth, with the "Rebel yell," dashed at the solid ranks of the enemy over a barricade of abattis. For a while they stood firm and received the charge. Now it was man to man and hand to hand. Pistol and sabre were busy in slaughter, while the shrieks of the stricken and the shouts of the victors mingled with the roar of battle.

The fierce onset of the Confederates did not slacken. On pressed the whole brigade, crowding to the front. The Federals gave way and retreated across the river Po. On the other side they made a gallant stand, but the Confederates, now flushed with victory, pressed forward, and again drove them, in spite of the efforts of the officers to hold the men in line.

With great coolness, the enemy kept selecting new positions for their artillery, which enabled him to shell the advancing column, but nothing could keep back the horsemen in the road.

The Federal retreat, however, was orderly, and at every favorable point the enemy again made efforts to rally. Although the attempts were ineffectual, they were successful enough to allow their artillery to withdraw and escape capture. Finally a good position was reached, where there was little timber, and posting squadrons with supporting squadrons on both sides of the road, the Federals poured a deadly fire from carbines into Rosser's advancing column. Most bravely did the Twelfth charge, rally and charge again, but the Federals stood like a rock.

Rosser now ordered the Seventh and Eleventh to charge. Says Lieutenant Vandiver, who commanded Company F of the Seventh, that day: "At length we reached a point where the enemy had evidently made a stand. Coming to an old field grown up in scattering pines and sumac, we found the Federal cavalry formed. General Rosser stood on a slight eminence to our left, and as the organized supporting column emerged from the timber he ordered the charge. My company came up in good shape. It seemed to me that the enemy was then weakening, and in spite of efforts of brave officers to hold them in line, were breaking up. About that time, the Eleventh Regiment, which followed us, came into the open ground, and Maj. E. H. McDonald led it into action, heading the charge. Our boys joined in, and the body went like a solid shot into the ranks of the Federals, who now broke and ran. Many of them were captured in the pursuit, which was continued for several miles."

During this retreat the Federals made several attempts to rally, selecting new positions for their guns, and stationing fresh squadrons of carbineers on the flanks to annoy the oncoming Confederates.

But the Confederates only halted to reform, and charging the flanking parties drove them away.

Rosser's men had begun the fight with a scant supply of ammunition, the ordnance train in the march from the Valley not having kept up with the column. As prisoners were taken their ammunition was eagerly seized, but this was not sufficient, and after several hours of fighting some of the men became discouraged.

White's Battalion was drawn up on one side of the road, and as a regiment of Yankees galloped down in their front Captain Meyers, commanding Company A, turned to Colonel White and asked, "Colonel, how can we fight those fellows with no ammunition? We'd as well have rocks as empty pistols." But the Colonel replied so grimly, "What are our sabres for?" that the men drew their blades without further hesitation, and charged square at the Yankee column, which wheeled about and retired faster than it came.

White's Battalion had been christened by Rosser "The Comanches" on account of the wild and reckless dash with which they usually bore down upon the enemy.

After pursuing the Federals to the vicinity of Todd's Tavern, Rosser halted and began to retrace his steps.

Meantime Wilson, reinforced by Gregg's division, assumed the offensive and began to harass Rosser's rear. The skirmishing was slight, but continued until the Confederates had crossed the river Po. In this fight Rosser's loss was considerable, but not nearly so great as it was the next day; yet it seems to be remembered with greater pride. It was a sort of duel between a Confederate brigade and a Federal division, in which the former had come out victorious. The superiority of the enemy in numbers, clearly seen by the men, instead of dispiriting only roused them to more energetic action. There was, too, a good deal of disorder on both sides, and more than once the scales of victory were turned by the prowess of a few.

Whether Gregg came up before Wilson had retired, does not appear.

General Grant, in his memoirs, says: "During the afternoon, Sheridan sent Gregg's division of cavalry to Todd's Tavern in search of Wilson. This was fortunate. He found Wilson engaged with a superior force under General Rosser supported by infantry, and falling back before it. Together, they were strong enough to turn the tables upon the enemy and themselves become aggressive. They soon drove the Rebel cavalry back beyond 'Corbin's bridge.'"

Grant was evidently misinformed and, if we are to compute the historical value of all the "Personal Memoirs" by the measure of truth in this statement, it would amount to very little. There was no infantry with Rosser and his force was greatly inferior to that of Wilson. It was not known for a long time afterwards, by the men at least, that Gregg had reinforced Wilson, or they would have been still more proud of the work done that day.

The general impression among the survivors is that then for the first time the command assumed the name of the Laurel Brigade. Whether, as some say, it was due to the fact that several soldiers conspicuous on the field wore laurel on their hats, or that Rosser, proud of his victory, dubbed the command the "Laurel Brigade," does not appear. Certain it is that from and after that date the name of "Laurel" was first used by the men themselves.[1]

General Wilson, in his official report of this fight on May 5th, says:

"By eight A. M. the Second Brigade, with the First Vermont Cavalry, Colonel Preston commanding, in advance, had arrived at Craig's Meeting-House. Just beyond they encountered the enemy's cavalry, Rosser's brigade, and after a very sharp fight and several handsome charges, drove it rapidly back a distance of two miles, taking some prisoners. About noon Chapman's ammunition became exhausted, and, fearing to press the pursuit too far, I directed him to hold the position he then occupied and observe closely the movements of the enemy's troops. Having observed the menacing disposition of the enemy in front of Chapman's brigade, I directed him to collect his dismounted men and be prepared to fall back if the enemy should press him too severely. Soon after this, having received reinforcements, the enemy advanced and compelled Chapman to retire. It was now apparent that the Rebel force was considerably superior to ours, and, being short of ammunition, I directed Chapman to fall back rapidly beyond the Meeting-House, and reform in rear of the First Brigade. My headquarters having been located at Mrs. Faulkner's house, when the Rebels arrived at that place my escort, composed of about fifty men of the Eighth Illinois Cavalry, commanded by Lieutenant Long, Third Indiana Cavalry, gave them a severe check, and in conjunction with a heavy fire from Pennington's and Fitzhugh's

---

[1]Quite a number of survivors of the brigade insist that the name was given by General Rosser, at an earlier date, in the Valley, which is probably true; the name, however, was not immediately adopted by the men.

batteries, enabled everything to withdraw from the main road to the position occupied by the First Brigade. I had scarcely arrived there, however, when I was informed by Colonel Bryan that the enemy had made his appearance, at an early hour in the forenoon, in his rear, on the road to Parker's Store, and that none of my couriers to General Meade had succeeded in getting through. Surprised at this, and fearing for the safety of my command, I immediately determined to withdraw by a blind road by Todd's Tavern to Chancellorsville. I had scarcely taken this resolution, when I perceived that the enemy was pushing rapidly down the Catharpin Road in the same direction. The march was begun at once; the Second Brigade in advance, followed by the batteries and the First Brigade. The Eighteenth Pennsylvania Cavalry, Lieut.-Col. W. P. Brinton commanding, was left to cover the rear. The main column crossed the river Po near its head, and struck the Catharpin Road just beyond Corbin's Bridge. It had scarcely got upon the road when the Rebels made their appearance on the hill west of the bridge. I succeeded in reaching the road with my escort just in time to prevent being cut off. The rear guard found the road occupied by the enemy, but Colonel Brinton made three brilliant and determined charges, breaking the enemy's cavalry; but finding he could not succeed in getting through without heavy loss, he struck off to the left and joined the division late in the evening.

"At Todd's Tavern I found Brigadier-General Gregg, with his division, and passing behind him, formed my command to assist in holding the place. Gregg moved promptly out, attacked the enemy, and after a sharp fight repulsed him."

General Davies of Gregg's division, in his report, says:

"On the morning of the 5th we marched to Todd's Tavern, and on arriving there relieved the Third Division. We fought until dark and succeeded in driving the enemy. Lost sixty-one men, mostly from the First New Jersey and First Massachusetts Cavalry."

Col. John W. Kester, of First New Jersey Cavalry, reports:

"When we arrived at a village called Todd's Tavern, we met the Third Cavalry Division, commanded by General Wilson, rapidly retreating before the enemy's cavalry in a very disordered state. General Davies' brigade was immediately thrown forward, and having repidly moved a half mile, we met the advance of the enemy's cavalry pressing forward on the rear of General Wilson. Captain Hart, with the First Squadron, was ordered to charge, which he did with such impetuosity that the enemy in turn was routed, and the gallant First Squadron pressed them back on their main body, until they in turn were met by the charge of a Rebel regiment, which again turned the tide of battle. At this critical juncture, I hastened to his support with three squadrons of my regiment, the remaining two being sent on the flanks. Hastily forming these squadrons in line of battle, the whole line moved forward and gave the enemy such a sharp volley, followed by a rapid fire at will, that they desisted from their charge and endeavored to keep back the advancing line of my regiment, but without success. Forward we moved as steadily as a parade, the Rebels endeavoring to check us with showers of canister, but with no avail; and they hastily limbered up their guns, and fell back just in time to prevent their capture."

Maj. John W. Emmett, assistant adjutant-general on staff of Genl. Thos. L. Rosser. This gallant gentleman and officer, so well and favorably known to the men and officers of the Laurel Brigade, was severely wounded in the body in the battle of the Wilderness, on the 5th of May, 1864, and again was wounded in the foot in one of the battles with Sheridan in the Valley of Virginia, by which he was disabled for the rest of the war.

From the foregoing official reports of the Federal officers in command of the opposed forces, it will be seen that the Laurel Brigade, consisting of three regiments, one battalion, and Chew's Battery, had repulsed the whole of Wilson's division, and driven it beyond the Po River, compelling Wilson to seek shelter and reform his command in the rear of Gregg's division, which had been sent to his support. It was not until the Laurel Brigade was assailed by the combined forces of Wilson and Gregg, numbering seventeen regiments of cavalry and six batteries, that it was forced to fall back beyond the Po River.

General Lee, in his report to the Secretary of War, says: "A large force of cavalry and artillery on our right flank was driven back by Rosser's brigade."

The brigade, in this all-day conflict, had more than sustained its previous reputation, and earned the name of "Laurel," by which it was thereafter known. It had opened the ball of the Wilderness campaign, the most noted in the annals of modern warfare, the campaign in which, more than in any other, the marvelous generalship of Robert E. Lee was demonstrated, and had protected the right flank of his army against an overwhelming force of Federal cavalry.

Its loss in killed, wounded, and missing was 114, the larger part in killed and wounded. It had inflicted upon its antagonist, as admitted by Federal reports, three officers and ninety-four men killed, twenty-seven officers and 389 men wounded, and 187 men missing.

Weary with the hard day's work and the excitement of battle, the men slept an unbroken sleep, little dreaming that the morrow would prove for them the bloodiest day of the war.

At break of day on the 6th all was astir, and by sunrise the bugle called to horse. The sun was just glinting through the pine-tree tops as the column marched out to its place in the battle line.

Lee's infantry was already engaged, and on the right could be distinctly heard the ceaseless roll of musketry, which rose and fell like the distant roar of a mighty torrent.

White with his battalion led the advance, with Company A, commanded by Captain Myers, in front. After crossing the river Po, and passing the Chancellor plantation, the brigade entered the open pine country bordering the Wilderness. Rosser sent orders to White to run over everything he came to. "How far must I go?" inquired White. To this the officer bearing the order could not well reply, and at White's suggestion went back for more explicit instructions. "Tell him," said Rosser, "to drive them as far as he can." In obedience to which, White immediately closed up his ranks and moved briskly forward. Soon the enemy's pickets were encountered and driven rapidly back upon their reserve. White pushed them all before him, the whole brigade following at a gallop. Above the rush of the column could be heard the shouts of the "Comanches" as they dashed upon the flying Federals.

White, in the ardor of the pursuit, which carried his command some distance in advance of any support, came suddenly upon Federal infantry and dismounted cavalry in a pine forest, who promptly opened upon him with volleys of musketry and carbines, inflicting some loss among the "Comanches."

He would probably have been pursued by the mounted cavalry, which had reformed, had not Rosser quickly put in the Eleventh to cover his retreat.

The Eleventh, under Major McDonald, now charged in fine style, and again the pines resounded with the "shout of the captains" and the roar of battle.

The Federals were now better prepared, and the rattle of the musketry grew louder. The Eleventh pressed on into the pines and turned back the advancing column of Federals, driving them through the pines until it came suddenly upon Grant's entrenched infantry. Though the Eleventh had delivered a staggering blow, yet it quailed before the tremendous fire then poured into it, and began to retire.

Now the Twelfth, under Colonel Massie, tried it, closely followed by the Seventh under Colonel Dulany. Into the pines, murky with the smoke of battle, they charged. Every step forward revealed new bodies of the enemy. The timid recoiled, but a few of the bravest pushed on until forced to retire to avoid capture.

Rosser now ordered a piece of artillery, which was the first of Thompson's Battery to reach the field, and was commanded by Lieutenant Carter, to open. Carter hastily pulling down a rail fence, brought his piece at a gallop into the field, and planted it on the rising ground before mentioned. He delivered his fire into the pines over the heads of the few struggling Confederates who,—at the edge of the woods, still faced the foe. The enemy did not advance. Not a bluecoat rode out of the pines. For a brief space, the broken regiments attempted a stand on the hill upon which Carter's piece was planted. But the Federals had now quickly placed in position to the left of the pines, on a slight eminence opposite to Carter, five or six guns. These swept the hills with a terrible fire. Before it went down men and horses, and the ground was strewn with the dead and dying. The horsemen now fell back into a woods behind Carter's piece in much confusion. There they halted and began to reform. Rosser hastily strengthened his left with about 150 dismounted men under Maj. E. H. McDonald.

The enemy lined the ridge-like eminence opposite with infantry or dismounted men, whose continuous volleys, uniting with those of their well-served artillery, swept every part of the Confederate position. A little to the right and rear of Carter's piece, White had gathered about thirty of his men, and a little further to the right was a small portion of the Eleventh, probably a dozen men, under Lieut. Isaac Parsons, still facing the foe. Carter stood his ground, answering with great rapidity the Federal shots. Now and then the enemy concentrated his fire on Carter, raining bombs around him. But he and his men, like salamanders, seemed to revel amidst the fire. Enveloped in the smoke of bursting shells the brave gunners worked their pieces, Carter encouraging them with cheering words and with shouts of triumph as he saw his well-aimed shots take effect.

The truth is that the Federal artillery was making great havoc, though the foe could not see it. Most of the bombs aimed at Carter's gun passed over him, so close was he to the enemy, and burst in the woods where the Confederate cavalry regiments were attempting to reform, falling right among them, killing and wounding a great many.

The care of the dead and dying, and the plunging of the wounded and frightened horses, created unavoidable confusion. Under the circumstances, it seemed impossible to form column. Stuart was there, riding among the men and officers, and calling upon them to be steady. The ordeal was a terrible one for cavalry, and though apparently deaf to orders amidst the thunder of bursting shells, yet most of the men stood firm. The number of killed and wounded was considerable.

Meantime Rosser sat on his horse near Carter's gun, expecting every moment to see a regiment of Federal horse burst over the crest of the opposite hill. None came, however, and it was evident that the splendid and well-maintained charges of the Laurel Brigade, together with the incomparable service of the horse artillery, which had charged with the cavalry, and discharged canister into large bodies of the enemy at close range, had severely punished the Federal cavalry and dampened the ardor of Wilson.

On the 7th, there was little fighting along any part of Lee's line. White's Battalion had a light skirmish at the bridge over the river Po, in which it defeated an attempt of the Federals to take and hold it.

Towards evening General Hampton met a reconnoitering force of the enemy, and drove it back. In this engagement the brigade participated to some extent.

On the night of the 7th, Grant began his movement by the left flank towards Spottsylvania Court House, and on the 8th, Lee's infantry began a movement to the right.

On the morning of May the 8th, Rosser with the Laurel Brigade joined Genl. Wade Hampton at Shady Grove, and from that time to the 1st of September, the brigade formed a part of Hampton's division.

When Stuart fell and Hampton was put in command of the cavalry corps, his division was commanded by General Butler of South Carolina.

The enemy now appeared, May 8th, in full force in front of Hampton's division, then consisting of Young's and Rosser's brigades. By means of the artillery's well-directed fire his advance was soon checked.

Receiving orders from Lee to attack the enemy vigorously, in order to co-operate with Early, who was about to attack their left at Todd's Tavern, Hampton sent Rosser to attack their right and rear, while he with Young's brigade pressed their front. Both movements were executed handsomely and vigorously, and the attack was a complete success. The enemy fell back rapidly, abandoning his camp and newly-issued rations.

The fighting had been mostly against the enemy's infantry, little or no cavalry having been seen since the 6th.

This was the first engagement of the Laurel Brigade under Genl. Wade Hampton, and was fought mainly by dismounted men. It was Hampton's favorite method, to use cavalry as mounted infantry and carbineers, wherever the nature of the country, such as that of the Wilderness, made it practicable; the horses being of use primarily for quickness of movement from one point to another, the fighting being done on foot with carbines. By adopting this use of cavalry, Hampton had by several decades anticipated the universal modern use of mounted soldiers. The introduction of the long-range repeating carbine having rendered the cavalry charge with sabre and pistol almost entirely impracticable and obsolete.

The cavalrymen realizing the usual success of Hampton's method, especially where there was to be long-maintained opposition to the enemy's infantry, were willing to dismount and accepted the use of carbines, which many of them had heretofore despised, preferring to dash in upon the enemy with sabre and pistol.

The fighting on the 8th being mainly skirmishing with the infantry, most of whom were behind breastworks and abattis, the day was destitute of incidents worthy of mention.

Next day the enemy drove in Hampton's pickets and after a sharp fight obtained possession of the main road leading from Shady Grove to Spottsylvania Court House, and also held the bridge over the river Po.

On the 10th Early was sent to dislodge them. In this attack, which was successful, Hampton's division participated.

On May the 12th, the great and bloody battle of Spottsylvania Court House was fought. Hampton took position on Lee's left, with his sharpshooters in the trenches, and his artillery posted so as to seriously annoy the right flank of the Federals.

On the 15th, Rosser made a forced reconnoissance as far as the Poor House, in the direction of Fredericksburg, driving in all the cavalry he met, and developing the position of Grant's right flank. In this movement the Eleventh was in front and suffered some losses. Among the wounded was Lieut. B. Funsten, adjutant of the regiment.

On the 16th, news came of the fight at Yellow Tavern and the fall of Gen. J. E. B. Stuart. The effect of the news, at first, was greatly to depress the men of the Laurel Brigade, who had followed the plume of Stuart on many a hard-fought field, and had been extricated by his genius and daring, from frequent situations of imminent peril. But recognizing such fatalities as the inevitable and looked-for incidents of war, they steeled themselves to the performance of present duty for sake of the cause, which, with the noble example of Stuart, still remained.

Grant was now moving rapidly towards Spottsylvania Court House, and Lee's infantry, in order to confront him, moved speedily in the same direction, leaving the Laurel Brigade to protect the left wing of Lee's army.

Sheridan with his cavalry corps continued his march towards Richmond, and on the 9th had gone around Lee's right with a heavy force of cavalry, and on the 11th, was confronted at Yellow Tavern by Stuart with greatly inferior numbers. Sheridan pressed his whole front vigorously, while he sent one brigade to make a dash upon Stuart's left. To this point, as the one of greatest danger, Stuart rode. Before he got there, nearly the whole left had given way, but he found a few men still holding the ground, and these he joined. With these men he fired into the enemy's flank and rear as they passed and repassed him, for they were driven back by the First Virginia Cavalry. As the Federals retired "one man who had been dismounted in the charge, and was running out on foot, turned as he passed the General and discharging his pistol, inflicted the fatal wound."[2] While a few still held the enemy in check Stuart was borne from the field in an ambulance. When he noticed the disorganized ranks of his men he cried out: "Go back, go back and do your duty as I have done mine,

---

[2]McClellan's "Stuart and His Campaigns."

and our country will be safe. Go back! Go back! I had
rather die than be whipped."[3] These were his last words
on the battlefield. On the evening of the following day he
died.

Few, if any, of Lee's great captains had won more
fame than Stuart, and none was more beloved by the
cavalrymen. Perhaps, his most distinguishing characteristic, and the one which endeared him most to the rank
and file, was his self-contained and buoyant manner in the
presence of the greatest danger, and his personal courage
and dash. The brilliant and successful charge, being in
the nature of what he expected, often seemed unnoticed by
him; but if there was a repulse or a threatening of disaster,
right in the deadly breach was to be seen the waving plume
of Stuart, where with burning words and flashing sword he
strove to wrest victory from defeat.

In the bloom of manhood and the noontide of his fame,
this brilliant soldier, superb cavalier, and Christian patriot
gave to his State the libation of his blood, and his life a
noble sacrifice on the altar of his country.

---

[3]McClellan.

CHAPTER IX

June, 1864

Hampton takes command of cavalry—Milford—Haw's Shop—Atlee's Station—Depleted condition of brigade—Scarcity of food and forage—Grant develops his wearing out policy—Assails Lee's lines of communication—Wilson attempts to cut the Virginia Central Railroad—Fight at Ashland—Heroic act of Maj. Holmes Conrad—Wilson defeated and pursued—Another affair at Haw's Shop—White's Comanches charge Federal breastworks—Hampton sent to meet Sheridan's raiders—Battle of Trevilians—Pursues Sheridan to the North Anna—Hard fare for men and horses—Some types of vandals—Skirmishing near White House—Cavalry against infantry and gunboats—Hanging on Sheridan's flank—White's Battalion detached—Sheridan entrenches at Samaria Church—Is driven out of entrenchments, leaving dead and wounded—Col. Thomas E. Massie of the Twelfth wounded—Pursuit of Sheridan to Charles City Court House.

On the 19th of June Hampton, taking with him Rosser's brigade, co-operated with Ewell in his attack on the enemy. Moving around Ewell's left, he drove in some Federal cavalry and succeeded in planting two guns in the rear of the enemy's right flank, which did good service. This good service was rendered by two guns of Thompson's Battery. Their well-aimed shots drew the attention of the enemy, who sent a force of infantry to capture them. At first Thompson checked them with grape and canister, but upon discovering the magnitude of the attacking force, he withdrew, having been ordered by Rosser to do so. Ever since the battle of May the 12th, when Grant suffered such heavy loss in his attempt to break through the Confederate lines, there had been a continuous movement of the Federal army towards Lee's right. This necessitated a corresponding movement of the Confederates.

On the 21st of May, Hampton proceeded towards Milford, and encountered some cavalry at Wright's Tavern, within two miles of Milford. Rosser charged at once and drove them back on a strong force of infantry and artillery, thus developing Grant's movement to Hanover Junction. Placing his division in front of this column Hampton fell back slowly to the Junction, skirmishing with the enemy and checking him at the bridge near the Junction, until relieved by infantry. The division was then posted on Lee's left.

On the 25th and 26th there were heavy rains, which made the roads very muddy. On the 27th, at eleven o'clock in the night, the brigade mounted and marched towards Anderson's Ford, passing through Ashland and camping near Atlee's Station, with the whole division within six miles of Richmond.

At Atlee's Station Hampton, now commanding all the cavalry, was ordered to ascertain if all the infantry of the enemy had crossed the Pamunkey River. Accordingly, on the morning of the 28th, taking with him William H. F. Lee's division, Wickham's, Butler's, and Rosser's brigades, he moved towards the enemy and encountered his pickets within two miles of Haw's Shop. These were at once driven in on the main body.

Rosser's and Wickham's brigades led in the assault and a heavy engagement ensued. Only dismounted men and the artillery were engaged, and the ground was stubbornly contested by both sides, with mutual loss, for some hours.

After much bloodshed the Federals gave way but, being heavily reinforced, they soon recovered their lost ground, and became the attacking party.

Hampton hearing from some of the prisoners that Sheridan's whole cavalry force, besides a large body of infantry, was opposed to him, determined to withdraw.

With an aggressive and superior force in his front this was no easy matter, and the difficulty was increased by the too sudden withdrawal of Wickham's brigade, which, being in the line between Rosser's and Butler's brigades, left a gap that exposed their flanks. The enemy was quick to take advantage of this. "Rosser's men being veterans," says Hampton, "withdrew without loss and in perfect order under their able commander," but Butler's troops, many of whom were raw recruits, were not so easily handled. Vigorously attacked on the flank before they had begun to retire, though up to this time they had fought admirably, they now fell into disorder and suffered heavily. Being without any general officer in command, for Butler was absent from a previous wound, Hampton went in and brought them out.

The Confederate loss in this engagement was quite serious, though that of the enemy was probably greater. Rosser's loss was eight killed and about twenty wounded.

By this time the number of men fit for duty in the brigade was much less than on the 5th of May, though not a few recruits had come to fill up the depleted ranks. More than 300 had been killed, wounded, or captured since the beginning of the campaign. A still greater number of horses had been killed or disabled, and the ranks of the dismounted men continued to swell. The scarcity of forage was severely felt. Little was furnished and the cavalrymen had to rely mainly upon the pastures they chanced to find at the places of temporary rest. Often, after a hard day's fight, they were occupied long after dark in hunting food and forage. The rations, too, were poor and supplied in scant quantity.

Grant had already discovered, that the only way to overcome Lee was to destroy his means of subsistence, and accordingly, by means of his numerous and well-appointed cavalry, he began to assail Lee's lines of communication.

On the 31st of May, Wilson with his division was sent to seize the Virginia Central Railroad and destroy it as far back as possible.

On the 1st of June this raiding column attacked William F. Lee's command near Hanover Court House, and forced it to fall back towards Ashland. Hampton at once went to his assistance with Rosser's brigade, and struck the rear of the Federals. Having notified W. F. Lee that Rosser would attack as soon as he came up with the enemy, this column was charged as soon as it was discovered and thrown into confusion. Following up his success, Rosser pressed the enemy vigorously, and in a series of brilliant charges, some of which were over dismounted men, he drove Wilson into Ashland, capturing prisoners from eight regiments, about 200 horses and many arms.

Wilson now made a stubborn stand, posting his artillery in the village of Ashland, and his men behind the houses and the railroad embankment.

"Meeting Lee on the Telegraph Road near Ashland, I directed him to attack at once. The North Carolina Brigade was dismounted for this purpose, and in the first volley fired against them, Brig.-Genl. P. M. B. Young, who was temporarily in command of the brigade, received a severe wound. Deprived of the direction of this gallant officer, the brigade failed to dislodge Wilson in the first assault. Lee immediately formed his troops for another attack, whilst I took the Tenth Virginia and a squadron of the Third North Carolina of his division, together with a squadron of the Seventh Virginia, Rosser's brigade, to attack on the right flank."[4]

Simultaneously with these assaults Rosser pressed his front. The Federals, though now vigorously attacked, for some time stubbornly held their ground. Hampton's well-formed plan of attack, seconded by the persistent valor of the Confederates, finally forced the enemy to give way at all points, leaving his dead and wounded and many prisoners in the hands of the victors.

In the beginning of this action, when Rosser first struck the enemy on his left and rear, the Twelfth was in front under Col. Thomas Massie, the leading squadron consisting of Companies B and I under Lieut. George Baylor. They first reached the led horses and pushed through them until they came up with the marching column. This they struck with so much vigor that the enemy, surprised and broken, fell back rapidly upon Ashland, where dismounted men, strongly posted in some houses of the village, received the Confederates with a galling fire. In the effort to dislodge these men some lives were lost, and there were many instances of valor that we have no space to record.

---

[4]Hampton.

In the fight that now ensued, both the Seventh, under
Colonel Dulany, and the Eleventh, under Colonel Beal, bore
conspicuous parts. Colonel Dulany had two horses shot
under him. At one time during the battle the enemy, having placed dismounted men with artillery behind the railroad embankment, poured deadly volleys into the ranks of
the Confederates.

Taking advantage of an apparent confusion in Rosser's
brigade, their mounted squadrons made a dash at a column
that Rosser was bringing up. The day was hot and the
dust fetlock deep. Coming up to within pistol shot the
Federals, seeing Rosser's defiant attitude, halted and began
firing their carbines. On both sides there was apparent
hesitation, the men moving about restlessly instead of
remaining in their places ready to obey the word of command. Rosser, as usual, in the forefront, was exhorting the
men to prepare to charge; while on the other side, the
Federal officers were urging their men to hold firm. The
smoke of the small arms, mingled with clouds of dust from
the moving horsemen, added to the confusion of the scene.

At this juncture it was evident that the action of one man
might turn the scale of victory. Maj. Holmes Conrad,[1] on

---

[1]Maj. Holmes Conrad, major and inspector-general of the Laurel
Brigade, when the State of Virginia seceded, enlisted in a company of
cavalry from Frederick County, Va., commanded by Capt. Jas. W.
Drake, which was later Company A, of the First Virginia Cavalry.
The same day he was made first lieutenant of the company; was made
adjutant of the Seventeenth Battalion August, 1862. The Seventeenth
Battalion was the nucleus upon which was developed the Eleventh
Regiment of the Laurel Brigade.

In 1864 he was commissioned major and assistant inspector-general
of Rosser's Cavalry Division.

Major Conrad was a familiar figure to the men who were at the
front in the battles of the Laurel Brigade.

Rosser's staff, taking in the situation, seized the flag of the Eleventh Regiment and exclaiming, "Men, save your colors!" rode straight at the Federal column. With banner waving he penetrated the first files, and turning to the left he escaped unharmed. Partly from the clouds of dust, and partly from astonishment and admiration of the audacity of Conrad, the foremost Federals failed to assault him. Their attention was immediately engaged by the onset of the grey troopers, who followed closely upon his heels.

The "Bath Squadron," under Captain Dangerfield of the Eleventh, was in front. Aroused by the desperate valor of Conrad, with a shout they charged, and soon drove the enemy in confusion upon his main body.

When Wilson withdrew beaten from the field of Ashland, Hampton pushed him until night, when he drew off. By what route Wilson withdrew in the night is not certainly known, but from Grant's memoirs it is found that he rejoined the Army of the Potomac on the 3rd of June.

On the same day, Hampton with his division assaulted the enemy strongly posted behind earthworks near Haw's Shop. Dismounting his North Carolina Brigade, under Colonel Baker, and attacking promptly, Lee carried the outer line. In this engagement Rosser with the Laurel Brigade seems to have borne a part, though the main work of the day was performed by Lee's North Carolina Brigade.

On the next day Rosser moved with the brigade to the same point with the purpose of gaining information. Colonel White with his mounted squadrons was ordered to charge the earthworks. With great gallantry the "Comanches" rode up to and along the fortifications, discharging their pistols at the enemy. The Federals, astonished

at the audacity of the Confederate horsemen, abandoned
the works, and some of White's men climbing over, or at
points riding through, pursued them for a short distance.
So daring a charge excited the admiration of the rest of
the brigade, and Rosser's cheers for the "Comanches"
were joined in by the whole command.

There was now for some time a calm along the front.
Grant's punishment at Cold Harbor, had strengthened his
conviction that Lee's lines could not be broken through, no
matter what sacrifice of life he was willing to make in the
attempt. What, therefore, bullet and steel could not accomplish he thought starvation might. He, therefore, planned
to menace Richmond with sufficient force to keep Lee's
army near by; while, with light marching divisions of
infantry and cavalry, he would destroy the railroads, and
devastate the country from which Lee drew his supplies.

The vandal Hunter was at this time in the Shenandoah
Valley burning and destroying. News of his outrages had
reached the camp of the Laurels, and there was manifested
a great desire to go to the defense of their homes. They
also had heard of the capture of Staunton, and the death
of their former commander, Genl. W. E. Jones. But, there
was soon quite enough close at hand, to engage their attention.

On the 7th of June, "Sheridan was sent with two divisions to communicate with Hunter, and to break up the
Virginia Central Railroad and James River Canal."[5] The
intention, as was evident from papers which fell into the
hands of the Confederates afterwards, was that Sheridan
should destroy Charlottesville and Gordonsville, with the

---

[5] Grant's Memoirs.

railroads near those places, and then unite with Hunter in his attack on Lynchburg. He had with him about 8,900 effective men, well mounted. With flanking squadrons scouring the country for fresh horses, he proceeded on his mission of destruction with fine promise of success.

Early on the morning of the 8th, Hampton with his own division and that of Fitz Lee, and several batteries of horse artillery, was sent to look after this raiding column. The enemy had a day's start. To follow in his wake would have been to invite destruction from famine, unless he could be overtaken before the pursuers' rations gave out, for the track of Sheridan was like that left by a cyclonic hailstorm; what man and beast did not devour or take away, was burnt or destroyed. He even shot his own broken-down horses. Hampton, therefore, with characteristic foresight, sought by celerity of movement to get ahead of the raiding column and post his force right on its projected line of march. As soon, therefore, as the order was received from Lee, Hampton with his own division moved out at once to get between Gordonsville and the enemy, ordering Fitz Lee to follow as soon as possible.

Outmarching Sheridan, Hampton got ahead of him, and encamped the night of the 10th in Green Spring Valley, three miles beyond Trevilians Station, on the Virginia Central Railroad. Fitz Lee encamped the same night near Louisa Court House.

There was a road from this place to Trevilians which Sheridan was expected to march into and along it approach the station.

Hampton, having learned during the night that Sheridan had crossed the North Anna, determined to attack him at daylight. Fitz Lee was ordered to attack on the road leading from Louisa Court House to Clayton's Store, while Hampton, with his own division, intended to move against the enemy on the road leading from Trevilians Station to the same point.

"By this disposition," says Hampton, "I hoped to cover Lee's left and my right flank, and to drive the enemy back if he attempted to reach Gordonsville, by passing to my left, and to conceal my real design, which was to strike him at Clayton's Store after uniting the two divisions."

At dawn Hampton was ready with Butler's and Young's brigades to go forward, Rosser with his command having been sent to cover a road on Hampton's left.

Soon a message was received from Fitz Lee that he was moving out to attack, and Butler immediately advanced to engage the enemy, supported by Young.

According to Hampton's report, the Confederates repulsed the enemy and drove him behind his breastworks. According to Sheridan, the contrary was the case. Up to nine o'clock, at any rate, Hampton pressed the enemy. All seemed to be going well. Fitz Lee was momentarily expected to join on the right, but Custer's dash materially changed the Confederates' plans. Instead of waiting to be pressed by Fitz Lee, Custer, finding an unguarded road leading around Hampton's right to Trevilians Station, followed it blindly. Coming upon the ambulances, caissons, and led horses of the division, he fell upon them with his accustomed alacrity, and then looked around to see what else he could do. Near him on the right was Thompson's Battery, behind Butler's line, and ignorant of any hostile

movement in the rear.   Custer at once made preparations to
take it.

Says Col. R. P. Chew, commander of the horse artillery,
who was present:

"I had gone to the position occupied by General Butler, to
select a position for artillery to aid him in his fight, and returning about nine o'clock I met General Hampton, and was
informed by him that the enemy was in our rear, and had
captured our caissons and led horses, and was told by him to go
back and do the best I could with the guns.

"Butler was at this time hotly engaged in front. I went back
rapidly and found Custer's men advancing from the rear to
capture the guns.

"Fortunately a company of South Carolina cavalry was
formed near our position, which charged and drove back the
enemy. I then moved the guns to a hill north of and facing
the station. They were without support.

"At this stage of affairs Rosser, who was on the Gordonsville Road some distance off to the left, was quickly recalled by
Hampton to oppose Custer. He returned rapidly, but Custer
was now trying to escape with his captures, by going off the
Gordonsville Road around Butler and Young and the horse
artillery, and getting through on their left."

From his new position Chew opened fire on the column
and drove them back on the station, and by a well-directed
fire delayed its escape by crippling the horses and stopping
the wagons. After considerable delay Custer again attempted to escape by the same route, but Rosser hearing
the firing, brought his brigade at a gallop down the Gordonsville Road, and wheeling to the left struck Custer's column and doubled it back on Fitz Lee, who was coming up
on the other side of the station, and who attacking vigor-

ously, pushed that part of Custer's column back, recapturing many wagons and taking five caissons. Some idea may be formed of the vigor of Lee's attack from the desperate charge of one company of the Sixth Virginia, known as the Clarke Cavalry, which lost in a single charge upon a Federal battery more than half its number.

The well-timed assault of Rosser was made in double column, the Eleventh in front on the right of the road, and White in front on the left.

To the Laurels, success meant more than victory. The enemy had captured the division trains and many prisoners. His presence for a moment in Hampton's rear meant general disaster. What was to be done, had to be done quickly. Seldom did a duty of heavy responsibility where promptness of decision in the leader, and ready valor in the men was needed, fall upon a command better fitted to perform it. With well-closed ranks and steady gallop, the Laurels followed Rosser towards the point where the firing indicated the presence of the enemy. A glance at the victorious Federals, accompanied with captured trains and ambulances filled with prisoners, only quickened the rush as the brigade swept with shouts to the rescue.

The bluecoats, who, following the adventurous Custer, had by a wild dash created a momentary panic in the Confederates' rear, were now in their turn surprised, and the impetuous charge of the grey troopers soon put Custer to precipitate flight. Wagons, prisoners, and precious plunder were now quickly abandoned, and the marching column soon scattered in many directions. The pursuit of the fugitives, many of whom had taken for shelter to the woods, left Rosser's force somewhat diminished. The main body of the enemy fell back towards the station, hotly pursued by the Confederates. Here, forming his men with artillery commanding the approaches, Custer stood at bay, while Rosser, putting his regiments in order and gathering his men, made ready to attack him.

Colonel Chew, who had counted Custer's men as they passed in front of his battery, now informed Rosser that Custer had only about 1,200 men, and that by promptly charging he could capture them.

Rosser, especially eager to discomfort the vainglorious Custer, ordered White to charge. Just then Hampton rode up and forbade the movement.

Custer remained at Trevilians assisted, doubtless, by the advance of Sheridan's whole force on Hampton's right flank.

Butler and Young fell back, and they, with Rosser, were posted by Hampton along a new line to the west of the station and facing Sheridan.

The enemy in the evening made several attempts to dislodge Hampton from his new position, but without success.

After the repulse of one of these assaults Rosser, still believing that a bold charge would drive Custer from his position, had just begun the perilous task when he was badly wounded.[6] This put a stop to the movement. The command of the brigade now devolved upon Col. R. H. Dulany of the Seventh. The remainder of the day was spent in repelling Sheridan's assaults upon Hampton's new line.

---

[6]Says Hampton in his report, "In the list of wounded was Brigadier-General Rosser, who received a painful wound whilst charging at the head of his brigade."

Night closed the scene, and after dark both sides began to entrench preparatory to the next day's decisive struggle.

At dawn the combatants were in position, and until twelve o'clock stood facing each other.

Fitz Lee, who on the previous day attacked Custer beyond the station, and recaptured many wagons and prisoners, now swung around and about twelve o'clock connected with Hampton. His division was placed in a position to support Hampton's division in case the enemy attacked Hampton's right.

About three o'clock Sheridan began a series of heavy assaults. His dismounted men, armed with repeating rifles, had an immense advantage over the Confederate sharpshooters, who had to be content with the ordinary carbines or muskets. Many of their carbines were of Confederate make, and were nearly as dangerous to the man behind as to the enemy in front.

As the fighting this day was chiefly on foot, and the woods at places furnished good cover, the incessant fire of the assailing Federals, called for heroic powers of resistance on the part of the poorly-armed Confederates. The brunt of the fight fell on Butler's brigade and the horse artillery, and they proved equal to the occasion, repelling with stubborn courage all the assaults of the enemy.

The nature of the ground prevented much use of the enemy's artillery, while the Confederate position was excellent in this respect, though from its being in the open field and near the enemy, the gunners were much exposed to the deadly aim of the sharpshooters.

A space of only 250 yards was between the lines. The Confederate gunners lay close to the ground, and only rose when the Federals charged. The colors of Thompson's Battery were riddled with bullets, and around a single piece nine men were killed or wounded, among them the color-bearer.

The fighting continued until after nightfall, when the flash of the guns lifting for a moment the veil of darkness, revealed the position of the on-coming enemy.

In the meantime Fitz Lee, directed by Hampton, reinforced Butler's left with Wickham's brigade, while he took Lomax's brigade across to the Gordonsville Road, so as to strike the enemy on his right flank.

Says Hampton with laconic brevity, "This movement was successful."

Desperately did Sheridan struggle to force Hampton from his path. But with greater resolution did the Confederate leader maintain his ground against the superior numbers of his opponent.

Under the cover of darkness Sheridan began to retreat, and by morning was far on his way back to Grant's army, leaving behind him his dead and many of his wounded. Grant explains in his memoirs (Vol. II, page 302) that "Sheridan went back, because the enemy has taken possession of a crossing by which he proposed to go west, and because he had heard that Hunter was not at Charlottesville." This, however, will hardly explain his hurried retreat, and the abandonment of his dead and wounded.

He could not have thought of going to Charlottesville, when it was as much as he could do to give Hampton the slip, and get back to Grant's infantry. This, however, he did without being vigorously pursued by Hampton, though it was evident that the Federals had retreated very hurriedly.

Hampton, in his report, says:

"In the meantime Fitz Lee reinforced the left with Wickham's brigade, while he took Lomax's brigade across the Gordonsville Road to strike the enemy on his left flank. Sheridan now heavily pressed in front and attacked on the left, fell back *hurriedly*."

Sheridan's report is disingenuous, and indeed lacks the internal evidence of truth. For instance, he accounts for the loss of some caissons by saying, "When the enemy broke they hurried between General Custer's command and Colonel Grigg's, capturing five caissons of Remington's Battery."

This is perhaps the only instance in the annals of war, where the victor lost caissons because the enemy ran away.

On the 13th, the brigade with Hampton followed on after Sheridan to the North Anna, and down the river to a point opposite Frederick Hall.

As an evidence of what the cavalry suffered now for lack of food and forage, the following extracts from the diary of a soldier of the Laurel Brigade will be of interest.

"May 14th. Lay still all day; no rations. Ewell is at Frederick Hall.

"15th. Crossed North Anna at Caws Bridge, moved along very slowly, reached our stopping place after dark, and fooled around till late hunting grass. No rations yet.

"16th. Drew two crackers and a little meat; nothing for the horses. Marched all day on the county roads; borrowed a few rations from another command for us. No corn tonight and not a particle of grass; camped after dark.

"17th.   Grazed the horses a little this morning; wagons with corn and rations expected, but no one seems to know anything definite about them.   The dust is three inches deep everywhere, and the sun broiling hot.

"18th.   No wagons yet, the men are suffering very much for rations, and have been for several days.   Drew plenty of corn.   Moved back on Wickham's Farm on the Pamunkey River, where we found the long expected wagons with four days' rations.   Two squadrons have been without rations since the 12th."[6]

While Sheridan failed to unite with Hunter, or to do much damage to the Virginia Central Railroad, there was one part of Grant's program for crushing the Confederacy which Sheridan never failed to carry out.   That was to ravage the country through which he passed, destroying or carrying off everything possible to be removed.   Grant's object, as a war measure, was to starve out the men whom he could not beat in the field, reduce Richmond to the point of starvation, and thus decrease the efficiency of Lee's army.

Whatever may be said of Sheridan as a fighter, no one can deny that as a ravager he was not wanting in the elements of success.   While he had not yet quite mastered this method of restoring the amity of a disunited country, he was learning fairly well, from those two past masters in that art, Generals William Tecumseh Sherman and David Hunter.   It is fair to say, by way of classification, that the ravaging of Sheridan was somewhat systematic and purposeful, being part of an avowed military plan.   That of Sherman in his march through Georgia was brutal and wanton; while that of David Hunter in the Valley of Virginia was absolutely heinous and devilish.

[6]From the Diary of Private Joseph L. Sherrard.

Hampton did not give Sheridan much time to make way with property as he went along, but he did the best he could under the circumstances. He gathered up all the horses his flanking column could find, and when one of his own gave out he had it shot, lest some one of the farmers he had tried to ruin might use the animal to raise a crop for his family.

On the 20th Hampton reached the vicinity of the White House, and had a small engagement with some infantry and cavalry of the enemy, assisted by their gunboats on the Pamunkey.

During the night Sheridan crossed over and marched towards the James, with his force much increased by infantry.

Hampton, after skirmishing with him the best part of the day, withdrew towards evening and encamped at Bottom's bridge, on the Chickahominy.

Sheridan, who was in full retreat, was acting as rear guard for Grant, who on the night of the 21st began the operation of transferring the Army of the Potomac across the James River, the bulk of which was already on the south side.

For two or three days Hampton hung on Sheridan's flank, but without accomplishing any serious results. The starved condition of the Confederate horses had greatly reduced the efficiency of the brigade. The sore-backed and broken-down animals were sent to the rear for rest, and with the remainder of the command, a large portion being now dismounted, Colonel Dulany, commanding the brigade, had to engage in almost daily fights with the enemy.

On the 24th the command was roused up at two o'clock, and lay in a field near Samaria Church until morning. The pickets had been driven in and there was expectations of an advance of the Federals.

Sheridan, however, had begun to throw up earthworks with the obvious design of holding his ground, and Hampton immediately formed his plan of attack; arranging to have the brigades of Gary and Chambliss to assault in flank, while the rest of his command pressed in front.

As soon as Gary had engaged the enemy, Chambliss was thrown forward, and by a movement handsomely executed connected with him. At the same moment the whole line, under the immediate command of Maj.-Genl. Fitz Lee, charged the works of the enemy, who, after fighting stubbornly for a short time, gave way, leaving his dead and wounded on the field.

This advance of our troops was made in the face of a heavy fire of artillery and musketry, and it was most handsomely accomplished.

In the charge of the works, the Eleventh and the Seventh regiments participated, White's Battalion being absent on detached service.

The Twelfth, being mounted, joined in the pursuit of the retreating Federals, driving them for three miles. In this charge Lieut.-Col. T. B. Massie, commanding the Twelfth, was wounded while gallantly leading his men over the works of the enemy.

Sheridan was completely routed, and his broken and flying columns pursued to within two and a half miles of Charles City Court House. Hampton captured 157 prisoners, including one colonel and twelve commissioned officers, while a considerable number of Federal dead and wounded was left on the field. Thus foiled and defeated at Trevilians, severely punished at the White House, and routed at Samaria Church from a chosen position defended by earthworks, Sheridan very wisely concluded to rejoin Grant as soon as possible. This he speedily did, falling back to the James River under protection of gunboats, and crossing to the south side.

The loss in Hampton's division was six killed and fifty-nine wounded.

CHAPTER X

June 1864

Hampton marches towards Richmond—Federals cross to south side of
James River, and Hampton follows, crossing near Drury's Bluff—
Moves below Petersburg—Camp near Reams Station—Intercepts
Wilson's raiders, and sharp fight near Sapony Church—Lieutenant Vandiver's account of the engagement—Ruffian marauders—
Wilson escapes after punishment and loss—A short rest, water-
melons and hospitality—Brigade recuperates by return of men
from hospitals and horse furloughs—Fitz Lee with his division
sent to the Shenandoah Valley—Hampton kept to hold the lines on
Lee's right—Grant creates a diversion on the north side of the
James—Hampton ordered to Culpeper, but was recalled when he
reached Beaver Dam—Fight at White Oak Swamp—Brigade
returns to south side—Monk Neck's Bridge—Hatcher's Run—
Reams Station—The newspaper raid—Hampton's cattle raid.

On June the 25th Hampton withdrew, moving towards
Richmond, but following the farm roads lest the dust on the
highway might subject his column to a shelling from the
gunboats on the James.

Passing by Frazier's Farm and Malvern Hill the weary
soldiers halted and encamped within five miles of Rich
mond. Next day they crossed the James near Drury's
Bluff.

On the 27th the brigade moved towards Petersburg.
That city was now invested by Grant and was being vigorously shelled. The brigade did not pass through the town,
but around it, on account of the bombardment. Some of
the soldiers ventured to pass through and were astonished
to find people going about on the streets as if nothing was

going on. Such incessant warfare, bringing grief into almost every home, had inured even the women and children to its dangers and hardships.

The trains running out from Petersburg were regularly shelled, but they moved along on schedule time, apparently indifferent to the shots of the Federal artillery.

After dark the brigade went into camp near Reams Station, on the Weldon Railroad. The horses had nothing but one sheaf of green oats apiece during the day, and were also much jaded with the long and dusty march.

Early next morning the command moved out and halted in an oat field to feed. It was now known to the soldiers that Hampton was making an effort to intercept a raiding column of two brigades under Wilson which had been destroying a part of the Weldon Railroad and devastating the surrounding country. Wilson was known to be on his return and endeavoring to rejoin the army of Grant. The difficulty was to ascertain by which route he was coming.

Hampton, however, had his plans well laid, and with pickets on all the roads and scouts scouring the country around, the men were ordered to sleep on their arms. There was not much sleep for some of them. The brigade had halted near Sapony Church, and soon after dark picket firing was heard, and every one knew that Wilson was trying to break by.

His first assault, which was on a part of the line held by Chambliss' brigade, after some stubborn fighting was repulsed. The Seventh seems to have been the only regiment of the Laurel Brigade that participated in the repulse.

Says Lieutenant Vandiver of Company F, Seventh Regiment, who lost an arm in this fight: "Mounting hurriedly and forming in line the Seventh went forward at a trot, while the distant picket firing on the road south of Sapony Church told what was going on. The Federals had forced the pickets in at a gallop, and the Seventh was ordered to dismount and fight on foot. The regiment had barely time to get in position on the left of the road and church, in fact it formed under fire. It was then dark, and the bullets and shells went over the heads of the men. The men carried rails and everything movable in reach to make breastworks, and in less than thirty minutes after the dismounted men were in the midst of one of the hottest battles of the campaign."

Lieutenant Vandiver was at that time commanding Company F of the Seventh, being the only officer with the company, Captain Kuykendall and Lieutenant Parker then being prisoners. On account of the absence of the regular commander Lieutenant Vandiver was assigned the command of the second Squadron dismounted.

The battle raged furiously, and the Federals were so near the Confederate lines that their forms could be seen by the flash of the discharges, and the commands "Forward!" "Close up!" etc., given by their officers were distinctly heard. But they would not advance to closer quarters, although outnumbering the Confederates three to one. The continual discharge of small arms was interspersed with artillery firing, and the shells exploding over the heads of the men caused great confusion among the led horses and mounted men in the rear of our line of battle.

The attack on Chambliss continued until nearly daylight. At one o'clock, and again at three, the brigade was aroused by the noise of the combat.

About daylight all was astir and the men formed in line dismounted. Colonel Dulany swung his command around and participated in a vigorous assault on the Federal left flank. They were driven in disorder, many falling into the hands of the Confederates.

In the meantime White's Battalion went with General Butler to fall upon the enemy's rear; and simultaneously with Chambliss' attack in front and that of Dulany and others on the left flank White's mounted men charged. Pressed in front and flank, the Federals scattered through the pines, and broke away to the right, leaving 800 prisoners in the hands of the victors.

The plunder thrown away by the fugitives was of many kinds, and is worthy of notice as indicating, not only that these raiding columns had all the license of pirates, but that plunder was one of the chief objects of their raids. The license to plunder served to swell the ranks of the raiding regiments for the time being with professional marauders and cutthroats. Over the field of flight were found shawls, silk dresses, mantles of velvet, jewelry, and every kind of light valuables to be found in the houses of well-to-do people.

The war, now that the Confederacy was declining, had become popular with the ruffian classes of the North, and many entered the army for no other purpose than to steal and plunder.

After pursuing Wilson's column for some eight or ten miles the command returned to Stony Creek.

On the morning of the 30th the pursuit was again taken up, but Wilson, after running against infantry and cavalry

in turn, and retreating by way of obscure country roads, at
last got by with a remnant of his division and rejoined
Grant's army.

From the 4th of July until the 30th there was little more
than picketing. Quiet reigned along the lines and the cavalrymen had time to rest and recruit. The fishing in the
streams was fine and the country abounded in melons and
luscious fruit. The land of that section appeared sterile to
the eye, but nevertheless it furnished bountiful supplies for
the table, and in the plain but spacious homes of the land-
holding people there was dispensed a generous hospitality.
Three weeks of comparative rest did wonders for the men
and horses. Many of the sick and wounded had returned.
Many of the dismounted had returned from "horse furlough" with fresh horses. The improved appearance of
the command was noticeable, and once more the men were
in good spirits. What if Grant was besieging Richmond,
was not Early at the gates of Washington? The vandal
Hunter had done his worst in the Valley, and was now with
his stolen goods flying through the hills of West Virginia.
The dark cloud in Georgia was then no bigger than a man's
hand, and few dreamed to what dimensions it would grow
before another winter set in.

The 30th of July was the day selected by Grant for blowing up a part of the Confederate works and the capture of
Petersburg.

In order to divert a considerable part of Lee's army
away from the south side of the James River, Grant now

Maj. F. M. Myers, of the Thirty-fifth Battalion, was formerly
captain of Company A, Thirty-fifth Battalion, and afterwards promoted to major of the battalion, succeeding Maj. Geo. N. Ferneyhough.
He was a courageous and efficient officer.

began a demonstration on the north side with Hancock's corps and Sheridan's cavalry. The news of this called most of Lee's cavalry into the saddle, but the collapse of the scheme in a few days restored the soldiers to their camps. Every attempt of Grant to assault Lee's lines ended in complete discomfiture.

In the early part of August Fitz Lee was sent with his division to the Shenandoah Valley, and Hampton with his own division and that of W. F. Lee was left to hold the lines to the right of Lee's infantry.

On the 11th of August Hampton was ordered by Lee to proceed with his division to Culpeper and report to Genl. R. H. Anderson, commanding in that quarter. Lee's object was to threaten the enemy's flank and rear should he move across the Blue Ridge.

In obedience to command Hampton marched his division northward, passing through Richmond August 13th. At Beaver Dam he received a telegraphic despatch from Lee recalling him. Before daylight on the 14th he began to retrace his steps, and at ten o'clock the next day brought his command to the support of Genl. W. F. Lee, who was then being heavily attacked at White's Tavern, eight miles below Richmond.

Grant, in order to prevent Lee from sending reinforcements to Early, had made another demonstration north of the James.

W. F. Lee's right was being forced back when Hampton arrived and took a small part in the repulse of the enemy by W. F. Lee's division. It was here that General Chambliss was killed while gallantly rallying his men.

On the morning of the 18th it looked as though serious work was at hand. The bugle called to horse at two o'clock A. M. At seven the brigade moved out, the Eleventh Regiment in front.

Lee had ordered Hampton to attack the enemy in his front. General Fields, commanding the left of the infantry, was directed to co-operate in the movement.

W. F. Lee's division attacked on the Charles City Road. Butler with his own and Rosser's brigade, under Col. R. H. Dulany, on the left, while Fields with his infantry pressed the enemy in front. Delay occurring in getting the forces in position, the attack was not begun until evening.

W. F. Lee drove the enemy some distance in his front, and Butler made a most successful attack on his right, when with the assistance of Rosser's brigade, under the command of Col. R. H. Dulany, he drove the Federals from their breastworks and pursued them two miles. There were captured in this affair 167 prisoners. The Federals during the night withdrew and recrossed the James, and Hampton was accordingly ordered by Lee to return to the south side and re-establish his picket line in front of Reams Station.

Grant having extended his left flank far enough to get possession of a part of the Weldon Railroad, was now attempting to destroy the part south of him. For this purpose Hancock's corps and Gregg's division of cavalry, on the 21st of August, were sent to the neighborhood of Reams Station.

Hampton's division was moving towards the same point when on the 23rd of August the enemy was encountered at Monk Neck's Bridge, two miles west of the station, on the Rowanty Creek. Butler here attacked them in position and had a severe engagement. He succeeded, however, in driving back the enemy, a division of infantry, and in establishing the picket-line.

As this was a pitched encounter between Confederate cavalry and Federal infantry aided by cavalry, in which the latter after a stubborn contest were badly worsted, it deserves full space. But the story can only be told from the standpoint of the Laurels, some of whom speak of the contest with great and commendable pride.

In this action the brigade was still commanded by Col. R. H. Dulany, General Rosser not having sufficiently recovered from the wound received at Trevilians to resume command.

On the 23rd the command moved down the Stage Road to meet the enemy. Upon reaching Hatcher's Run there were the usual signs of a recent fight. Broken ambulances and dead horses lined the road.

Very soon the enemy was found, and the Seventh Regiment, which was in front, was forced back. The bulk of the Seventh and Eleventh regiments and a part of the Twelfth, under Lieut. George Baylor, were now dismounted and deployed on each side of the road, White's Battalion and the Twelfth remaining mounted.

White's First Squadron joined General Butler on his right. The dismounted men of the Eleventh, under Maj. E. H. McDonald, advanced on the left side of the road, while the Seventh, under Col. Thomas Marshall, advanced on the right.

The movement at first was through a woodland, and the Federals being mounted, retired before the Confederate advance. After following them for half a mile the latter

reached the end of the woods, and before them lay an open
field across which at a distance of 500 yards, was distinctly
seen a line of breastworks occupied by infantry. Halting
at the edge of the woods behind a dilapidated rail fence,
the Seventh and Eleventh lay down.

For half an hour the Federals waited for an attack. Then
a considerable force, apparently a brigade, moved out and
took position on the left of the line occupied by the Eleventh. The design of the enemy was plainly to execute a
flank movement and take the Eleventh in reverse; but there
were no orders to fall back and the Confederates grimly
awaited the issue.

Presently the enemy advanced in heavy force beyond
their breastworks to within a short distance of the fence
behind which lay the Confederates. A withering fire met
them, but they fell flat on the ground and, partly concealed
by the grass, poured volley after volley into the thin lines of
the dismounted men. Attacked by greatly superior numbers, and threatened by the brigade of infantry on their
left, the Confederates fell back through the woods. Soon
they met General Butler bringing up a South Carolina brigade. Hastily reforming they resumed their old position
under a heavy fire, and the battle raged furiously.

The flanking brigade of Federals swung around on Butler's left, and the South Carolinians, pressed in front and
flank, after heroic efforts were forced to retire. This necessitated the falling back of the Confederate line of dismounted men which was under command of Maj. E. H.
McDonald.

The Federal commander, seizing his opportunity,
ordered forward a squadron of horse that now rode among

the disordered Confederates, and pressed on, endeavoring to stampede Dulany's reserves. But this proved not so easy a task. Their charge was met with a countercharge, and the beaten Federals in a few moments were seen by the dismounted men returning hotly pursued by the grey troopers.

Butler, now readjusting his lines, forced the Federals behind their breastworks, where they remained. He was unable to dislodge them without the aid of infantry, although the fighting continued until after dark, heavy volleys of musketry at intervals breaking the stillness of the night.

The next day was one of comparative quiet.

The success of Butler at Monk Neck's Bridge suggested to Hampton the feasibility of driving the Federals from their works at Reams Station. His plan of attack was communicated to General Lee and concurred in.

General Heth's division of infantry was ordered to co-operate with Hampton, and Genl. A. P. Hill was sent to take command of the expedition.

On the morning of the 25th, Hampton moved out with his two divisions of cavalry under Generals Butler and Barringer. After disposing part of his command so as to cover Hill's advance, with the remainder, including the Eleventh and Twelfth regiments, and White's Battalion, he crossed Malone's Bridge at nine A. M. and drove in the enemy's pickets. Following up these he encountered a heavy force of Federals strongly posted. After a sharp fight the enemy fell back rapidly towards Malone's Crossing, hotly pursued by the Confederates.

Near Reams Station Federal infantry came up and took the place of their cavalry, while the latter attempted to turn

Hampton's flanks. "In this," says Hampton, "they were foiled and I held my ground steadily."

Hill, whose advance was masked by some of the cavalry, was not yet ready for the assault. He requested Hampton to retire slowly and draw the enemy after him, so that he with his infantry might take them in rear. This Hampton proceeded to do, but the Federals followed with great caution.

At five P. M. the boom of Hill's artillery indicated that all was ready, and Hampton at once ordered forward his battle line of dismounted men. Before them were the serried ranks of veteran infantry, with strong works to retire behind; while the enemy's cavalry was threatening their right. Unskilled in the maneuvers of infantry, and knowing little beyond keeping an even front, the dismounted men moved steadily forward. The sharp volleys of Federal musketry were only answered by the rattle of Confederate carbines, but the grey line kept steadily advancing while delivering its fire, and soon the bluecoats fell back in confusion, seeking safety behind their works at Reams Station.

Up to this point of the engagement, Hampton's line had been extended across the railroad, occupying both sides. Discovering now that Hill, approaching from the west side, was driving the enemy, he moved his force to the right and east side of the railroad. Pivoting his left on this, and with his right far extended, he ordered the line to advance and swing around so as to envelop the enemy's rear.

Rosser, who had returned to the field the day before, though still suffering from the wound received at Trevilians, was in command of his brigade.

The Eleventh, under Colonel Funsten, and a portion of White's Battalion formed part of a second line supporting Young on Hampton's right, while the extreme right of the assaulting column was occupied by the Twelfth under Colonel Massie, the two right companies, B and I, being armed only with pistol and sabre.

As the advancing line moved on, it was obliged to pass over ground naturally rough and broken, and now made still more difficult of passage by felled trees that had been cut down for purposes of defense. The right was obliged to go forward more rapidly than the center and left, and besides, it encountered a body of the enemy until then unassailed, and in position outside of the entrenchments.

It was now nearly sundown, when amid the roar of cannon, bursting of bombs, and the pattering of the deadly bullets through the foliage, Hampton's line, clambering through the branches and over the trunks of the fallen timber, drove the last line of the enemy behind his fortifications.

The circle around the enemy was now complete. The Twelfth Virginia Cavalry, on Hampton's extreme right, as it formed anew for the final rush, found itself alongside of the Twelfth Virginia Infantry, that, on Hill's extreme left, had swung around from the opposite side of the works. When it was discovered that there were two Twelfth Virginias side by side salutations were interchanged, and there was not a little bantering and boasting as to which of the two, the Twelfth Infantry or the Twelfth Cavalry, would be the first to reach and scale the ramparts in front of them. It was quite understood that there was to be a contest of valor, and bracing for the struggle, each regiment waited anxiously for the command to go forward. The enveloping lines were dressed and presented a steady front. The Federal gunners were at their posts, and the last beams of the setting sun glanced along the musket barrels of the awaiting enemy. It was only the stillness that usually heralds the storm-burst.

Hill opened with deafening roar, and above the din were heard the shouts of his gallant soldiers, and the whole line now moved forward.

The two Twelfth regiments at the word "Charge!" went forward with noble rivalry, facing undaunted a heavy fire from the Federal artillery. For a brief space the race for glory was an even one; but, when near the works, the Twelfth Infantry halted to deliver its fire before rushing on. The Twelfth Cavalry never stopped, but with cocked pistols in hand, made straight for the breastworks, and leaping over them fairly won the race. The Federals fired one volley and, then throwing down their arms, fled precipitately.

In the meantime the Seventh Regiment, under Col. R. H. Dulany, had been engaged in masking the advance of Hill's column of infantry. The following is Colonel Dulany's account of the same:

"I was ordered by General Rosser to report with my regiment, Seventh Virginia, to Gen. A. P. Hill near Reams Station August 24th, 1864. When I found General Hill, he told me that he was very anxious that the Federal forces who were entrenched at Reams Station should not know of his presence until he attacked their earthworks, and to that end he wished me to drive in all the cavalry in his front. Not knowing what was before me, I ordered Colonel Marshall to advance with a squadron and attack any forces he came up with. I followed with the rest of the regiment. We had not advanced more than a mile when I heard firing, and Colonel Marshall was brought back badly wounded. I immediately rode to the front, and taking command of the advanced squadrons, charged the enemy and drove them behind their earthworks. We were so close on their heels that two of my men, unable to control their horses, followed the Federal cavalry into their fortifications. One of the men was Pendleton of Baltimore, the other I do not remember—fell dead in the trenches. I do not recollect what other loss was suffered. General Hill was repulsed in his first attack with a heavy loss.

"On the morning of the 25th Hill ordered me to protect his flanks with the assistance of a portion of Wright's command, while he made his second attack when he carried the earthworks, capturing twenty-six or eight hundred men and six or eight new three-inch rifle-guns. During the fight the Federal cavalry made three efforts to get at his flanks, but we drove them back every time. As Hill sent his prisoners to the rear, the Federal cavalry again attempted a flank movement, and with more stubbornness than at their first attempt. We had a number of the Henry sixteen-shooters recently captured from Wilson's cavalry, and our fire was so rapid that Hill became uneasy, supposing we had run up against infantry, and sent to me an aid to see if we needed any assistance. I asked for two howitzers, which he sent me, and immediately after a portion of General McCowan's command. They came at a double-quick and the General, being a large man, was pretty well blown. He asked me to put his men in position, as he did not know the ground. As the howitzers were all the help I wanted, and I desired my own men to have all the credit of the frequent repulses of the enemy, I told General McCowan, that there was a stream in the woods in our rear, where, if he would take his command, he would be near enough if we required his assistance. After this General Hill ordered me to move forward and take possession of the battlefield, to secure the guns and ammunition left by the enemy, and bury the dead. While carrying out these orders, a squad of Federal cavalry under a flag of truce came, asking permission to bury their dead. I had orders to refuse such applications and they retired."

General Hill wished to get back to the army before the enemy should know that he had left Reams Station.

After dark Hampton with seven regiments of his command, including the Twelfth Virginia and White's Battalion, remained in the trenches to cover the withdrawal of the infantry. For there was still a force of the enemy outside of the works in the direction of Grant's army, and there was some apprehension of its attempting to recover the station.

After a twelve hours' battle an almost sleepless night followed. The ground in front of the trenches was strewn with dead and dying Federals, and the shrieks of the wounded banished slumber. At midnight a terrific storm burst forth, deluging all with a downpour of rain, and bringing much relief to the wounded. The dreadful patter of the elements with the sharp rattle and deafening roar of the thunder was appalling, and the bright flashes of lightning, that revealed the ghastly features of the dead and of others in the agonies of death, added to the horrors of the scene.

During the night the Federals withdrew from the vicinity, and next day were followed and harassed by Hampton's cavalry, with which was the Twelfth Virginia.

While the battle around the station was going on the Seventh, as we have seen from Colonel Dulany's report, had been doing some good work. It had been ordered to report to Gen. A. P. Hill to mask the movement of his infantry, which it did by driving in all the Federal cavalry in his front. Lieutenant-Colonel Marshall, leading in this attack, was badly wounded, and so vigorous was the charge which was pressed by Colonel Dulany that two of his men rode over the enemy's entrenchments, one of them being killed inside of them.

On the 24th the Seventh repulsed several bold attempts of the Federals to turn the flanks of Hill, blocking their way at every attack until, foiled and disheartened, they finally withdrew.

The engagements before Reams Station on the 25th, in which the cavalry did most of its fighting on foot, co-operating and forming parts of the fighting line with the infantry, a large part of them armed only with pistols and sabres, tended greatly to inspire the infantry with admiration for the dash, and confidence in the staying qualities of the cavalry, which arm of the service they had heretofore affected to belittle. It was shown that they were capable of attacking infantry in entrenched positions with such inferior weapons as carbines and pistols and this, not only on foot, but in some instances mounted.

There were engaged in this fight on the part of the Confederates about 8,000 men under command of Genl. A. P. Hill, consisting of McRae's, Cook's, and Lane's brigades, with Pegram's Artillery, and the cavalry division of Hampton and Barringer; while the Federal force under General Hancock was composed of the Second Army Corps, Mills' and Gibb's divisions, fifty regiments, the two cavalry divisions of Gregg and Kautz, and the whole supported by Wilcox's division in reserve, numbering from 16,000 to

20,000 men, the Federals having advantage of fortified positions.

The victory of the Confederates was decisive, nine guns being captured and some of them turned upon the enemy. According to the official report of General Hill the captures were, "Twelve stands of colors, nine pieces of artillery, ten caissons, 2,150 prisoners, 3,100 small arms, thirty-two horses. My own loss, cavalry, artillery and infantry, being 720."

The Federal official reports on the 26th, of the engagements near Reams Station on the 25th, are interesting reading mainly for their inconsistencies, contradictions, and general inaccuracy, though some are wonderfully candid; Grant being misinformed by his subordinates.

General Grant reports:

"City Point, Va., August 26th, 1864, 10 A. M.
Major H. W. Halleck,
                    Washington, D. C.
I have no report of the casualties yet from operations yesterday near Reams Station. Orders were given during the day for General Hancock to return, but being pressed by the enemy he could not do so until night. Frequent assaults were repulsed, but just before night the enemy carried one point of the line and captured eight pieces of artillery.

The staff officer, who gives the only report I have, thinks the enemy were very severely punished, and that our loss in prisoners will be small.

During the night General Hancock returned to his place in line without opposition.   *   *   *
                                   U. S. Grant,
                                   Lieutenant-General."

August 26th, 1864, ten A. M., Genl. George D. Meade reports to General Grant:

"Hancock's troops were withdrawn without molestation or being followed. He is now near the Williams house. He reports his command at present unserviceable. A report from General Gregg, commanding cavalry on Warren's left and Hancock's rear, reports the enemy pressing his pickets a little this morning with a view, he thinks, of picking up stragglers."

At half past twelve P. M. Meade reported to General Grant: "A safeguard that was left on the battlefield remained there until after daylight this morning. At that time the enemy had all disappeared, leaving their dead on the field unburied. This shows how severely they were punished, and doubtless hearing of the arrival of reinforcements, they feared the result if they remained."

Again at one o'clock P. M. Meade despatched to Grant as follows:

"Since sending my last despatch, I have conversed with the safeguard referred to. He did not leave the field until after sunrise. At that time nearly all the enemy had left, moving towards Petersburg. He says that they abandoned not only their dead but their wounded also. He conversed with an officer, who said that their losses were greater than ever before during the war.

"The safeguard says he was over a part of the field, and it was covered with the enemy's dead and wounded. He has seen a great many battlefields, but never saw such a sight. Very few of our dead, nearly all of the enemy.

"All of our wounded are brought off, but our dead unburied. I have instructed Gregg to make an effort to send a party to the field and bury our dead.

"I should judge from all accounts the enemy will most likely
be quiet for some time."

The absurdity and absolute falsity of the statement of
this "safeguard" is so apparent that it is a wonder that
Meade should have forwarded it to General Grant and with
remarks indicative of his having given credence to it. We
have seen from Meade's report to Grant of ten A. M. of the
same day, two hours before he forwarded this statement of
the "safeguard," that Hancock had fallen back in such condition that he reported his command as "unserviceable." We
have seen also that after the discomfiture of Hancock, in
which he lost 2,724 men, of whom 2,150 were prisoners,
nine guns, ten caissons, 3,100 small arms and twelve stands
of colors, A. P. Hill, wishing to return unobserved by the
enemy to the army near Petersburg, left Col. Richard
Dulany with the Seventh Regiment, Laurel Brigade, of
Cavalry, to screen his movement, to occupy the field, secure
the captures, and bury the dead.

Colonel Dulany, in his modest report, has said: "While
carrying out the order a squad of cavalry under flag of
truce came asking permission to bury their dead. I had
orders to refuse any such applications, and they retired."

The people of the North, as well as the Northern Government, having raised magnificent armies, supplied with
the most modern and approved equipments of war, demanded, with good reason, that their generals should win
victories. In order to satisfy this demand, victories won
only by peculiar processes on paper, were very often sub-
stituted in the place of real ones in the field. So a first-class
official report could easily convert a serious defeat into a

victory of very respectable proportions. It was a victory of
this kind that General Meade, upon the statement of the
"safeguard," reported to General Grant. It is not likely,
however, that Grant was enthused with the report of the
victory in which he knew that Hancock had fallen back
hors de combat, leaving guns, colors, prisoners, etc., in the
hands of the Confederates.

General Miles, commanding the First Division of the
Federal Second Army Corps, says in his report:

"At five P. M. the enemy drove in the skirmishers of the
consolidated brigade, who made feeble resistance, debouched
from the woods in front of that and the Fourth Brigade,
advancing through the slashing, which was thirty yards wide.
At first he was met by a sharp fire from these brigades, part of
the First Brigade which fired to the left oblique, and the
Fourth New York Artillery to the right oblique. Although he
pushed forward with determination he was repulsed at several
points, and his organization greatly broken up by the severity
of the fire, and the obstacles in his front; but unfortunately,
just as his entire repulse seemed certain, a portion of the consolidated brigade, consisting of the Seventh, Fifty-second and
Thirty-ninth New York regiments, broke and fell in confusion.
At the same time a break occurred in the same brigade—the
One Hundred and Twenty-fifth and One Hundred and
Twenty-sixth New York regiments. I stood at the time on
the banks of the railroad cut, and saw a Rebel color-bearer
spring over our works and down into the cut almost at my
feet. But few of the enemy had reached the works, and a
determined resistance of five minutes would have given us the
victory.

"I looked for Lieutenant-Colonel Rugg, but not at the
moment seeing him, I directed his regiment to rush into the
gap and commence firing. Not a minute's time was lost before
giving this order, but instead of executing it, they either lay on

their faces or got up and ran to the rear. I then rode down the line of the Fourth Brigade, ordering them to move toward the right and hold the rifle-pits. These troops were then fighting gallantly, their brigade commander, Lieutenant-Colonel Broady, being conspicuous, encouraging and directing the men. Finding the enemy had gained the angle and flanked my line, I rode to the Twelfth New York Battery and directed Lieutenant Dandy to fire canister at that point, which he did with great effect, working his guns gallantly until the enemy was upon him. His horses were killed, and it was impossible to limber up and draw off his guns in the breaking of the line. The enemy pushed forward, and taking possession of them, turned one of them and opened fire with it upon our troops.

"The One Hundred and Fifty-second Regiment, Captain Brent commanding, when the assault was made, was directed to attack the enemy in flank and rear. The regiment had changed front and was moved up to within 200 yards and directed to open fire. Captain Martin, division inspector, a very cool and reliable officer, reports that not a shot was fired at it, but the men broke from the ranks and fled in the most disgraceful manner, only two men in the regiment discharging their pieces. The panic had become somewhat general, and it was with the greatest difficulty that my line could be formed."

General Gibbon, commanding the Second Division of Hancock's corps, in his official report, states the following:

"About five P. M., the enemy having placed his batteries, opened a heavy fire, most of which took my part of the line in reverse. Soon afterwards he made his assault on General Miles' line, from which a portion of the First Brigade had been withdrawn to strengthen mine, under the impression that an attack was to be made there. The enemy broke through General Miles' line and, pushing forward his troops, appeared to be for a time carrying everything before him. His fire taking my line in reverse, I shifted my men to the opposite side of the parapets to resist his further advance, but there was checked by the steadiness of a portion of Miles' division, and my division was then ordered forward by General Hancock to attack the enemy and re-take the breastworks. In attempting to obey this order, that portion of the division with me did not sustain its previous reputation, and demoralized, partly by the shelling and musketry firing in its rear, and partly by refugees from other parts of the line, retired after a very feeble effort and very slight fire, in great confusion, every effort of myself and staff failing to arrest the rout until the breastworks were reached. Soon after this the enemy attacked my line, the men shifted to the inside of the parapet. Besides the fire from the front which, however, was very feeble, they were subjected to a musketry and artillery fire from the right flank, when the enemy turned our guns upon us. The men soon gave way in great confusion, and gave up the breastworks almost without resistance, and were partially rallied in the woods behind the right wing. The result of this action was a source of great mortification to me, as I am confident but for the bad conduct of my division, the battle would have terminated in my favor, even after the enemy had broken through General Miles' line."

The minuteness and candor of the two foregoing reports indicate their truthfulness, and corroborate the accounts of the engagement made from the Confederate standpoint.

Genl. Robert E. Lee, in his report to the Secretary of War, says:

"Gen. A. P. Hill attacked the enemy in his entrenchments at Reams Station, and at the second assault carried the entire line. Cook's and McRae's North Carolina brigades, under General Heth, and Lane's North Carolina brigade of Wilcox's division, under General Conner, with Pegram's Artillery, composed the assaulting column. One line of breastworks was carried by the cavalry under General Hampton with great gallantry, who contributed largely to the success of the day. The loss of the enemy in killed and wounded is reported to be heavy, ours relatively small. Our profound gratitude is due to the Giver of all Victory, and our thanks to the brave officers and men engaged."

General Lee, in his letter replying to a communication to General Hampton of date August 26th, 1864, says:

"I am very much gratified with the success of yesterday's operations. The conduct of the cavalry is worthy of all praise. I wished you to be near them because I feared that as Gregg was so much in the background in yesterday's operations, he might be preparing for a raid on the Danville and Southside Railroad."[1]

There was now a few days of rest, but on the 1st of September Rosser had the men again in the saddle for the purpose of making a reconnoissance. This expedition was called by the troopers the Newspaper raid, because it was believed by them that it was made for the purpose of getting the latest Northern papers.

About four miles beyond Reams Station Rosser drove in the enemy's pickets, and the whole brigade galloping in pursuit ran the fugitives into their camp close by the infantry fortifications. The surprised Federals stoutly defended their camp, and for a brief space there was hot work with pistol and sabre. After securing some prisoners and a good deal of plunder Rosser withdrew. In this charge the Eleventh was in front and lost two killed and several wounded. It does not appear that a newspaper was secured, nor is

---

[1]United States War Records, Series I, Vol. XLII.

there any intimation of the nature of the information expected to be obtained.

The brigade had continued in camp resting and recuperating after the fight at Reams Station until the 14th of September. That morning, with five days' rations in haversacks, the brigade under Rosser started with Hampton on his celebrated Cattle raid. The rest of the column consisted of Maj.-Genl. W. H. F. Lee's division, Dearing's brigade, and 100 men from Young's and Dunnavant's brigades under Colonel Miller of the Sixth South Carolina Regiment, and the horse artillery under Col. R. P. Chew.

The object of the expedition was to capture and secure for the use of Lee's army, a large herd of cattle belonging to the Federals, grazing in security on the James River near Coggin's Point, in the rear of Grant's army. The location of the cattle being well within the enemy's lines, it became necessary to force the lines at the most practicable point.

Hampton had been well informed as to the exact location of the cattle, and the position and approximate number of the force guarding them, by intelligent scouts under Shadburn of the Jeff Davis Legion; John G. McCleur of Company B, Twelfth Virginia Cavalry, being one of them. Upon their information, Hampton selected Sycamore Church, in Prince George's county, as the point at which to make the attack.

The first night the whole force bivouacked near Wilkinson's Bridge, over the Rowanty Creek. Early next morning the march was continued. The region through which the expedition passed was flat and marshy. The road wound along through occasional pine forests that helped to conceal the strength and design of Hampton's force. Few houses were seen, and almost unperceived they stole along towards Grant's rear. Early in the evening the Blackwater was reached at a point where Cook's Bridge, recently destroyed, had stood.

Hampton purposely took this route because the absence of a bridge averted suspicion of any approach that way. Here he halted and fed, while the engineer corps built a new bridge, finishing it before nightfall.

At midnight the column crossed over, and each subordinate command proceeded to perform the part that had been assigned to it.

Lee was ordered to move up the Stage Road, drive in the pickets, force back the Federals, and occupy the roads leading from the direction of Grant's army to Sycamore Church. Dearing was to proceed to Cox's Mill and remain there until the attack had been made at Sycamore Church, when he was to charge across and attack the picket on the Minger's Ferry Road.

To Rosser was assigned the duty of carrying the outpost position of the enemy at Sycamore Church, and then to push on and capture the cattle which were corralled about two miles from the church and guarded by another considerable force of cavalry.

When within a mile and a half of the church, Rosser halted and waited until morning. At the first streak of dawn, while darkness yet lingered, the column moved forward and the enemy was soon discovered in a strong position. This was the outpost of the force protecting the cattle, the approaches to it being protected by felled trees and abattis. This position was occupied by about 400 men of the District of Columbia Cavalry, armed with sixteen-shooter Henry rifles. The narrow roadway leading through the abattis into the camp, which the scouts had reported to be open was now found to be well barricaded, which fact indicated that the Federals had become suspicious of Hampton's approach, and had prepared in a measure to receive him, but were, perhaps, somewhat deceived as to his numbers.

A squadron of the Eleventh Regiment was ordered to charge, which it did promptly, the men riding up against the barricade, where heavy volleys were poured into them, it being too dark to see the enemy except by the flash of the discharges. A number of casualties occurred as the result of this gallant charge. The horse of Adjutant Funsten was killed, falling across the narrow roadway. A portion of the Seventh Regiment was dismounted and attacked and removed a portion of the barricade in the roadway.

The Twelfth Regiment was now ordered to charge mounted, the First Squadron, Companies B and I, in front. The opening in the barricade was carried, a number of men and horses being killed there.

The enemy, covered by darkness and from behind trees, kept up a rapid fusillade with repeating rifles upon the front and flanks of the charging column, the streaks of flame from their guns now and then revealing their forms to the aim of the assailants. Quite a number of them were killed and wounded and about 300 captured, besides a number of horses and ten wagons. They had, however, inflicted a heavy loss upon the brigade. The Seventh, under Colonel Dulany, had three men killed and fifteen wounded; among them Lieut. G. P. Smith of Company A, who fell leading a charge.

Among the killed and wounded of the Twelfth, were Lieutenant Lucas of Company D and Private Richard Timberlake, a gallant soldier of Company B.

The horse of Orderly-Sergt. Seth Timberlake, known as the "Fighting Sergeant" of Company B, was shot dead, and falling upon him, it required several comrades to remove the animal and extricate the rider.

The Eleventh also had some losses, as well as White's Battalion, which, however, was mostly in reserve and not engaged until later.

Daylight had now appeared, and the brigade pushing on without much organization for a mile further, came suddenly upon a line of cavalry composed of a few squadrons mounted, and in the rear of them the coveted prize—the cattle—in close corral.

General Rosser, riding at the head of the brigade, directed a soldier to ride in advance and demand the surrender of the opposing force.

Private Cary Seldon of Company B, Twelfth Regiment, with a white handkerchief hanging upon the point of his sabre, riding a little in advance, called to the Federals, "General Rosser demands your surrender." The officer in command replied, "Go to h—l!" Which defiance was instantly followed by a volley from his men. With a yell the brigade fell upon them, White's Battalion taking the front. The Federals fled in disorder through their encampment, firing into the cattle as they passed and yelling in order to stampede them. A few of the beeves at the farther end of the corral stampeded, but were overtaken and rounded up, not one escaping. The net result of the capture was 2,486 large, fat young steers, 304 prisoners, a considerable number of horses, arms and equipments, including several hundred of the Henry sixteen-shooter rifles. The camps of the enemy were burned, the stores being first secured and brought off in several captured wagons.

The following is an account of the capture of the cattle. written by General Rosser, which appeared in the Philadelphia *Times* some time after the war. It was written from memory without consulting any official reports or other data.

"Our army had been for some time on short rations, and as our cavalry was stronger than that of the enemy, we determined to forage in the rear of the enemy's position. Scouts reported a large herd of beef cattle near Coggin's Point, and on the morning of the 14th of September, General Hampton took Dearing's brigade and mine, and W. H. F. Lee's division, and by making a long detour, crossing the Jerusalem Plank Road at Belcher's Mill, and marching the 14th and 15th and night of the 15th, we halted near daylight on the morning of the 16th, as we were nearing the enemy's line, to dispose of our troops for the attack upon the enemy and the capture of the beeves. W. H. F. Lee was sent off to the left towards Prince George Court House to amuse Gregg and keep him off. Dearing was sent to threaten Cabin Point, and I was ordered to break through the line at Sycamore Church and secure the cattle.

"These preliminaries all arranged I resumed the march. The moon had set, and although the sky was cloudless, the night in the woods was very dark. My men were ordered to march in silence, but the road was hard, and in the profound stillness of the night the tramp of the horses could be heard a long distance, and I knew it would be impossible to surprise the enemy, and therefore made my arrangements to fight. I knew that I would find a regiment of cavalry at Sycamore Church, and I knew that every man of them would be in position and ready for me on my arrival there, and I brought up the Twelfth Virginia Regiment and gave orders to the commander, Major Knott, a very gallant officer, to charge just as soon as he was challenged by the enemy.[2]

"My guide reported that we were near the church, and I was riding by the side of Knott, telling him how to proceed in the event of his being able to dislodge the enemy, when, as if by the flash of lightning, the front was all ablaze by the flash of musketry, but the gallant Twelfth was not the least staggered by the sudden discharge in its face, but as quick as thought the charge was sounded, and the noble old regiment went thundering upon the enemy. But a strong abattis had been thrown across the road, over which cavalry could not pass, and when it was reached the men were dismounted and put to work clearing it away; and, seeing this, I dismounted the next regiment, the Seventh, and ran it up in line as skirmishers, and soon cleared the way for the mounted men of the Twelfth, who were followed by the Eleventh and Twenty-fifth battalions, and before the enemy could mount and escape, or communicate with the guard over the cattle, they were our prisoners.

"When we captured the regiment at Sycamore Church it was barely light enough to see the road, and leaving a strong guard with the prisoners, I pressed on in search of the cattle.

"I had proceeded about a mile, when in the dim light of the early morning, I saw a line of cavalry—about two squadrons—drawn up on a hill in front of me. My command was not closed up, and I had to halt for a few minutes, but a portion of White's Battalion coming up, we made a dash at this little

---

[2]Col. Thomas E. Massie, and not Major Knott, was in command of the Twelfth on this occasion, and received the order referred to by General Rosser, and executed it with great gallantry, which the heroic Knott would have done had he been in command. The mistake is an inadvertence of General Rosser.

squad, which broke on our approach, and pursuing we soon came upon the beeves.

"When I came in sight of the beeves they were running rapidly in the direction of the James River. The herders had thrown down the fence of the corral, and by firing pistols and yelling Indian fashion, had stampeded the cattle, and they were running like mad. I ordered the Seventh Virginia, which had just overtaken me, to run their horses until they got in front of the herd, then to turn upon it and stop it. This order was not easily obeyed, for the young steers ran like buffalo, and it was requiring too much of jaded cavalry to force it into a race like this. But after running a mile or so the steers slackened their pace, and the cavalry was thus able to get in front of them, and then to round them up, and quiet them, then turn them about and start them to the pens of their new masters on the Dixie side of the line. When the excitement was all over and the herd was obediently following 'the leader,' I had them counted and found that our haul amounted to 2,486 head, and all fat young steers."[3]

The cattle having been captured had to be taken care of, and moments now were precious, for the overwhelming cavalry force of Grant's army was in striking distance and could intercept Hampton by several roads unless the captures and escort could be hurried past the roads intersecting the line of retreat, and these approaches successfully defended.

The situation was a dangerous one for cavalry without encumbrance, but to escape successfully with an additional column composed of the cattle, wagons, and prisoners made it more than doubly difficult, and taxed to the fullest both the genius of Hampton and the steadiness and courage of his command. Hampton, however, was equal to the occa-

---

[3]Taken from the Southern Bivouac, page 417.

sion, and before making the attack had made his arrangements and prepared for almost any contingency.

W. H. F. Lee and Dearing had attacked the enemy at the opportune time, with success, and had established themselves at the points they were ordered to secure on the roads leading to Grant's army.

By eight o'clock A. M. Hampton had secured everything, destroyed the enemy's camps and immovables, withdrawn his forces and started upon the return.

It is not to be supposed that all the hubbub created so near the main body of the Federal army, in its very rear, only five miles from its base of supply at City Point, and in sight of the gunboats at Cabin Point, and the capture of so much valuable property, had not caused a stir at Grant's headquarters, and that vigorous efforts were not instantly put forth to make a recapture, and punish the Confederate raiders for their insolence and audacity. In this connection, some of the Federal reports and despatches are of interest.

On the 16th General Kautz reports to General Grant:

"General Hampton has captured all the cattle and taken them away on the road leading south from this point. I shall pursue and endeavor to annoy them as much as possible. About 150 of the First District of Columbia Cavalry have been captured."

General B. F. Butler to General Grant, September 17th:

"Yesterday three brigades of Hampton's cavalry turned our left and struck the cattle corral about seven miles below City Point, and captured about 2,000 cattle and our telegraph construction party."

Grant despatches to General Davies, commanding cavalry near Williams' house:

"September 16th. I send you despatch just received from City Point. The Commanding General wishes you to strike the enemy on their return, if they are now in return.
(Signed)   A. A. Humphries,
                                          Chief of Staff."

General Davies the same day replies:

"Major-General Humphries,
    Chief of Staff, Army of the Potomac.
    General: Upon the information in your last communication I will move all the available force of this division down the Jerusalem Plank Road, instructing General Kautz to move out in pursuit with a view of cutting them off between here and the river."

September 17th General Kautz despatches to General Grant from Baxter's Mills:

"I have returned thus far from the pursuit of Hampton's forces. I followed him to the Jerusalem Plank Road, and my advance skirmished last night with what I presumed to be his rear guard. I thought it possible it might be Gregg's forces and fell back about two miles. * * * This morning I sent a scout to the Plank Road and found no enemy. * * * He drove the cattle more than thirty miles, and very few were left in the road. I was disappointed not to effect a junction with General Gregg's forces."

It will be seen from the following from Grant to Kautz of the 16th that Kautz, besides his division of cavalry, had been reinforced by a brigade or more of infantry.

"Headquarters of the Army of the Potomac,
Sept. 16th, 1864. 8.40 A. M.
Brigadier-General Kautz,
    Commanding Cavalry Division:
    Colonel Smyth, commanding Second Division, Second
Corps, is ordered to send you a brigade of infantry immedi-
ately, and to hold the remainder of the division ready to fol-
low. General Hunt will send you a battery of artillery. * * *
                                        A. A. Humphries,
                        Major-General and Chief of Staff."

The success of Hampton in securing the cattle and
defeating the forces sent to intercept him, had to be
accounted for by the Federal subalterns to their superiors,
especially to the commander-in-chief. Hence Meade
attributes it to Hampton's superior numbers, which he
estimated to be 6,000. Kautz had it from a reliable citizen
that the Confederates numbered 14,000, of whom a large
part was infantry.

From the various reports and despatches relating to the
Cattle raid, which fill not less than fifteen pages of Volume
XLII. Series I, of the United States War Records, from
which the foregoing reports and despatches have been
taken, it can be shown that, while the Confederate raiding
column largely outnumbered the force protecting the cattle,
the forces of Gregg and Kautz sent out to intercept Hampton outnumbered his available forces two to one. Besides
Hampton's losses in killed and wounded in the attack near
Sycamore Church, a considerable number of his troopers
were sent with the captured prisoners and cattle, greatly
reducing his force opposing Kautz and Gregg.

While the divisions of Gregg and Kautz had been quickly
despatched to intercept Hampton on the Jerusalem Plank

Road, this had been expected and prepared for by Hampton, who had ordered Rosser, with the artillery under Chew, to hold that road at a point east of the Weldon Railroad some distance below Petersburg. W. H. F. Lee's division was assigned to protect his rear, Dearing's brigade and Miller being ordered to support Rosser.

Rosser sent White ahead with his battalion to look out for the enemy on the Plank Road. White had hardly gotten into position before the Federals appeared in heavy force—a whole division.

White with characteristic audacity blocked the way with an attitude of defiance that suggested that he had strong backing. It was a fine play of bluff. The Federals moved slowly and cautiously forward. White now fighting and falling back, but moving his men from point to point, deceived the enemy as to his numbers. Soon Rosser came up with the rest of the brigade, and the Federals were attacked and driven back. Ordered by Hampton to make a firm stand at Ebenezer Church, Rosser promptly took position there. Behind him about three miles the captured herd was crossing the Plank Road. Everything now depended on his keeping the enemy back. On pressed the Federals in a heavy column with flanking parties. It was Kautz reinforced by the division of Gregg. Their artillery, numerous and well handled, swept the road and the adjacent fields with shot and shell, and under cover of this fire their whole line advanced. Rosser with dismounted men on his flanks and mounted squadrons in the road never yielded an inch, but hurled his regiments against them shattering the head of the blue column and driving it back some distance.

The Federals, realizing that this was the only opportunity to recapture the valuable prize in Hampton's possession, made an effort to break through his line at this point. But Rosser held his ground steadily until reinforced by Dearing and Miller, Lee also having been ordered to form on the right. Colonel Chew had already taken position with his guns, and the Federal artillerists were soon forced to give him their attention. "After a heavy cannonade of an hour he completely silenced the guns of the enemy."[4] Being repulsed repeatedly the Federals withdrew after dark. Hampton, fearing a movement towards his left, also retired, and the whole command bivouacked for the night near Wilkinson's Bridge.

Next day the subdivisions of the raiding column returned to their respective camps, the mighty, bellowing drove of fat beeves that preceded them having already conveyed to the army the news of their brilliant success.

The expedition had been absent three days, during which time it had marched upwards of 100 miles, defeating the enemy in two fights, and bringing from behind his lines in safety 2,486 cattle, a large amount of captured property, together with 304 prisoners. The Confederate loss was ten killed, forty-seven wounded, and four missing.

Genl. Benjamin F. Butler, on the 17th, sent a despatch to General Meade saying:

"The cavalry sent in pursuit of the captured cattle have returned, having found all avenues of approach so strongly held by the enemy as to prevent any attempt on their part to recapture the cattle."

---

[4] Hampton's Report.

September the 20th General Grant, in a communication to General Meade, says:

"General Lee claims in an official despatch that in driving back our pickets they captured ninety men from us. In the cavalry fight he claims to have captured 300 prisoners, a large amount of horses and some arms, besides 2,500 cattle. The ease with which our men of late fall into the hands of the enemy would indicate that they are rather willing prisoners."

The caution with which Hampton conducted this expedition, his frequent halting of the column waiting information from his scouts as to the latest situation within the camp of the enemy, the silence enjoined upon the men, and the stealthiness generally that marked his approach, together with the careful assignment of each subdivision of his command, providing as well for his return as for the attack, marked him as a cavalry leader of the most commanding genius. While great praise is due to Generals Lee and Dearing, and to Colonel Miller, for their hard fighting in keeping the way open and protected against the vastly superior forces of Kautz and Gregg, yet the most conspicuous service, the central attack and capture of the cattle, devolved upon the Laurel Brigade, and was duly acknowledged by Hampton in the following report:

"The enemy had a strong position, and the approaches to it being barricaded, he had time to rally in the woods around his camp, where for some time he fought as stubbornly as I have ever seen him do. But the determination and gallantry of Rosser's men proved too much for him, and he was completely routed, leaving his dead and wounded on the field."

The success of the expedition was highly gratifying to Genl. Robert E. Lee, and expressed by him to General Hampton, who in just pride promulgated the following order:

"General Order No. 2.
HEADQUARTERS CAVALRY CORPS,
ARMY OF NORTHERN VIRGINIA.

The Major-General commanding takes pride in communicating to his command the praise which their recent achievement has won from the Commanding General, who, in acknowledging his report of the successful return of his command from the rear of the enemy's army, says: 'You will please convey to the officers and men of your command my thanks for the courage and energy with which they executed your orders, by which they have added another to the list of important services rendered by the cavalry during the present campaign.'

To such praise the Major-General Commanding would only add the expression of his own appreciation of the gallantry of his officers and men, whose conduct in battle is all he could desire, and inspires him with pride and perfect confidence in such a command.

By command of MAJ.-GEN. WADE HAMPTON.
H. B. McCLELLAN, Assistant Adjutant-General."

CHAPTER XI

September, 1864

The return to the Valley—Tedious march and wornout horses—Eager
to avenge the outrages of Sheridan—Federals devastate the
Shenandoah Valley—Fitz Lee having been wounded, Rosser com-
mands the Cavalry Division—Fight at Mill Creek—Toms Brook—
A much-mooted night attempt to surprise and bag Custer—Cedar
Creek—Brent's Farm—Fighting on the Back Road—Death of
Lieut.-Col. Thomas Marshall—Brigade camps and rests at Fisher's
Hill and Timberville—Kershaw's division and Crosby's brigade of
cavalry withdrawn from Early's army—Sheridan with superior
numbers hesitates to attack Early.

After the Cattle raid the Laurels had a week of rest, during which time came the pleasant rumor that the brigade
would soon be ordered to the Valley. News that reached
camp from that section was depressing. Sheridan was
reported as marching through the Valley counties with fire
and sword; and the letters from home telling of the desolation made by his soldiers kindled a strong desire among the
men to go and defend their firesides and punish Sheridan.

On the 26th of September orders were issued to prepare
to move to the Shenandoah Valley. The preparations were
made with much rejoicing. Little attention was given to
the details of packing, all being absorbed with the single
thought of getting off as soon as possible.

On the 27th the brigade moved under the command of
Col. R. H. Dulany; Rosser and his staff going in advance
by rail, via Lynchburg to Staunton.

By the 30th the column had reached Lynchburg, and thence continuing through Lexington arrived late in the evening of October 5th in front of the enemy at Bridgewater. The march had been a long and hard one. When the brigade went into camp at Bridgewater the ranks had been thinned by the length and fatigue of the journey.

On the morning of the 6th the troopers awoke somewhat refreshed by deep slumbers, and though needing more rest, the sight of the burning barns and stack-yards banished everything from their minds but thoughts of vengeance. The fires of destruction were partly visible. Clouds of smoke hung across the Valley, extending from the Blue Ridge to the North Mountain, hiding the movements of the incendiaries, but clearly showing the fiendish character of their work.

Fitz Lee had been badly wounded at Winchester, and was still absent from the field. To his division, consisting of Wickham's and Payne's brigades, the Laurels were temporarily assigned, and the whole put under the command of General Rosser, Col. R. H. Dulany taking command of the brigade.

Rosser found Fitz Lee's division thinned and exhausted by a long and unequal contest with Sheridan's greatly superior force of Federal cavalry. His own brigade was much reduced in numbers by the toilsome forced march from beyond Petersburg, but the men, many of whom lived in the Valley and were now on their native heath, were eager to engage the enemy.

It was soon discovered that Sheridan was retreating, and the Confederates moved rapidly in pursuit. As they advanced the sight of the burnt barns and stack-yards, and occasionally of dwelling-houses, inflamed them with rage. Groups of houseless women and children, who had been robbed of every means of sustenance, stood near the wayside bemoaning their fate.

With zeal quickened by such new scenes of desolation, the Laurels galloped forward and late in the evening overtook the rear guard of Custer's cavalry near Brock's Gap. Here a spirited skirmish ensued, and the Federals being worsted withdrew across Dry River. Custer posting his artillery on the high ground on the other side, kept Rosser at bay until night, and then under cover of darkness continued his retreat in company with Sheridan's whole army.

During the whole night the work of destruction went on. Every kind of provender for cattle and food for men was burnt, while the live stock of every kind was driven off. The burning parties distributed across the Valley swept it with the fire of desolation. Every home was visited, the proud mansion and the humble cottage feeling alike the blasting and savage hand of war.

At dawn the next morning Rosser's whole force was in the saddle, and straightway began a vigorous pursuit of the enemy.

To understand the several cavalry actions in which the Laurels participated in the weeks following, some knowledge is necessary of the relative positions of the main roads that traverse the Valley between Harrisonburg and Winchester. Three roads run nearly parallel the whole length of this tract, the Valley turnpike along the eastern border, the Back Road skirting the foothills of the North Mountain, and the Middle Road between the two. The last two are hilly and rough, but the Back Road, which occasionally

hugs the jutting spurs of the North Mountain, is especially
so. It was along the latter that Custer retired with the
flocks and herds and other movables he had taken from the
doomed inhabitants of the burnt district. The broken and
steep approaches to the crossings of the mountain streams
afforded admirable positions of advantage for defense.

About three o'clock in the evening Rosser's pursuing
column overtook the enemy at Mill Creek, the Laurels
under Colonel Dulany in the lead. On the opposite bank of
this stream the Federals were discovered in force and
strongly posted. Colonel Dulany was ordered to take a
part of the Seventh and White's Battalion and cross at a
lower ford. This he accomplished without molestation,
but it quickly appeared that the flanking column was not
unobserved. No sooner had it crossed than it was confronted by a body of Federal horse which, though it had
come too late to hold the ford, stood ready to block the way
of the Confederates.

Dulany at once ordered a charge. Capt. Dan Hatcher,
commanding the First Squadron of the Seventh, led with
his customary dash, and executed a movement that quite
disconcerted the enemy. While advancing he adroitly
turned to the left, then quickly wheeling to the right, struck
the Federals on the half flank just as Dulany with the rest
of his force charged full in front. The Federals taken by
surprise, after a feeble resistance turned and fled up the
creek, halting on a hill near their main body. Beyond them
could be seen their wagon train and droves of sheep and
cattle, a prize worth fighting for.

White's Battalion, under Captain Myers, now charged
the force on the hill, while Rosser, pressing forward his

column, with the Eleventh and Twelfth regiments in front, burst across the ford and assaulted the main body.

The Confederates, eager to get within sword range of the detested barn-burners, rode at them furiously. The Federals fought bravely, but could not withstand men who were seeking vengeance rather than victory.

The fight that began at Mill Creek lasted until night, being renewed whenever the Federals attempted a rally, and the loss of the enemy was considerable. Darkness coming on, Rosser ceased to pursue, while Custer moved on.

It was not until noon the next day that the Confederates again overtook the Federals, who, as before, fell back down the Back Road all the way to Toms Brook and across it. Rosser followed Custer more than twenty-five miles beyond New Market, where Early had halted his infantry.

Beyond Toms Brook Custer doubled and attempted to get in Rosser's rear, having first moved off towards the turnpike. Rosser, already perilously far in Sheridan's rear, divined Custer's purpose, and turned back in time to prevent its accomplishment. With a dashing sabre charge Custer's column was again driven off the Back Road, and the Confederates recrossed Toms Brook and went into camp.

For two days the Confederates had been driving and chasing Custer's detested barn-burners. The Laurels, blinded with rage at the sight of their ruined homes, had struck with savage fury. Impelled by a sense of personal injury, they had dashed on counting no odds and taking all risks. Custer's men had repeatedly quailed before their onset, and seemed to severely avoid an encounter with the men whose families had suffered so much at their hands.

But now that bloody punishment had been inflicted upon the enemy, though a sense of superiority remained, the passion for revenge, somewhat satiated, began to cool; and when the Laurels first began to retrace their steps, they found occasion for sober thought. That night, when gathered around their camp-fires on the high ground south of Toms Brook, they could not avoid thinking of their situation. All knew the country well, and were not ignorant of the fact that Early with his infantry was twenty-five miles away to the rear, while Sheridan's whole army was camped near by.

The numerous camp-fires of the Federal cavalry indicated, without much if any exaggeration, the greatly superior strength of Sheridan's mounted force.

Says Pond in his "Shenandoah Valley in 1864":

"The assurance with which Rosser challenged Custer all the way down from Harrisonburg, showed that he had no conception of Sheridan's mounted strength, though his fatal zeal was probably due in part to the excitement of his men at seeing their barns and houses in flames; for many of Early's cavalrymen were from this region. Their eagerness to exact retribution brought upon them double mortification and suffering."

Perhaps the Laurels did feel some pangs of remorse for the bloody retribution they had exacted. At all events they lay down that night with a sense of insecurity, which only yielded to a strong faith in the genius of their fearless commander. Rosser himself was not without misgivings. At one time he thought seriously of withdrawing during the night. Some of his officers tried to pursuade him to do so; but regarding Early's orders as imperative, he determined to stay where he was, thinking that if pressed by an overwhelming force on the morrow, it would be quite easy to retire in good order before an enemy whom he had driven pell-mell for two days.

At dawn on the morning of the 9th, the Federals were in the saddle and were observed to be moving into position along Toms Brook.

In the fights of the two preceding days the greatly superior numbers of the enemy had either not been noticed or were disregarded. Now, as squadron after squadron deployed in full view, the inequality of the contest was manifest. Rosser had all told less than 2,000 men, probably not more than 1,500, while opposed to him were at least 4,000 Federals, freshly mounted and armed with the Spencer seven-shooter carbines, which were effective at over 1,000 yards.

Wickham's brigade, under Colonel Munford, held Rosser's left, resting its right on the Back Road. Near by on the right of this road were posted two pieces of Thompson's Battery under Carter, supported by William Payne's small brigade of about 300 men. The right of Rosser's line was held by the Laurel Brigade under Col. R. H. Dulany. The Seventh occupied the center of the brigade line, supporting the dismounted sharpshooters of the Eleventh. On its right was the Twelfth mounted in single battle line, with White's Battalion mounted on its left.

The fighting began all along the front with little preliminary demonstration. Sheridan had ordered General Torbert commanding Merrit's and Custer's divisions of cavalry, "to start out at daylight and whip the Rebel cavalry or get

whipped himself." The command was imperative for the
the Federal horse to assume the offensive, and it went to
the work with promptness and activity. A heavy line of
sharpshooters advanced, supported by numerous bodies of
mounted men. Every opening disclosed moving masses of
bluecoats, and soon they advanced, covering the hill slopes
and blocking the roads with apparently countless squadrons.

It needed but a glance at the oncoming foe to start Carter's guns to action. The intervening woods at first partly
obscured them from view, but at every flash of blue through
the trees, Carter sent a shot of defiance. The enemy's guns,
greatly superior in number and admirably posted, now
challenged his attention, and the Federal horse, taking
advantage of this diversion, in dense swarms moved steadily
forward. The sharpshooters on both sides were busy, those
of the enemy pressing on with confidence.

On Dulany's front their audacity was severely punished
by charges from the Twelfth and White's Battalion, which
drove them back in confusion. Confident in numbers and
heavily supported, they reformed and again advanced.
Meantime they were getting near Carter's guns on Dulany's
left.

While their long and heavy battle line began to envelop
Rosser's left flank, held by Wickham's brigade, Carter saw
his danger and worked his guns with redoubled energy.

From several directions mounted and dismounted bodies
of the enemy were coming eager to seize the prize, while a
superior number of Federal pieces, from positions of security, sent bomb after bomb at the doomed battery. But
Carter never flinched for a moment. Often before his wonderful pluck, and the gallantry of his men, had saved the

guns. Perhaps it could be done again, at least they thought it worth the effort, and their well-directed shots made the enemy waver. But Custer had gotten around Rosser's left flank, Wickham's brigade had withdrawn, and the Back Road near by, and to the left of Carter's position, was swarming with bluecoats.

With a shout the Federal squadrons that had recoiled before Carter's fire renewed their efforts to take his guns, which continued to send grape and shrapnel into their ranks. It was a desperate chance, but the gallant Payne made a heroic effort to save the guns. Straight across the slope, with banner flying and sabres flashing, rode his men right at the crowding Federals, Payne and Rosser in the forefront. It was too late; the enemy was among the guns, and Payne, almost surrounded, fell back.

But the Laurels, under Dulany, were holding the enemy at bay.

White's men, under Lieut. N. Dorsey, had met the onset of the bold Federals with a countercharge. The Eleventh dismounted as sharpshooters, presented a steady front, while the mounted men of the Twelfth repulsed all efforts of the enemy to advance upon them. At this juncture Colonel Dulany was wounded and had to leave the field, but the Laurels were still facing and threatening the enemy. After the artillery on the left had been taken, and the enemy in pursuit of Munford's brigade were far past their front and towards the rear, nothing remained for Rosser but to retire, which he did after covering the dismounted men until they had gained their horses.

About this time Captain Emmet, a gallant officer of Rosser's staff, was seriously wounded.

Custer pushed his advantage vigorously, and was only prevented from producing a panic by Rosser's coolness in handling his rear guard, which, by dashing charges, repelled the most aggressive of the enemy's advance squadrons.

About two miles from Toms Brook Rosser attempted to make a stand and retrieve his fortune, but the numbers and activity of the Federals forced him back in some confusion, and he withdrew his division as far as Columbia Furnace.

In this fight, the greatest loss the Laurels suffered was the two guns of Thompson's Battery, and it was a source of great regret and some mortification to them. Although they were not to blame, they chafed greatly under the disaster and were anxious for revenge, while Rosser was still more eager for an opportunity to get even with Custer.

With this end in view he had his scouts watching Custer's division and making daily reports of his camping-ground. He was waiting for a chance of finding him bivoucking away from Sheridan's infantry.

At last it seemed as if the longed-for occasion had arrived. Custer was reported to have gone into camp near Old Forge, a point several miles distant from Sheridan's main body, and easily approached without discovery by a column moving along the blind roads at the foot of North Mountain.

Rosser, after obtaining Early's consent, took 500 picked men from his cavalry, and mounting Grimes' brigade of infantry behind them, started out after dark to "bag Custer." It was on the night of the 17th of October, eight days after Toms Brook.

No moon was shining, and the light of the stars was dimmed by fleecy clouds that floated across the sky. The column seemed to move with muffled tread over the stony road, that wound with snakelike curves around the spurs of North Mountain. Upon reaching the place where it was necessary to turn to the right and cross the low ground towards the enemy's rear, a halt was made. Here Rosser had arranged for a trusty scout to meet him and make further report of Custer's position. The scout was near by, but did not make himself known. for some reason he mistook the Confederates for Federals, and remained concealed in the bushes by the roadside. This was a disappointment. Rosser moved on cautiously. Upon coming near what was supposed to be Custer's camp, the Confederate force was divided in order that the assault might be made from two directions. When everything was ready, at a given signal, both divisions of the force went forward with a rush, to find Custer gone and nothing but a small picket left in his old camp. This was captured by the force under Rosser, but owing to the darkness, some of the men in the other column, under Colonel Funsten, ignorant of the state of affairs, mistook Rosser's column for the enemy, and a brisk skirmish between them for a short space ensued. A plucky bugler of the Eleventh, noticing the hesitating manner of the men on his side, increased the difficulty by blowing a vociferous charge, for he drowned the voices of the officers commanding the fire to cease. At last, after several were wounded, quiet reigned and the command soon set out for camp.

On the return the column passed several bluffs from which the outposts of the enemy fired down upon the tired and disappointed raiders.

This bold attempt of Rosser to capture Custer by a night
attack, convinced the Federals that the spirit of the Confederate horse had recovered from the defeat at Toms
Brook. The effect, however, as the sequel showed, was a
bad one for the Confederates, for it put the enemy on the
alert; and when, two days after, Rosser advanced with
Early across Cedar Creek, the cavalry on Sheridan's
right flank was the only part of Sheridan's army that was
not surprised.

On the memorable 19th, the day that opened with so
much promise and closed with so much disaster for the
Confederates, Rosser with Wickham's and his own brigade
crossed Cedar Creek before daylight, and attacked the
enemy's cavalry; Colonel Funsten commanding the Laurels, and Colonel Owen of the Third Virginia Cavalry, commanding Wickham's brigade, which was dismounted. The
enemy was in heavy force and fully prepared. Still the
vigorous advance of Rosser alarmed the Federal chief of
cavalry. "Torbert's first effort was to check Rosser, who
appeared on the Back Road and attacked Custer."[1] After
some hard fighting, mainly done by Owen's dismounted
men, Rosser steadily advanced, driving the enemy, who
left his camps, killed, and wounded in our hands.

Early's successful attack had routed Sheridan's infantry,
and Rosser pressed forward on his left until the foot soldiers of the enemy could be plainly seen flying in great confusion down the Valley turnpike towards New Town. In
sight of their broken columns Rosser halted, for in front of
him was a greatly superior force of Federal cavalry.

---

[1]Pond's "Shenandoah Valley," page 23.

For several hours there was now a profound lull all along the battle front, and many wondered what it meant.

The brigade with the rest of the division halted massed in squadrons, some in the timber and some in the fields in low valleys. Not a few of the men got off their horses and, exhausted by the morning's work, fell asleep.

In the meantime the Federals were not idle. The complete rout of their left called for reinforcements there. Torbert moved the greater part of his cavalry force thither, leaving only a few regiments in front of Rosser.

This transfer was, however, unperceived by Early as well as Rosser, and both remained under the conviction that all day long there was an overwhelming force of cavalry in Rosser's front.

About three o'clock, the ominous stillness was broken by rapid artillery firing near Rosser's front, where Colonel Funsten with the brigade was resting in careless security. The enemy seemed to be advancing with great confidence. The bombs from their guns fell among Funsten's squadrons, and were the first intimation of their nearness in force.

Of course great confusion ensued, and there was mounting in hot haste. Rosser assuming that Custer's whole force was moving down upon him, ordered his two brigades to fall back. Colonel Funsten was doing his best to retire in order, but the shrieking bombs were bursting in his half-formed column, and a number of the men broke ranks. Besides a heavy column of the enemy was close at hand, who, at the sight of disorder among the Confederates, were encouraged to come on at a charge.

Maj. E. H. McDonald, commanding the Eleventh, fearing a panic might ensue, hastily formed about fifty men of the Eleventh in battle line and, without waiting to receive the onset of the Federals, advanced to meet them, obliquing first to the right so as to take them in flank.

It looked as if this small Confederate band was inviting destruction. Behind them was the division falling back, before them a force of the enemy ten times their number, actually encouraging them with shouts to come on, so confident were they of capturing them.

But the Federals themselves were in some confusion, a few of the bravest far in advance. As McDonald's men came on in battle line they presented a steady front, increasing their speed when they saw the foremost Federals begin to hesitate. For when the latter stopped, for the rear of their column to close up, the whole column stopped; the men of the Eleventh now pressing on with shouts, the Federals turned and fled and were chased back over the hill upon which was planted their artillery.

Rosser now withdrew the greater part of his division across Cedar Creek, and when, later in the evening, Sheridan, heavily reinforced, routed Early's infantry, Rosser held the Back Road against Custer's cavalry.

After dark Colonel Funsten was ordered to hold the infantry trenches at Fisher's Hill. Here the brigade spent the night, and in the morning marched out and formed the rear guard of Early's retreating army.

Everything now looked extremely blue, and the cavalry were jaded for lack of rest and loss of sleep.

The enemy, content with his great victory, made but a feeble pursuit.

At Edenburg his advance column first appeared. Here it halted and, after exchanging a few shots, turned back.

About three miles beyond Edenburg the brigade went into camp, and for three weeks afterwards formed a part of Early's cavalry line on Stony Creek.

In spite of heavy disaster, the indomitable Early began to reorganize his beaten army with renewed hope and energy. A more rigid discipline was enforced, among the cavalry at least, and there were now frequent reviews and inspections.

On November the 9th, orders were issued to the brigade to be ready to march next morning at daylight, with corn for horses and three days' rations. Sheridan, it seemed, was falling back and Early was about to follow him. On the 10th the brigade moved down the Back Road. On the 11th Rosser, leaving the Eleventh Regiment at Cedar Creek, marched with the rest of his command towards New Town. Near this place, encountering a force of Federal cavalry, he charged and drove it as far as the Opequon, where a large force of Federal infantry was posted. After a brisk skirmish he withdrew, encamping out of range of the enemy's guns.

The Eleventh Regiment, under Maj. E. H. McDonald, left a squadron on picket at Snyder's Church. About nine o'clock on the morning of the 12th this squadron was driven in, but the rest of the regiment arrived in time to check the Federals at the ford.

Being ordered to advance down the Back Road, the Eleventh was just on the point of starting, when a strong column of Custer's command came in view, moving up the road with confidence.

A sharp fight ensued. The high bank on the south side of Cedar Creek furnishing vantage-ground, the Eleventh held the Federals at bay until the Twelfth and Seventh, coming up from the direction of Middle Town, attacked the enemy vigorously on the flank. After a stubborn resistance the Federals gave way, and were followed for several miles by the victorious Confederates.

The Seventh and Twelfth were now withdrawn, and joined Rosser with the rest of his division on the Middle Road, where a formidable body of Federal cavalry was threatening an advance. The Eleventh only was left on the Back Road, Rosser supposing that the main body of the enemy was on the Middle Road, where they appeared in great strength, and threatened to overwhelm him with superior numbers.

In the Toms Brook fight, Rosser had to contend with Custer's large division and one of Merrit's brigades, but on the 12th of November both of these divisions confronted him, each nearly double his own.

Between Rosser and the Back Road, was a wooded ridge not easily crossed by cavalry. Beyond it was a fair valley, through the middle of which ran the Back Road, flanked on either side with small, well-cultivated farms; each house amid a cluster of trees, with garden and orchard attached.

While Rosser with his whole division except the Eleventh remained, observing the heavy force in his front, Custer with his full division advanced up the Back Road. There was nothing to intercept him but the Eleventh, under Maj. E. H. McDonald, which met him about a half a mile in advance of Rosser's left. Hastily disposing his small regiment into four squadrons, Major McDonald prepared to do the best he could against a superior force, by deploying two companies as skirmishers on his flanks, holding the others, formed into three squadrons, across the road.

Custer moved forward with great confidence. To the thin array of Confederate skirmishers he opposed almost a battle line. His numerous squadrons, arranged in echelon, extended entirely across the valley, while the road was crowded with his main column.

The rattling fire of the skirmishers began; the volleys of the Federals answered by the scattering but well-aimed shots of the Confederates.

The Federals pressed forward, but the Confederates, taking advantage of the trees and outhouses, held their ground with persistent valor.

Custer's main column now moved forward, the foremost squadrons advancing at a charge. They were met by the Second Squadron of the Eleventh, under Captain Dougherty. For a brief space the weight of the heavy column and the vigor of the assault seemed resistless. The Confederates were borne back, and some had turned to retreat, but the gallant Dougherty recalled them to duty. They now wheeled and turned upon the foe. At their fierce onslaught the Federals gave way. Soon Dougherty was wounded and his men faltered. The Federals, seeing their hesitation, again pressed forward, and the First Squadron was broken and pursued. But the victory was not yet gained. The brave skirmishers on the flanks were still against great odds, keeping back the enemy. As the Federals galloped forward McDonald hurled at them the First Squadron, commanded by Capt. Foxhall Dangerfield. It was composed of two veteran companies from Bath county, men accustomed to victory. Mounted on good horses, these strong-armed and martial sons of the mountains, dashed like a thunderbolt at the head of the pursuing column. The bluecoats recoiled before this furious onset, and in spite of the efforts of their brave officers, began to give ground. The Bath men pressed on, dealing deadly blows until the enemy, turning, fled in disorder, carrying along the fresh squadrons sent to their aid. For several hundred yards the Federals were followed. Such was the fury of the assault, that it seemed as if Custer's whole division was about to fall back. The main body in the road appeared staggered and vacillating, while from the squadrons on the flank many men broke ranks, and were beaten back into line by the sergeants with their swords. But it was now evident to Custer how small was the force opposed to his division. Fresh squadrons were put to the front, the broken ones reformed, and the whole division moved forward. The Bath men were pushed back, and though the Third Squadron came to their aid, it too was driven, and the Eleventh fell back in disorder.

In the meantime, Rosser had sent the rest of the brigade, the Twelfth and Seventh, under Funsten, to McDonald's help. They reached the field just as Custer had forced the Eleventh into a hasty retreat. But in passing over the ridge along a blind road crossed by deep gutters, the column broke into single file, at points, and reached the field in bad shape. Custer was already beyond Rosser's left, and they had to make a circuit to get around the enemy and pass to his front. Had Funsten moved directly against their left flank the result might have been different.

Pennington's whole brigade was now advancing, flushed with success. The gallant Col. Thomas Marshall, ever ready to lead a forlorn hope, at the head of the Seventh, now much scattered, was the first to give aid. With the part of the Seventh that had gotten up he charged the Federals and checked them for a moment. It was like breasting the rush of waters; the waves rolled around him, and Marshall with a few men at his side was almost surrounded. To avoid capture he turned and, after going a few yards, was mortally wounded, amid confusion, much increased by the fall of their colonel. None was more beloved for his virtues; surely his fall was a heavy blow.

Colonel Funsten withdrew across Cedar Creek and attempted to hold the ford. The stand made here was successful, until portions of the Federal force, crossing below and above the ford, attacked both flank and rear.

While the fight at the Creek was still going on and the enemy was trying to force his way across, Rosser, leaving General Payne to watch the enemy on his front, attacked Pennington's flank and rear with Wickham's brigade. It was commanded by Col. William Morgan, who put his regiments into the fight with so much promptness and decision, that Pennington's rear column was soon driven in towards the main body, which was now forcing its way across Cedar Creek, and pushing the Laurels in front of it. As some of Morgan's squadrons swept through the fields and woods towards the Back Road, they fell in with small parties of Federals either skulking or lost, and took many prisoners.

Rosser himself, while galloping through the bushes, came suddenly upon a tall Federal major, who seemed to rise up out of the earth. Hardly had the Federal given up his arms, when a shout near by disclosed the fact, that six or seven bluecoats were coming with lifted sabres to the rescue of the prisoner. They were already unpleasantly near when up rode a body of Morgan's men, until then concealed by a clump of trees, and captured the would-be rescuers.

Custer's men, pushed by Morgan's brigade, had crossed Cedar Creek, and from the high ground there were keeping off the Confederates.

But a few minutes before, the Laurels had abandoned the position, owing to the enemy's having crossed below the ford and gotten in their rear. Now the Federals must hold it, to protect Pennington's rear while he was pursuing the Laurels.

The Fourth Virginia, under Colonel Owen, attempted with great gallantry to carry the position. From the high bank on the other side the Federals delivered a galling fire, but the Fourth pushed bravely on. Twice at the ford they hesitated under the volleys that came from the enemy securely posted. Once more with loud cheers they rushed forward. The ford was passed and they galloped up the hill, and drove the Federals in wild rout before them.

Retreating rapidly up the Back Road, Custer's beaten vanguard rejoined his division. It was now nearly dark, and both sides were exhausted. Custer, gathering up his command, made off to the right, and by a mountain road returned to Sheridan.

This fight was counted by the Federals among Custer's victories, because he drove the Laurels back upon the Back Road. If the punishment inflicted by Wickham's brigade upon Custer be considered, honors were about even. The loss of the Confederates in this affair was trifling in numbers, but in the death of Colonel Marshall there was a heavy loss not to be expressed in mere numerals. He was one of those rare men, nature's noblemen, who, on account of extreme modesty, seldom shine in time of peace; but when forced into action by a sense of duty, as in time of war, attain often to enviable distinction. In him there was so much goodness blended with aggressiveness and high ability, that he could have shone in any sphere of action. But as a soldier only was he known to the men of the brigade, and by common consent he was recognized as the knight without fear and without reproach. Endowed by nature with all the qualities that excite the love and command the admiration of our race, he yet added to these the graces of meekness and Christian charity. Deeply religious, he exemplified the highest type of the Christian soldier. He suffered without murmering; while in word and deed he helped others to bear the hardness of their lot. Whether in camp or field it was his happiness to "go about doing good." To his men, though firm, he was tender and considerate, and they repaid him with an affection that had grown with the lapse of time. His absorbing desire was to follow duty's path, and even if he wandered from that straight and narrow way, it was on honor's side, so full of martial spirit was his generous and noble nature.

After the fight at Brent's house the brigade went into camp at Fisher's Hill, and on the 20th they moved to Timberville.

Early had again fallen back, for which he assigned the following reasons:

"Discovering that the enemy continued to fortify his position and showed no disposition to come out of his lines with his infantry, and not being willing to attack him in his entrenchments after the reverses I had met with, I determined to retire, as we were then beyond the reach of supplies."[2]

In spite of Early's many disasters Sheridan, though greatly outnumbering him, was still afraid of the audacious Confederate leader. No defeat could break his spirit, and calamity but strengthened his resolution to maintain with desperate valor the unequal struggle.

About the 20th of November, Early's force was much diminished by the departure of Kershaw's division for Lee's army, and Crosby's brigade of cavalry to Breckenridge; but Sheridan still insisted upon keeping the Sixth Corps of Infantry with him.[3] The doughty conqueror of the Valley must, forsooth, still have the odds of nearly three to one in his favor, before daring again to face his oft-beaten opponent.

----

[2]Early's Memoirs, page 116.
[3]Pond's "Shenandoah Valley," page 247.

CHAPTER XII

November, 1864

Difficulty of supplying subsistence for Early's army—Plenty beyond the mountains westward—Rosser starts out for New Creek with the Laurels and Payne's brigade—New Creek a Federal stronghold—Rosser joined by McNeil's Partisan Rangers—McNeil defeats Federals at Parsons Ford—Some unexpected happenings—A council of war—Rosser decides—The surprise—A successful ruse—Capture of New Creek—Homeward bound with captures, flocks, and herds—Brigade camps near Timberville—Moves to near Swopes Depot—Custer with large cavalry force threatens Staunton—Rosser and Payne make night attack on Custer's camp—Back to old camp at Swopes Depot—Lack of forage—Companies detached in order to subsist—Beverly.

Small as Early's army was, the difficulty of supplying it with food and forage was a serious one, so complete had been the devastation made by the Federals.

Though there was little left for man or beast in the Valley below Staunton, it was well known that there was an abundance beyond the North Mountain, especially in the fertile valley of the South Branch of the Potomac.

On the 26th of November Rosser, with Early's consent, set out for this land of milk and honey. He had with him his own and Payne's brigade and a few of the choice spirits of the cavalry and artillery left behind, among whom were Capt. James Thompson, Maj. Robert Mason, Lieut. Charles Menegrode, and Maj. James Breathed.

While the open purpose of the expedition was to secure supplies, Rosser intended to try the capture of New Creek. The place is now called Keyser. It is the county-seat of

Mineral county, West Virginia, and is romantically situated at the foot of the Alleghanies, on the Baltimore and Ohio Railroad, about twenty-two miles west of Cumberland, Maryland.

It is now a growing town of 2,000 inhabitants, and is remarkable for the neatness of its appearance, the number of its cosy dwellings, and the picturesque beauty of its landscape. Forty years ago the scene was quite different. Then it was a mere railroad station, with a few houses in the vicinity. But it was regarded as a military point of great importance by the Federals. Two forts on commanding hills overlooking the depot were erected, one of them manned with heavy ordnance. A garrison varying from 800 to 1,500 men held the place and guarded immense stores of food, forage, and ammunition placed there for the convenience of troops stationed in the counties of Hardy and Hampshire. With mountains on three sides, and its natural strength being increased by military art, it was a most formidable stronghold of which to contemplate the capture with cavalry.

Its large garrison, and the facility with which reinforcements could be poured into it from Maryland, demanded the greatest secrecy in any movement against it. If warning was given, its frowning castles could laugh a siege to scorn, and with their guns sweep out of existence all attacking columns. The position was deemed impregnable. A much greater force than Rosser's under General McCausland had previously failed to take it. Fitz Lee not long before had gotten within eight miles of it, and turned back discouraged after learning the character of its defenses.

Rosser had been watching for an opportunity to try his fortune upon it. Some time before, as a preparatory step, he had sent two reliable scouts, John T. Pearce and James L. Williams, to spy out the land and bring him a map of the fortifications. Their reports encouraged the hope that a bold dash might succeed; and when he marched across the mountains, his plans were already matured. Notwithstanding its strong defenses were rather formidable, the place was thought of by Rosser as an object of attack—for he had planned a surprise.

Moving through Brock's Gap the column reached the vicinity of Moorefield about noon on the 27th. Halting his command at the fork, Rosser with a small force went ahead to Moorefield. Shortly after reaching there, he learned that a body of Federals with one piece of artillery was at Old Fields. With about seventy-five men taken from Captain McNeil's command of partisan rangers and from Company F of Seventh Virginia Cavalry, he moved in the direction of the enemy and soon encountered him at Parsons Ford.

Captain McNeil with his detachment was sent to pass around the enemy's flank and cut off his retreat through Reynolds' Gap. The movement was soon discovered by Lieutenant-Colonel Fleming, the Federal commander, and resisted. Before the rest of Rosser's men had gotten up, McNeil had beaten the enemy, capturing his piece of artillery and twenty men, and chasing the fugitives through Reynolds' Gap. Fleming had under him in the fight, according to his own official report, 120 men. Those who escaped from McNeil rode straight for New Creek. The affair occurred about six o'clock P. M., and by quarter past nine P. M. Colonel Latham, commanding at New Creek, twenty-one miles distant, had learned of Fleming's defeat. He at once telegraphed to General Kelly at Cumberland the result of the skirmish. The latter replied, "Put your post in the best possible position for defense, as it is probable that the Rebels will attack you." To this Colonel Latham responded, "I am prepared for them."

To explain the situation it is necessary to state that another scouting party of Federals, under Maj. P. J. Potts, had been sent from New Creek on the 26th of November. On the evening of the 27th, the same day of Rosser's arrival at Moorefield, it camped a few miles north of the town. The next morning Major Potts, learning of the near presence of the Confederates, made off by a mountain path, and after wandering through the mountains, reached New Creek the day after its fall. It does not appear that Rosser was aware of the existence of this scouting party, but the sequel shows that its absence from New Creek had much to do with his successful surprise of the garrison.

The unlooked-for meeting with Fleming's detachment at Old Fields was discouraging. It was highly probable that before sunrise the enemy at New Creek would be informed of Rosser's arrival at Moorefield, and would make preparations to receive him. Instead, however, of changing Rosser's plans, these unexpected events only made him act with more celerity. He determined to march at once against the enemy. Possibly he might reach New Creek before the fugitives; at any rate he would go forward and see what fortune awaited him.

Moving his command from Moorefield after dark, he proceeded by way of the Alleghany and Moorefield turnpike to the head of Patterson's Creek. There he followed the road leading down the creek to the northwestern turnpike. When within a mile of Burlington, situated at the junction of the road upon which he was marching and the northwestern turnpike, he turned to the left. He had now to follow, at times, little more than a bridle-path, which led up Mike's Run to a point on the northwestern turnpike five miles west of Burlington and near Harrison's Gap in the Knobley Mountain. Thus far he had missed all scouting parties, and was within six miles of New Creek station. Here the seriousness of Rosser's design was apparent to all. The men had been marching all night and were exhausted. The sun was just rising, gilding with its beams the lofty peaks of the Alleghanies. The column was still in the woods; in sight was the turnpike along which at any moment a Federal scouting party might pass.

A council of war was held. The question was, Had not some of Colonel Fleming's fugitives already reached New Creek and put the Federals on their guard? Such was the opinion of not a few, and Rosser was urged to go back. Captain Pearce, the scout, reasoned that, without doubt some of the escaped Federals had given warning of Rosser's being in the neighborhood, but that information, in his opinion, would only make the Federals more careless, for they would think Rosser would not dare to approach the fort, knowing as he must, that they were informed of his being near at hand. This view struck Rosser as a sensible one, and offering as it did a fighting chance of capturing a famous stronghold, quickly obtained his approval.

Genl. W. H. Payne, the second in command, always ready to adopt a bold line of action, was of the same opinion. The result of the short talk was, that the column very soon moved forward across the turnpike towards New Creek, taking a near cut to the New Creek turnpike.

General Payne with his brigade, consisting of the Fifth, Sixth, and Eighth regiments of Virginia cavalry, took the front, the Sixth Regiment being in the lead. The Eleventh Regiment, under Maj. E. H. McDonald, was sent by another road leading down Limestone Branch, and approaching the station from the east. Traveling down it Major McDonald was to strike the Baltimore and Ohio Railroad a half mile east of the station, and after cutting the telegraph wire, advance and unite with the main body in the attack on the forts.

The main body had gone but a short distance, when an accident suggested the means of success. From a conversation with a wayside resident, it was discovered that a body of Federal horse had left New Creek on a reconnoissance, and that their return was hourly expected. It was resolved to make the most of this discovery. In order to mask his approach and deceive the Federal pickets, General Payne put twenty men in blue overcoats in advance under Captain Fitzhugh. They were instructed to go at a walk and, when in sight of the enemy's pickets, to approach them quietly after the manner of friends. These orders were executed with great coolness and admirable judgment by Captain Fitzhugh.

In a short time the New Creek turnpike was reached at a point about four miles from the station. Thence the road led along the bank of the creek, which with very slight meanderings washes the western base of Abraham's Ridge. The road was almost a dead level and nearly straight. On the right, the woody banks of the stream served partly to conceal the column; but it was the blue overcoats of the men in front, and the shrewdness of Captain Fitzhugh, that served most to disarm and assure the success of the movement.

The Union people, living near the line of march, came out of their houses to watch the column pass, supposing from the uniform of the advance that it was a body of Federal soldiers, and when the appearance of the main body in grey revealed the truth, it was too late for any of them to get away and give the alarm. Citizens, riding or driving out, and even a small scouting party of Federal horsemen, met the vanguard in the road, and passing it with friendly salutations, rode into the grey column behind and were "taken care of."

The same gait of careless assurance, enabled Captain Fitzhugh to ride up to the Federal pickets and capture them without the firing of a gun or of making any loud demonstration. When within a half mile of the town, it was necessary to lay aside the mask and make a dash at the enemy. A part of the command, with the Sixth in front, turned out of the turnpike to the left, and galloped up the hill upon the summit of which was the fort. Its big guns frowned savagely upon the grey horsemen, and though the gunners were away in the town, the sentinels standing by them being plainly seen gave the impression to many that the cannon were about to be fired. A minute's delay and all would have been lost. Steadily the column moved on, Payne and Rosser near the front. When close to the parapet, the Federal sentinels presented arms in token of surrender, and Payne, taking off his hat, shouted, "Three cheers for the gallant Sixth!" This was given with a will, for already, in the plain below to the right of the garrison, the enemy was seen running in great confusion towards the Potomac.

When Payne with his column turned out of the road to assail the fort, Rosser ordered another part of his command to move quickly down the road and take Church Hill, upon which was posted Mulligan's Battery of field pieces. Fortunately, a projecting bluff concealed them from observation until within a short distance of the station. Rounding the bluff, the Fifth suddenly appeared, and turning to the left charged up Church Hill, upon the top of which was the Federal battery. Here there was a momentary show of resistance. Some of the gunners had made out to load one piece. As the cavalry approached at a gallop the artillerymen fled, but a Federal lieutenant bravely seized the lanyard, and was about to fire, when Maj. James Breathed, of Stuart's horse artillery, cut him down with his sabre. The whole assault had been so sudden and unexpected that the garrison, though numbering more than 1,000 men of all arms, made no effort to recover from the panic that had seized them, but fled *en masse* towards the river. Most of the fugitives were captured, but some succeeded in crossing the river, and from the other side opened fire upon their pursuers.

The number of prisoners taken was about 800, and about 400 horses. A great quantity of forage, grain, and ordnance stores was burned. The guns on Fort Hill were spiked, and the four pieces of Mulligan's battery were carried off. The victory was almost a bloodless one.

Rosser, not content with his rich capture, now sent Maj. E. H. McDonald with the Eleventh Regiment to Piedmont to destroy the machine shops of the Baltimore and Ohio Railroad located there.

The place is about five miles west of New Creek station, and at that time was guarded by a small force of infantry. The road leading to it from New Creek followed the course of the railroad, and near the edge of the town passed through the mountain gorge made by the North Branch of the Potomac.

With a river on one side and a rocky and steep mountain on the other, the pass is easy to defend against a superior force by a small and resolute body. The news of the taking of New Creek had already reached Piedmont, and when Major McDonald got near the town, he found Federal infantry strongly posted in the gorge and ready to receive him.

Dismounting some of his men he engaged the enemy, and after a sharp fight, in which he lost two men killed and several wounded, he drove the enemy from cover, and pursued him with his mounted squadrons through the town to the Maryland side of the river.

Turning his attention now to the engines and shops, he burnt many of them, though his men were exposed to a galling fire from the Federals posted on the neighboring hills across the river.

After the work of destruction was finished, the Eleventh withdrew by a road through the mountains. They camped on the Alleghanies that evening, and learned in the morning that the Federal scouting party under command of Major Potts had passed near them during the night.

Rosser, after sending on in advance his prisoners, and many of the captured stores in wagons, without much tarrying turned his face homeward. Feeling sure that an effort would be made to intercept him on his return, he sent one regiment forward to hold the narrow pass between Petersburg and Moorefield, and went back by way of Petersburg, and not by Moorefield, as he had come. The regiment sent on to seize the pass between Petersburg and Moorefield, got there before the pursuing column of Federals, and Rosser was thus enabled to move on with his captures at a more leisurely gait, and free from molestation. His foraging parties had with great activity taken advantage of the march upon New Creek to gather up cattle and sheep, and Rosser went homeward taking with him a goodly quantity of these, to the relief and joy of Early's army in the Valley. While the capture of New Creek with its strong garrison was a ray of sunshine mid the general gloom caused by Early's repeated disasters, yet the tidings of victory were not received with near as much pleasure as was the arrival of the flocks and herds.

Upon their return the Laurels went into camp near Timberville, and for a few days enjoyed a rest much needed, with the exception of the necessary picket duty.

Very soon forage was not to be had. The cattle and sheep brought by the raiders supplied for a short time the wants of the men, but grain and long food had disappeared almost as completely as the pastures which the hard frosts had killed. Some of the horses died in camp from the effect of starvation.[1]

---

[1] Sherrard's Diary.

On the 16th of December Early broke camp at New Market and moved back to the vicinity of Staunton, so as to be near the Virginia Central Railroad.

Rosser's brigade moved to the neighborhood of Swopes Depot, seven miles west of Staunton, some of the companies being left on picket in front of New Market. There seemed to be now some prospect of relief, from hard service at least, though little from the miseries of want, cold and lack of warm clothing. The winter was severe, and to survive its rigors without sufficient clothing and food was an undertaking of some magnitude. Still the charms of repose were sweetened by thoughts of the recent victory, and the situation was not altogether without crumbs of comfort.

But hope and fortitude would not feed and clothe the men, nor keep alive the horses, upon which the usefulness of cavalry so much depends. Day by day the brigade was diminishing in numbers. Many went home, by permission, after fresh horses; many took "French leave," not as deserters, but for temporary absence without furlough. The remnant consoled themselves with the expectation of a short season of rest from their labors. It was soon discovered that Sheridan's 8,000 horsemen, splendidly equipped and armed, would give them little rest.

On the 19th of December Custer's division, 3,000 strong, advanced from Winchester towards Staunton. Sheridan, spurred on by Grant, was making a grand raid on the Virginia Central Railroad. The main body, consisting of Merritt's and Powell's divisions, crossed the Blue Ridge at Chester's Gap and marched towards Charlottesville. Custer's part of the movement was to go to Staunton and occupy the attention of Early.

On the 20th Early, learning through his signal corps of the Federal advance, with his usual pluck did what he could with the means at his command to foil the enemy.

In the midst of a hailstorm he moved Wharton's division towards Harrisonburg, and Rosser was ordered to the front with all the cavalry he could collect. Taking what could be mounted of his own and Payne's brigades, Rosser pushed forward through mud and rain and about ten o'clock P. M. went into camp below Harrisonburg.

There was nothing at all for the horses. Even the rations of straw obtainable at Swopes Depot could not be gotten.

After a halt of three hours the bugle called to saddle. Roused up at one o'clock the weary troopers mounted their jaded, half-starved horses and, forming column, moved out to seek the enemy.

Custer had gone into camp near Lacey's Springs, and if he remained undisturbed until daylight, his large and well-mounted division seemed likely to prove more than a match for Rosser's small force. There was nothing to do but to have it out before morning, and Rosser, ever anxious to meet Custer, started on a second expedition to surprise his camp.

The road, muddy from recent rains, was rendered more so by additional showers; a cold wind blew and the rain froze as it fell. The hats and clothes of the troopers soon became stiff with ice; while the horses were enveloped in frosty garments; the small icicles hanging from their bodies rattling as they staggered along. The road soon became icy smooth, and the horses not being rough shod, traveled with much difficulty.

Following the Middle Road the column struggled on. At Krotzer's Spring it turned to the right towards Lacey Spring.[2]

When near Custer's camp Rosser and Payne rode forward to reconnoiter. They speedily came in view of the enemy's campfires which, stretching away to a considerable distance, showed that it was impossible with the small force of Confederates present to surprise more than a part of the Federal force. There was, however, no other alternative but to try the chance of battle. Upon returning to the column they found the troops shivering with the cold, but ready to do their best. "Plans were hastily made, and without a yell or the sound of a bugle we swept down upon the half-sleeping foe like an avalanche."[3]

The camps first assailed were soon alive with fugitive Federals, but the report of the small arms roused the more distant sleepers, who hastily mounted and formed column.

A short and sharp fight now occurred, in which the enemy, being worsted, slowly withdrew down the Valley. Rosser, after pursuing a short distance, turned his face homeward, rightly thinking it no small victory to have forced into retreat a body of Federal horse outnumbering his own nearly five to one.

Custer had started to go to Staunton, but had failed to get within forty miles of it. Upon learning of Custer's discomfiture, Early moved Wharton's division back to Staunton. On the 23rd of December a portion of it was

[2]From Joseph Sherrard's Diary.
[3]Account by General Rosser.

sent by rail to Charlottesville. The same day Rosser was
ordered to the same point. An all-night march through
Rock Fish Gap brought him in its vicinity. Here he
learned that the Federals had gone back, and after a day's
halt the column moved for their old camp at Swopes Depot,
where they arrived on the 26th of December.

Shortly after Christmas winter set in cold and stormy.
The great activity, necessitated by the aggressiveness of an
overwhelming, mounted Federal force, had more and more
thinned the ranks of the cavalry.

There was hardly enough of forage to keep the horses
from starving, while the men were in miserable quarters
and on short rations. Many whole companies were permitted to go home and recruit.

On the 3rd of January the First Squadron of the Eleventh Regiment went off on leave to McDowell, the Second
Squadron to Lost River. White's Battalion had already
gone, January 1st, to their native counties east of the Blue
Ridge. Similar leaves were granted to many of the Seventh
and Twelfth regiments. So that, by the middle of January,
there was but a portion of the brigade left at Swopes Depot,
and this was suffering greatly for the means of subsistence.
Rosser, who was still in command of Fitz Lee's division,
began to cast about for some sort of relief. The country
around him was almost famine-stricken. The people had
been drained of their substance to support the soldiery.
The Government could do little. It was straining every
nerve to maintain Lee's veterans who, in spite of cold,
hunger, and constant assaults of Grant's multitudes, formed
a wall of defense for the Confederate Capital.

It was impossible to submit quietly to an environment that threatened to disband his command. As no help was to be expected from others, Rosser must strike a blow for himself. There was much to discourage any thought of campaigning in such a winter. His men were few, half-clothed and badly mounted; besides despondency was in the air.

It was plain, indeed, to the thoughtful that the sun of the Confederacy was near its setting, but to the brave hearts that defied fortune, it seemed only under a passing cloud. At the opening of spring, they thought, the gloom would vanish and victory once more perch upon the banner of Lee.

If the darkening prospect led many to despond and to falter in devotion to the cause of their adoption, in the more dauntless spirits it only awakened heroic constancy, and spurred them on to more daring achievements.

While seeking an opportunity to damage the enemy and help himself, Rosser through his scouts learned that at Beverly, a distant point west of the Alleghanies, was stored a large quantity of army supplies, and that the Federal garrison there did not exceed 1,000 men. Here was a chance to do something which might bring relief for a time, and for the want of a better opportunity Rosser began to think how he might capture the place.

Beverly is distant from Staunton, as the crow flies, about seventy-five miles. But the road traverses the steep ranges and winds through the gorges of the Alleghanies. For some distance it led through what was then a war-swept region, that could furnish little means of subsistence to either man or horse, and most of the way over almost impassable roads and across fierce mountain streams. It was blocked up, too, by the snows which for weeks had been falling, and in the gorges drifted to a depth of twenty-five feet. The people who lived along or near the road were as fierce and intractable as the rugged steeps among which they dwelt, and were, moreover, bitterly hostile to the Confederacy.

A sober estimate of the difficulties to be overcome did not furnish much reasonable hope for success, but necessity could not listen to judgment, and despair lent courage to hope.

Having gotten the consent of Genl. Fitzhugh Lee, who in Early's absence was in command of the Valley forces, Rosser took steps to prepare for the raid on Beverly. As the work to be done would make great demands upon the pluck and fortitude of those engaged in it, he deemed it wise to enroll for the expedition none but volunteers. A call for these discovered that more men were willing to go than there were horses fit for duty. Some wished to march afoot, but this was not permitted.

After some necessary delay a force of 300 men was gathered from the three brigades of Payne, Munford, and Rosser. These were divided into two detachments of 150 men each, commanded respectively by Colonel Cook of the Eighth Virginia Cavalry, and Colonel Morgan of the First Virginia Cavalry, of whom says Rosser, speaking of this diminutive force, "I can safely say that a more intelligent, more gallant, and more reliable 300 than composed my little army of invasion was never assembled in one command."

With the small force thus made up, a sort of forlorn hope, Rosser started for Beverly. The march was without important incidents except that, being in midwinter, and the weather exceptionally cold, the suffering of the troopers was intense. A deep snow was on the ground, and this was drifted in the mountain passes, in some places, to a depth of twenty-five feet.

While the direct road to Beverly was probably not over seventy-five miles, the route followed by Rosser was much farther, as his plan was to attack the Federal position from the north, it having been found that the road in that direction was not so well guarded, and also because the Federals would be cut off from their line of retreat. Beverly is located in Tygarts Valley, through which winds the Tygarts Valley River, and the mountain streams across Rosser's line of march flow into that river.

The night of the 10th of January the command bivouacked on a mountainside in Devil's Hollow, the road following the meanderings of a run that flowed into Tygarts Valley River, and intersected the Philippi turnpike in the rear of the Federal camp.

The attack was made before daylight on the morning of the 11th, most of the command being dismounted.

A thin line of battle was formed enveloping the encampment, and advanced over the frozen snow, the noise of the troopers' feet breaking through the crust being the first intimation of the approach of a hostile force. A sentinel near the encampment of huts and tents cried, "Who goes there?" several times. The only response to his challenge was the steady tramp of the advancing line. Thinking that he would fire and alarm the camp, a charge was ordered by the whole force. The mounted squadron dashed through the line and rode boldly up to the tents, demanding the surrender of the occupants. Being utterly surprised there was not much resistance, but some of the more resolute Federals fired at the men entering the doors of the tents, killing one and wounding several Confederates.

In a few minutes the place was in the hands of Rosser's force, and was quickly sacked by the half-starved Confederates.

The capture, however, did not turn out to be as valuable as General Rosser had hoped. The troopers indulged in the bountiful supply of the usual food and luxuries to be found in a Federal garrison; among them an abundance of liquor which, as may be supposed after the severity of the march, was freely indulged in.

The captures, according to the report of General Rosser, were 580 prisoners, which is corroborated by the Federal report, which admits 572 men and eight officers taken prisoners, six men killed and thirty-two men wounded; also 100 horses, about 600 arms and equipments, and 10,000 rations.[1]

The Federal force consisted of the Eighth Ohio Cavalry and the Thirty-fourth Ohio Infantry, about 1,000 in all.

The following is the report of the incident by the Federal general, George Crook, commanding that department:

---

[1] In a private diary preserved by Capt. Jno. S. Blackburn, ordnance officer of Payne's brigade, who attended the expedition, it is mentioned that Colonel Cook, a gallant officer commanding the Eighth Virginia Cavalry, lately attached to Payne's brigade, was left at Beverly, badly wounded in a leg, which was amputated. This is the only casualty mentioned, except the killing of private Hite.

"Headquarters Department of West Virginia,
January 25th, 1865.

Respectfully forwarded to Headquarters Middle Military Division.

Upon hearing of the surprise and capture of Beverly, I sent two trusty staff officers to examine into and report upon the affair. Their report has been forwarded. I herewith forward the report of Colonel Wilkinson, and recommend that Lieut.-Col. R. Yourt, Eighth Ohio Cavalry, and Lieut.-Col. L. Furney, Thirty-fourth Ohio Volunteers, be dismissed the service for disgraceful neglect of their commands, and for permitting themselves to be surprised and the greater portion of their commands captured, in order that worthy officers may fill their places, which they have proved themselves incompetent to hold.

George Crook,
Major-General Commanding."

The return of the expedition to Swopes Depot, which was necessarily slow on account of the large number of prisoners on foot, was attended with great suffering both to the troopers and to the prisoners, but particularly to the latter, who were taken many of them without overcoats and only partly clad. The frozen feet and hands of quite a number necessitated amputation.

Genl. Robert E. Lee reports to the Secretary of War as follows:

"Headquarters, January 15th, 1865.

General Early reports that Rosser, at the head of 300 men, surprised and captured the garrison at Beverly, Randolph county, on the 11th instant, killing and wounding a considerable number and taking 580 prisoners. His loss light.

R. E. Lee.

To Hon. J. A. Seddon."

The irony of fate is strikingly illustrated in an incident connected with the affair at Beverly.

Fontaine Hite, a private of Company D, known as the Clarke Company, of the Sixth Virginia Cavalry, being without a horse, followed the expedition all the way on foot, with the hope of capturing a mount for himself from the Federals at Beverly. He was killed while entering the door of a tent, the only Confederate reported to have been killed in the attack.

CHAPTER XIII

February, 1865

The capture of the Federal Major-Generals Crook and Kelly, in the
City of Cumberland by McNeil—The capture proposed and planned
by John B. Fay, formerly of Company F, Seventh Virginia Cavalry,
but at the time a member of McNeil's partisan company—Fay with
Ritchie Hallar reconnoiters in the neighborhood of Cumberland—
They locate the sleeping apartments of each of the generals, and
the outpost and reserve pickets—The hazards of the undertaking
—The surprise and capture—Two future Presidents of the United
States narrowly escape—A future judge not so fortunate—Federals
pursue but give it up—Prisoners transported to Dixie.

While this chapter is something of a digression, it contains an interesting item of history which, though it cannot
properly be claimed as belonging exclusively to the Laurel
Brigade, can be claimed in large part by members of the
brigade who participated in it, and contributed in a conspicuous way to its success; and the chronological order of
the history is best preserved by introducing it here.

The capture of two distinguished Federal generals—
Crook and Kelly—from their quarters in the center of a city
of 8,000 inhabitants, guarded with an army of 6,000 to 8,000
men, by a handful of Confederate cavalry, was an event
that excited the North with astonishment at its audacity, and
the South with admiration for its boldness and exultation
over its success.

The account is given in the words of John B. Fay, who
planned the enterprise and assisted in the execution of it.
Fay was a private in Company F, Seventh Virginia Cav-

alry, Laurel Brigade, from August 21st, 1861, until 1863, when he entered the partisan command of McNeil.

The account was written by him not long after the war, when his memory was fresh as to the details. Mr. Fay's account is corroborated by the Federal reports as far as they relate to it, and the accuracy of it is fully attested by his comrades in the enterprise.

Says Mr. Fay:

"Towards the close of the war, about an hour before daybreak on the cold, frosty morning of February 21st, 1865, a troop of Confederate cavalry, sixty-five in number, under Lieut. Jesse C. McNeil, having forded the Potomac and surprised and captured the pickets, quietly rode into the heart of the City of Cumberland, Maryland, then the headquarters of the military district of West Virginia, captured Major-Generals George Crook and B. F. Kelly, together with the latter's adjutant-general, Thayer Melvin; and without the loss of a man carried their distinguished prisoners back with them into the Confederate lines.

"Being a somewhat prominent actor in this affair, and to some extent responsible for its inception and success, and for the special purpose of subserving the truth of history, already violated by several erroneous accounts, I have undertaken in this article to narrate as fully and concisely as my memory will permit, the main incidents of the expedition.

"To enable the reader to properly understand the condition of affairs at the time, a slight retrospect at the outset will be necessary.

"The debatable ground which lay between the opposing armies in northern Virginia, both east and west of the Blue Ridge, covered an extensive territory running parallel with the Potomac, and embraced sometimes the breadth of two or more counties southward.

"During the latter part of the war this region was dominated by three famous partisan leaders, Mosby, Gilmor, and McNeil. Their forces sometimes intermingled, but the operations of Mosby were ordinarily confined to the country east of the Shenandoah, those of Gilmor to the Valley of Virginia; while McNeil's special field of action lay to the westward along the upper Potomac and the courses of the South Branch.

"McNeil's command was composed principally of volunteers from Virginia and Maryland, though nearly every Southern State, and not a few Northern States, had representatives in its ranks. Aristocrats of the bluest blood and their rough, unpedigreed comrades, lawyers, preachers, doctors, clerks, mechanics, sturdy farmer lads, college graduates, and hardy mountaineers, mingled in harmony.

"Moorefield, in the rich valley of the South Branch, was the principal headquarters of this command, and Harrisonburg, in the Shenandoah Valley, its reserved base of operations. In a daybreak attack on a camp of Pennsylvania cavalry at Mt. Jackson bridge on the Shenandoah, in the fall of 1864, Captain McNeil received a dangerous wound and died shortly afterwards. His son, Jesse C. McNeil, an officer of great courage and gallantry, though somewhat excitable and lacking the discretion of his father, was next in command. Some time in February, 1865, Lieutenant McNeil sent for me and, after alluding to a suggestion I had made his father a year before, to capture General Kelly in Cumberland, informed me that Generals Kelly and Crook were then in that city, and if I thought it practicable and could obtain the necessary information, he would make the attempt to secure them both as prisoners of war. As my home was in Cumberland, I was perfectly familiar with the place and its surroundings, and had found no difficulty in getting into it on several previous occasions, once remaining a week. I entered zealously into his project and gave him every assurance of success in case it was properly managed. I was then deputed to take someone, in whom I reposed sufficient confidence, and to go at once to

Cumberland or its vicinity and procure certain information deemed vital to insure complete success. Selecting as my comrade Ritchie Hallar, a lad from Missouri, not yet out of his teens, we started at once upon our mission. The understanding was, that McNeil should have twenty-five well-mounted men prepared to follow us within a day or two, making their way leisurely down the South Branch; while, in the meantime, I was to secure accurate information as to the situation at Cumberland, and the exact location of the sleeping apartments of Generals Crook and Kelly.

"Cumberland, which had then a population of 8,000, is situated on the north bank of the upper Potomac, at the confluence of that river and Wills Creek, and on the site of old Fort Cumberland. At the time of which I write, six or eight thousand troops were quartered in and around the city, under the immediate command of Brigadier-Generals Hayes, Lightburn, and Duval; the former since President of the United States.

"Sheridan's army lay at Winchester, and a considerable force of Federal troops were strongly entrenched at New Creek, now Keyser. The first-named point is southeast, and the second southwest, of Cumberland. These facts show the hazard of a trip to Cumberland, and the liability of being cut off, to which any force of Confederates would be exposed if discovered in that vicinity.

"Hallar and I proceeded with all due despatch, and a few nights after our departure found us about five miles west of Cumberland, on the south bank of the Potomac.

"After reconnoitering the ford we crossed and sought the humble home of a Celtic friend, which was close at hand. I had implicit faith in this man, and engaged him to procure what information we needed. We then recrossed the river, and by daylight were twenty miles away, taking breakfast near Romney. Selecting that point as a rendezvous, I sent Hallar to intercept McNeil and bring him there that evening. He arrived in time, and in addition to those of his own command had a number of men, probably a dozen, belonging to Company F, Seventh Virginia Cavalry, and Company D, Eleventh Virginia Cavalry, of Rosser's brigade. The men and horses were fed and rested, and the shades of evening saw us on our eventful journey.

"Our route lay over Middle Ridge and across the valley of Patterson's Creek, through the ridges beyond to the base of Knobley Mountain, where, taking a northeasterly course we came to a narrow gap, seldom used, leading up to open fields on the mountain-top. Over a road encrusted with ice we passed up this gap, and found the fields covered with snow-drifts of uncertain depths, causing us to dismount and lead our struggling horses.

"Having reached the road passing through a lower gap to the Seymour Farm, we descended the mountain into the Potomac Valley, made our way to the river, and this, our rubicon, being crossed, we found our faithful friend on hand with all needed information. At this juncture Lieutenant McNeil led the men into the middle of a neighboring field, and calling together a number of us, proceeded to the residence of S. S. Brady, where we held a little council of war. After stating that there was not sufficient time, before daylight, to enable us to reach Cumberland and carry out our designs there by pursuing the route laid down by me, McNeil proposed that that part of our expedition should be abandoned; but to prevent the trip from being an entire failure, he suggested that we surprise and capture the large picket at Brady's Mill near by. This proposition met with emphatic and almost unanimous dissent. The prizes for which we had traveled so far were estimated by quality and not by quantity, and we considered a company of infantry but poor compensation for the chance of capturing two major-generals. The attempt to pass quietly through two lines of pickets promised but doubtful results, but that being the only satisfactory alternative we determined to proceed.

"Lieutenant McNeil and Sergeant Vandiver, followed by Sergeant Kuykendall and myself, rode ahead as an advance guard. The rest of the troops, under Lieut. S. S. Welton, keeping close behind.

"A layer of thin, crusty snow was on the ground, and although it was about an hour and a half before dawn, we could see very well for a short distance. The New Creek or Cresaptown Road skirts the base of Wills Mountain, the railroad and river being on the right, and all three come close together at the mouth of a deep glen, about two miles from Cumberland, where the road deflects to the left, and winds up through the glen and over the hills to the city; the railroad reaching the same point along the river bottom. A mounted picket was stationed at the mouth of the glen, and as we reached this point, a solitary vidette was observed standing on the roadside. Upon noticing our approach he gave the formal challenge, 'Halt! Who comes there?' We responded, 'Friends from New Creek.' He then said, 'Dismount one, advance and give the countersign.' When, without a moment's warning, Lieutenant McNeil, putting spurs to his horse, dashed towards the vidette, and as he passed, unable to check his horse, fired his pistol at the man's head. We had nothing to do now but to follow rapidly and secure the picket, whom we found terribly alarmed at the peculiar conduct of his pretended friends. Two of his comrades, acting as a reserve, had been making themselves as cosy as possible before a few smouldering embers in a fence corner, about 100 yards in the rear, but hearing the commotion in front they hastily decamped, making towards the river. They got no farther than the railroad, for we were soon close upon them, and in response to our repeated threats of shooting, both halted and gave themselves up. They belonged to Company D, Third Ohio, and from one of the pickets, a German, the countersign for the night, 'Bulls Gap,' was extorted under menace of instant annihilation at the end of a halter. Mounting them upon their horses, which were found hitched to the saplings just off the roadside, we took these men into Cumberland.

"Naturally, our troops had been greatly provoked at the independent action of Lieutenant McNeil in firing, as he did, a shot which might have caused a general alarm and forced us to abandon our project. Sharing in this feeling, I insisted that Sergeant Kuykendall and myself should take the advance in the approach to the next and inner post. This was assented to, and we moved on determined that no more firing should be done on our part unless absolutely necessary.

"The inner post was fully a mile away, over the high intervening hill, and located at the intersection of the road we were on with the old Frostburg turnpike. The picket consisted of five men belonging to the First West Virginia Infantry, who were comfortably seated in a shedlike structure, a blazing fire in front, and busily engaged in a friendly game of cards. As we drew near the circle of light one of the number was observed to get up, reach for a musket, and leisurely advance in front of the fire to meet us. To his formal challenge, Kuykendall answered, 'Friends with the countersign.' We kept moving up in the meantime, and when the demand was made for one of us to dismount, noticing an impatient movement among our men behind us, in order to deceive the picket and enable us to get as near as possible before our intended dash was made, I shouted back in a loud voice, 'Don't crowd up, boys. Wait until we give the countersign.' We did not find it necessary to give it, however, as there was an open space around the picket, allowing them no chance to escape, and we were close upon them. In another instant a swift, forward dash was made and, without a single shot, they were surrounded and captured. The guns and ammunition of these men were destroyed, and they were left unguarded at their posts with strict injunctions to remain there until our return. On its face, this would appear to have been a very unwise thing, but it was the best we could do. We had no intention of returning that way, and we rightly trusted, that before the men could realize the situation and get where an alarm could be given, our work in the city would have been accomplished.

"We were now inside the picket-lines, and before us lay the sleeping city. We halted for a few minutes whilst Lieutenant McNeil hastily detailed two squads of ten men each, who were charged with the direct capture of the generals. Sergt. Joseph W. Kuykendall of Company F, Seventh Virginia Cavalry, Laurel Brigade, a special scout for General Early, a man of great courage and coolness, who had once been a prisoner in Kelly's hands, and had a personal acquaintance with him, was placed in command of the men detailed to secure that general. To Sergeant Vandiver, a man of imposing figure, a brave and gallant soldier, was given charge of the capture of General Crook.

"An interesting fact in connection with this latter squad is that among the number were Jacob Gassman, of the Laurel Brigade, a former clerk of the hotel where General Crook had his headquarters, and whose uncle then owned the building, and Sergeant Charles James Dailey, whose father was landlord at the time, and whose sister Mary is now Mrs. General Crook, and was probably then his fiancée.

"The duty of destroying the telegraphic communication was placed upon me, and Hallar was detailed as my assistant. These preliminaries being arranged, we moved briskly down the turnpike into Green Street around the Court House Hill, over the Chain Bridge across Wills Creek, and up Baltimore Street, the principal thoroughfare of the city, the men whistling such Yankee tunes as they knew, and occasionally bandying words with isolated guards and patrols whom we passed. Some of our men were disguised in Federal overcoats, but in the dim light no difference could be noted in the shades of blue and grey.

"Part of the command was halted in front of the St. Nicholas Hotel and Barnum House, now the Windsor Hotel. In the latter General Kelly slept. The rest of the command rode on to the Revere House, now the Lindell, where General Crook reposed in fancied security. Sentries paced up and down the pavement in front of the respective headquarters, but took little notice of our movements, evidently taking us for a scouting party coming in to report. Sprigg Lynn, of Kuykendall's squad, was about the first to reach the pavement, where he captured and disarmed the guard, who directed the party to the sleeping apartments of General Kelly. Entering the hotel, the hall of which and rooms occupied by the officers, they found lighted, the party first invaded a room on the second floor. This proved to be that of Adjutant Melvin, afterwards Judge Melvin. They soon aroused this officer, required him to dress and indicate to them the room occupied by his chief. Being informed they immediately entered the General's room, awakened him, told him he was a prisoner, and desired him to make as hasty a toilet as possible. With some nervousness the old general complied, inquiring as he did so to whom he was surrendering. 'To Captain McNeil, by order of General Rosser,' Kuykendall replied. He had little more to say after this, and in a very short space of time he and Melvin were taken down to the street and mounted upon horses, the owners of which gave them the saddle and rode behind.

"While these things were being done, an almost identical scene was being enacted at the Revere House. The guard there being taken and disarmed, the capturing party ascended the stone steps of the hotel and found the outside door locked. After knocking awhile the door was opened by a small colored boy and the party entered. The boy was terribly alarmed at the brusque manner of the unexpected guests, whom he evidently suspected of improper intentions. When asked if General Crook was in the hotel he said, 'Yes, sah; but don't tell him I tol' you!' And he afterwards made the inquiry, 'What kind o' men is you-all, ennyhow?'

"While Vandiver and Dailey were getting a light in the office below, Gassman went up to No. 46, General Crook's apartment, and thinking the door was locked, knocked at it several times. A voice within ased, 'Who is there?' Gassman replied, 'A friend,' and was then told to 'Come in.'

"Vandiver and Dailey had arrived by this time, and all three entered the room. Approaching the bed where the General was lying, Vandiver said in an authoritative tone, 'General Crook, you are my prisoner.' 'What authority have you for this?' inquired Crook. 'The authority of General Rosser, of Fitzhugh Lee's division of cavalry,' said Vandiver in reply. Crook then raised up in bed and said, 'Is General Rosser here?' 'Yes,' said Vandiver, 'I am General Rosser. I have 2,500 men with me, and we have surprised and captured the place.' That settled the matter as far as the bonafide general was concerned. He was intensely surprised at the bold announcement, but knowing nothing to the contrary, accepted Vandiver's statement as the truth, and submitted to his fate with as much grace and apparent cheerfulness as possible. Speaking to me afterwards of his sensations at the time, General Crook remarked, 'Vandiver was such a looking person as I supposed General Rosser to be, and I had no reason to doubt the truth of what he said. I was very much relieved, however, when I found out the real situation, and that the city and garrison had not been captured. In a few hours more I would have been on the train going to join Sheridan at Winchester, and I would have preferred being captured en route, and not taken out of bed as I was. But it is one of the fortunes of war. I expect to meet some of my old schoolmates of West Point in the Southern army, and I know I will be treated well.'

"General Kelly and his adjutant were secured some time before Crook was brought out and mounted, but when this was finally done, and the headquarters and other flags were secured, in a quiet and orderly manner the entire party moved back down Baltimore Street to the Chain Bridge. A large stable was located here, and under the leadership of Dave Barnum this was entered, and a number of fine horses taken, among them 'Philippi,' General Kelly's charger. The taking of these horses occasioned some delay, and Lieutenant McNeil, becoming impatient, directed me to lead them out of the city at once. Turning the column to the left down Canal Street I led it on to the bank which separates the creek and river from the Chesapeake and Ohio Canal, which has here its western terminus. At the locks, a few hundred yards below, we came unexpectedly upon a dozen or more guards, whom we surrounded and captured. We destroyed their guns and equipments, but did not encumber ourselves with their persons.

"From this point the column went at a gallop down the towpath, and as its front neared the Canal bridge on the road to Wiley's Ford, a mile below town, the men were halted by the picket posted there. The column not halting as ordered, one of the pickets was heard to say, 'Sergeant, shall I fire?' when Vandiver shouted, 'If you do I will place you under arrest. This is General Crook's bodyguard, and we have no time to wait. The Rebels are coming and we are going out to meet them.' This explanation seemed satisfactory, for not another word was said. We passed under the bridge beyond the picketpost, the enemy's outpost guard, and across the Potomac once more.

'McGregor was on his native heath, with McGregor's Clan around him.'

"We were four or five miles away before we heard the boom of a cannon giving the alarm. But what cared we? Although sixty miles from base and not yet out of danger, not a man among us but felt at his ease. No wonder we felt proud and happy as we rode back that cold winter morning over the snow-clad Virginia hills. Our expedition was a grand success, our every wish was realized.

"A mounted force from Cumberland in pursuit of us came within view on Patterson's Creek, but kept at a respectful distance in the rear. After passing Romney a few cavalry pressed our rear guard, but after the exchange of a few shots retired.

"On reaching the Moorefield Valley we came in sight of a battalion of the Ringgold Cavalry, then a part of the Twenty-second Pennsylvania Cavalry, sent from New Creek to intercept us. We were on opposite sides of the river in full view of each other, and soon our tired horses were being urged to their utmost speed. The Federals were endeavoring to reach Moorefield ahead and cut off our retreat; while on our side the great desire was to pass through the town with our prisoners and captured flags, and exhibit to our friends and sweethearts there the fruits of our excursion. It soon became evident, however, that the fresher horses of our competitors would win the race. Then at the very moment when prospects of success seemed brightest to our pursuers, to their infinite chagrin, like the clansmen of *Roderick* on the Highland pass—

> 'Down sunk the disappearing band,
> Each warrior vanished where he stood,
> In broom or bracken, heath or wood.'

"Convinced that the town could not be reached and safely passed, McNeil had suddenly ordered his men to enter the woods skirting the road, where, taking a trail well known to us, we passed through the ridge to a point seven miles east of Moorefield, on the South Fork, where we encamped for the night.

"In the previous twenty-four hours we had ridden ninety miles over mountains and streams, with little rest or food for men or horses, and, as may be imagined, heartily enjoyed the night's repose.

"Our prisoners received the best possible care, and next day were started for Staunton. The headquarters of General Early was there, to whom they were delivered, and who sent them from thence to Richmond under charge of a squad of their captors. They were fortunate enough to secure an early exchange, and were returned safely back into their own lines.

"The following are verbatim copies of the only official reports of the affair on record in the War Department at Washington, and have probably never before been published:

'Headquarters Army of Northern Virginia,
February 24th, 1865.
Hon. Jno. C. Breckinridge,
Secretary of War:
General Early reports that Lieutenant McNeil with thirty men, on the evening of the 21st, entered Cumberland, captured and brought out Generals Crook and Kelly, the adjutant-general of the department, two privates, and the headquarters' flag, without firing a gun, though a considerable force is stationed in the vicinity. Lieutenant McNeil and party deserve much credit for this bold exploit. Their prisoners will reach Staunton today.

R. E. Lee.'

'Cumberland, Maryland, February 21st, 1865.
Major-General Sheridan,
Winchester, Virginia:
This morning about three o'clock a party of Confederate horsemen came upon the New Creek Road, about sixty in number. They captured the picket and quietly rode into the town, went directly to the headquarters of Generals Crook and Kelly, sending a couple of men to each place to overpower the headquarters guard, when they went directly to the room of General Crook and, without disturbing anybody else in the house, ordered him to dress and took him downstairs and placed him upon a horse already saddled and waiting. The same was done to General Kelly. Captain Melvin, A. A. G. to General Kelly, was also taken. While this was being done a few of them without creating any disturbance, opened one or two stores, but they left without taking anything. It was done so quietly that others of us who were sleeping in adjoining rooms to General Crook were not disturbed. The alarm was given within ten minutes by a darkey watchman at the hotel, who escaped from them, and within an hour we had a party of fifty cavalry after them.

They tore up the telegraph lines, and it required almost an hour to get them in working order. As soon as New Creek could be called, I ordered a force to be sent to Romney, and it started without any unnecessary delay. A second force has gone from New Creek to Moorefield, and a regiment of infantry has gone to New Creek to supply the place of the cavalry. They rode good horses and left at a very rapid rate, evidently fearful of being overtaken. I am inclined to believe that instead of Rosser it is McNeil's company. Most of the men of that company are from this place. I will telegraph you fully any further information.

Robt. P. Kennedy,
Major and A. A. G.'

"But little remains to be told. Lieutenant McNeil secured at last his long deferred captain's commission, but the war closing soon after, he did not long enjoy his promotion, and some time in May, 1865, in accordance with the stipulations at Appomattox, he surrendered his command for parole. He then returned to the West, where for many years he has been a citizen of Illinois, whilst many of the captors have since passed from time into Eternity, and the survivors are scattered.

"Though a major-general of volunteers, General Crook's lineal rank in the regular army at the end of the war was captain in the Fourth Infantry. Since then he has risen to the grade of major-general, and is but three removes from full command of the Army of the United States. He is at present in control of the Military Department of the Missouri, and has his headquarters at Chicago. General Kelly, enjoying a sinecure post in the Civil Service and a modest pension, oscillates between Washington City and the mountains of Maryland, spending part of the year at the Capital and his summers on his farm in the Alleghanies; and Major Melvin is a distinguished member of the bar of West Virginia, who, since his creditable career in the army closed, has had the honor of presiding on the bench of the most important circuit court in that young and prosperous State. It was subsequently ascertained that there were in the hotel, in rooms not far from that of General Crook, two future presidents of the United States—

Brig.-Gen. Rutherford B. Hayes and William McKinley, the latter a major on the staff of General Crook. Had they, or either of them, been captured, it might seriously have affected the political history of our country.

J. B. Fay.

"July 11th, 1893."

The following members of the Laurel Brigade participated in the raid into Cumberland, several of them enacting the most prominent parts in the capture of the Federal Generals:

Joseph W. Kuykendall, Company F, Seventh Virginia Cavalry.

Jacob Gassman, Company F, Seventh Virginia Cavalry.

John S. Arnold, Company F, Seventh Virginia Cavalry.

George Everitt, Company F, Seventh Virginia Cavalry.

Leslie Davis, Company F, Seventh Virginia Cavalry.

George F. Cunningham, Company F, Seventh Virginia Cavalry.

George Harness Johnson, Company F, Seventh Virginia Cavalry.

Hiram R. Allen, Company F, Seventh Virginia Cavalry.

John Dailey, Company D, Eleventh Virginia Cavalry.

Joseph L. Sherrard, Company D, Eleventh Virginia Cavalry.

John W. Poling, Company D, Eleventh Virginia Cavalry.

John David Parsons, Company D, Eleventh Virginia Cavalry.

Joseph A. Pancake, Company D, Eleventh Virginia Cavalry.

Richard T. Merryman, Company G, Seventh Virginia Cavalry.

Jacob Gassman of Company F, Seventh Virginia Cavalry, was one of the party who went to the room of General Crook in the Revere House, being the first to enter.

The number of men in McNeil's party was sixty-five, and was erroneously reported as thirty in the report transmitted to General Lee, and so reported by him to the Secretary of War at Richmond.

The success of McNeil, in reaching Staunton with his prisoners, is almost as remarkable as the capture, when it is remembered that Sheridan occupied Winchester and vicinity with a large cavalry force, and was much nearer Moorefield than Cumberland; and that New Creek, also eighteen miles nearer Moorefield than Cumberland, was occupied by a considerable Federal force, including cavalry.

CHAPTER XIV

March, 1865

After the return from Beverly, Munford's and Payne's brigades ordered
east of the Blue Ridge—Wharton's division of infantry and Rosser's brigade of cavalry only force left under Early in the Valley
to face Sheridan—Government supplies almost fail, and home supplies no longer cheer the soldiers—Sheridan lays waste the Valley,
and with 10,000 sabres advances—Rosser meets him with 300 men
and, aided by high water, retards him at North River—Early withdraws towards Charlottesville, is overtaken, defeated, and his army
captured or dispersed near Waynesboro—Rosser attempts to recapture the prisoners, but fails—Rosser made major-general and
Dearing takes command of the Laurel Brigade—The trail of
Sheridan—Division under Rosser, not over 1,200 men, moves below
Petersburg—Federals capture Five Forks—Rosser's division forms
rear guard of Fitz Lee's column—Advancing Federals punished in
their onsets—Deep Creek—Brigade, April 5th, with rest of division
moves towards Amelia Court House—Soldiers depressed but resolute—Desperate charge of Dearing near Amelia Springs—Desperate
fighting by great fighters—Federals driven back into Jetersville—
Death of Captains Rutherford and Hugh McGuire—High Bridge—
Death of Dearing, Knott, Thompson and others and the wounding
of many—White takes command of brigade—Appomattox—The
last charge—Brigade disbanded near Lynchburg by Colonel "Lige"
White—Remnant of the Twelfth Regiment under command of
Lieutenant Wm. F. Anderson surrenders at Appomattox.

Not long after the return of the raiding column from
Beverly, the cavalry in the Valley was diminished by the
removal of Munford's and Payne's brigades to quarters
east of the Blue Ridge. To face Sheridan's army there
remained only Wharton's division of infantry and Rosser's
brigade of cavalry.

Want of every description, sharpened by the severities of
winter, proved a more deadly foe than the armed Federals.

The Government supplies almost failed, and what was almost equally as bad, the customary packages of clothing from the soldiers' homes no longer came to warm the bodies and cheer the hearts of the suffering Confederates.

Sheridan's policy of destruction had deprived the families of the soldiers, not only of the means of helping their sons and husbands in the field, but of the bare necessities of life. Their cows, fowls, hogs, and sheep, not to speak of horses and cattle, had been killed or driven off; their barns and outbuildings burned, their crops consumed or destroyed, and their winter supplies of food and clothing ruthlessly seized. In many instances their houses had been burned, and within the bare walls of these left standing, were not a few helpless families of old men, women, and children.

Most of the suffering wives and mothers in their letters suppressed the truth, or at least tried to conceal their destitution from the absent soldiers, by not writing at all, or by sending as cheerful reports as possible of their condition; but "camp rumors," and the failure of the home supplies, enabled the soldiers to read the truth between the lines.

In a few instances, the absent breadwinners were earnestly besought, by oral or written messages, to return home and save their families from destruction.

To remain idle in winter quarters, while wives and little ones were freezing and starving at home, or perhaps sick and dying from neglect, proved in many cases more than husbands and fathers could bear. Hence it was but natural that, as the grim winter progressed with unabated fierceness, Rosser's force continued to diminish in numbers. Amid so many difficulties Rosser kept his men together as best he could, deriving some comfort from the noticeable fact, that the desperateness of the situation had rendered the majority of those who remained with him the more eager for battle, and more determined to do bloody execution when the time for action arrived. He felt confident, too, that upon the first clash of arms most of the absent men would return to their commands.

When, therefore, about the 1st of March word was brought that Sheridan was again moving up the Valley, the report was welcomed as the harbinger of an agreeable change of scene and an opportunity for action.

Grant had been urging Sheridan for some time to renew his attempts upon Gordonsville and the Virginia Central Railroad. The last effort in that quarter had met with ignominious failure. Sheridan's grand column had been frightened away from Charlottesville by a handful of infantry and militia, while Custer's march upon Staunton with 3,000 sabres had been stopped by a small force under Rosser. But Grant was not satisfied, and with characteristic pertinacity continued to urge Sheridan to move forward. Sheridan, who never brought on a battle except where odds were more than two to one in his favor, seemed to have been made timid by his so-called brilliant victories. He appeared now to be waiting until there was no force left in the Valley to oppose him. At last, pushed on by Grant, Sheridan on the 27th of February, 1865, moved up the Valley from Winchester with a superb column of 10,000 sabres.[1]

Rosser with about 300 men met him at North River for the purpose of delaying his march until Early's small force

---

[1] Pond's "Shenandoah Valley," page 252.

of Wharton's brigades of infantry could reach a defensible position. Hastily constructing some breastworks near the bridge, he held Sheridan at bay for twenty-four hours, the river being swollen and past fording. Next day, the river had run down, or at any rate, a body of Federal cavalry crossed the river above the bridge and attacked the Confederates in flank. Sheridan now pushing across the bridge, a sharp fight ensued, that resulted in Rosser's being driven off with a loss of a part of his dismounted men, who were in the temporary breastworks near the bridge. Rosser now fell back towards Staunton, and was ordered by Early to hang on the flanks of the enemy.

In the meantime Early had withdrawn towards Charlottesville, and upon hearing of the near approach of Sheridan, he halted his command at Waynesboro, and drew them up in battle array on the west side of the river, having the stream in his rear. Here with characteristic serenity he awaited the foe.

General Custer, who led the Federal advance, did not hesitate to attack, adopting the plan that at Winchester, Fisher's Hill, Toms Brook, and Cedar Creek had uniformly brought victory to the Federal standard. Sending three regiments around to assail Early's left flank, with a strong force he attacked in front. Early's men, having little hope of success at the outset against Sheridan's superior numbers, when they saw the same old movement against their flank, that had so often before proved disastrous, at once despaired of making a successful resistance and threw down their arms. General Early escaped through the bushes, but nearly the whole of his command was made prisoners.

This was the last of that gallant army that had followed
Early so long, contending nearly always against more than
double its numbers, and though often beaten, yet had again
and again rallied and met the foe with intrepid front.
Under Early's leadership it had invaded Pennsylvania,
and had marched with victorious banner to the environ-
ments of Washington, creating consternation in the Federal
Capital, and alarm for its safety throughout the North.
Upon its withdrawal to the Valley, it had been almost constantly battling against the army of Sheridan, which was
always superior in numbers and equipment. If the persistent audacity of Early had served to make fame for
Sheridan, among those ignorant of the true conditions, it
had revealed to the historian a command composed of
heroic Southerners, unconquered by defeat, and unappalled
by disaster.

The common mind measures the merit of a general by
the splendor of his victories. To appreciate the conduct of
Early and his men, a different and higher standard must
be adopted. The leader who fights for glory only, and will
not hazard a battle without a double assurance of success, is
hardly to be compared to one who, for duty's sake, engages
in an unequal combat with hardly a chance for victory. The
prime object of Early and his command, was not so much to
beat Sheridan, as it was to hold him at bay, and by threatening Washington, compel a force greatly superior to his
own, to remain detached from Grant's army. This was
successfully accomplished. The wonder is not that Sheridan beat Early so often, as that he took so long to drive
him out of the Shenandoah Valley. And if Early often
fought with his adversary from a sense of duty and loyalty

to the Confederate cause, as he appears to have done, his very defeats are more glorious than Sheridan's boasted victories.

The capture of Wharton's two brigades at Waynesboro virtually closed the campaign in the Valley. Sheridan from Waynesboro moved towards Charlottesville, after sending his 1,100 prisoners back towards Winchester under a guard of about 1,200 cavalry.

When Rosser saw the long train of prisoners going down the Valley, he determined to try and rescue them. Following the column with about 300 men, he seized every opportunity to harass the guard. The enemy was on the alert, knowing his intentions. On the night of the 4th of March, near Harrisonburg, Rosser attacked the Federal camp. The attack was repulsed, but in the confusion a few of the prisoners escaped. Knowing that the Shenandoah was high, Rosser sent detachments ahead to hold the fords as long as they could. For two days the Federals were detained at Meem's Bottom.

During the evening of March 5th, in order to magnify his force in the estimation of the enemy, and create apprehension among the guard, as well as to excite the hope of the prisoners, Rosser sent detachments on the flanks, with orders to move continuously over the hill in full view of the enemy. Spies were also despatched to mingle among the captives and persuade them to revolt and co-operate with Rosser when he should make his attempt at rescue.

In the morning of the 6th, when the Federal column was in the act of crossing the river, Rosser charged the guard. The prisoners, either from indifference or despair, failed to co-operate, and though Rosser again and again attacked, all his efforts proved futile. For a short time there was great confusion, but the Federals succeeded in getting across the river without serious loss. Rosser giving up the hope of rescuing the prisoners, returned to the upper Valley.

Sheridan was over the ridge on his mission of destruction. There was nothing to do but to follow on his trail. After reaching Charlottesville the Federals had turned towards Lynchburg; one-half of the raiding column of 10,-000 sabres were engaged in tearing up the railroad track, the other in destroying the locks and culverts of the James River Canal. The business was one congenial to Sheridan. He had learned from Grant that the most effectual way of injuring Lee was to devastate Virginia, and he was doing it thoroughly, making his swath of destruction widespread and leaving utter desolation behind him.

Says Grant in his memoirs: "All mills and factories along the line of his march were destroyed. Negroes had joined his column to the number of 2,000, and they assisted considerably in the work of destroying the railroads and the canal."

To follow on the trail of Sheridan was difficult. The roads were rendered almost impassable, so badly were they cut up by Sheridan's column owing to the frequent rains. The country was stripped bare, and so far as food and forage were concerned it was like traveling through a desert. The havoc and ruin that met the eye at every step, suggested the end of all things, and often the scenes of wanton desolation, and the stories of brutal treatment, excited in the Confederate soldiers longing for revenge.

In the latter part of March, 1865, Brig.-Genl. Thomas L. Rosser was promoted to the rank of major-general, and placed in command of a division composed of his own brigade, consisting still of what was left of the Seventh, Eleventh, and Twelfth Virginia regiments and the Thirty-fifth Virginia Battalion, now put under command of Col. James Dearing, who was then made a brigadier-general; and a brigade consisting of the remnants of the Sixteenth, Seventeenth, Twenty-first, and Twenty-second regiments of Virginia Cavalry, under Brig.-Genl. John McCausland.

The new commander of the Laurel Brigade was a young Virginian not only descended from distinguished Revolutionary ancestry, but with a reputation of his own for valor and skill, well earned, through almost four years of continuous service in the Confederate Army.

Having been appointed to West Point in 1858, he with Rosser and other Southern cadets resigned arid tendered their services to Virginia and the Southern Confederacy. He was at first assigned to duty with the Washington Artillery, served a short time on the staff of General Beaureguard; and was later made colonel of cavalry. He was a man of soldierly appearance, and being a courageous and dashing soldier, and withal a man of winning disposition, during his short but eventful career as commander of the brigade, he became greatly endeared to the officers and men.

On the 16th of March Rosser's division reached Hanover Court House, and found there a part of Longstreet's corps on the lookout for Sheridan, who was then near Mangohick Church, on the north side of the Pamunkey. Effort was made to get the Confederate force across the river and put it in Sheridan's front, but the pontoon train failed to arrive and the bridge of boats and rafts was not complete until the morning of the 17th. A part of Longstreet's corps had already crossed, but the movement was put an end to by an order from Genl. R. E. Lee recalling the whole force to Richmond.

The division was now ordered to Petersburg, and the brigade once more went into camp near the sluggish Nottaway; the division taking position on Lee's extreme right.

In a few days there was fighting near Dinwiddie Court House between Fitz Lee and Sheridan, and Rosser's division was ordered to that point. A few days before White's Battalion had rejoined the brigade, but like most of the other commands, it was greatly diminished in numbers. Rosser's division of two brigades hardly numbered 1,200 men.

From Dinwiddie Court House Sheridan was attempting to reach Five Forks, by a road leading northwest, for the purpose of menacing Lee's line.

"My hope," says General Grant in his memoirs, "was that Sheridan would be able to carry Five Forks, get on the enemy's right flank and rear, and force them to weaken their center to protect their right, so that an assault in the center might be successfully made."

General Lee, knowing the strategic value of this point, was obliged to make a great effort to hold it; and accordingly, on the 30th of March, Pickett with five small brigades of infantry was sent thither.

In the meantime General Fitz Lee, now commanding the cavalry corps, with a greatly inferior force was disputing every inch of ground with Sheridan.

After an all-night march Rosser's division, on March 30th, reached the vicinity of Five Forks, where the main body of the cavalry had gone into camp. The resting spell was short, for about noon on the 31st Fitz Lee moved out to give battle to Sheridan.

Rosser's and W. H. F. Lee's divisions, followed by Pickett's infantry, moved by a concealed wooded road, to turn and attack the Federal flank, while Munford with Fitz Lee's old division held the lines in front of the enemy. The well-laid plan for surprising and assailing the enemy's flank seems to have been somewhat anticipated by Sheridan. Upon reaching Chamberlin's Creek, it was found that the Federals were on the opposite side strongly entrenched. Nevertheless the Confederates pushed forward, driving the enemy back some distance. The cavalry, dismounted, fought on the right and left of the infantry.

In the battle Rosser was wounded in the arm, but refusing to leave the field, and with his wounded arm in a sling, still continued at the post of duty.

"In this engagement," says Fitz Lee in his report, "the loss in Rosser's division was serious, but the details are unknown."

Darkness closed the contest, and Fitz Lee went into camp holding the ground he had won. During the night, having received the information that his left flank was menaced by a Federal corps of infantry that had come to Sheridan's assistance, Fitz Lee early on the morning of April the 1st began to withdraw and again returned to Five Forks.

Here Pickett drew up his men in line of battle with W. H. F. Lee's and Munford's divisions of cavalry on his right, and one regiment of Munford's division on his left.

Rosser was placed just in the rear of the center as a reserve, Hatcher's Run intervening between him and our line.[2]

About three o'clock P. M. a Federal corps of infantry, Warren's, marched up and menaced the Confederate left, and Munford was sent with two small brigades to meet it. Warren's forest of bayonets stretched far beyond the right and left of Munford, enveloping the Confederate position, and with overflowing numbers swept onward.

Munford after a brave but vain resistance withdrew, and Pickett, now assailed by Sheridan in front and Warren's multitudes on his left flank, was driven rapidly towards the right of his line. "Before Rosser could cross Hatcher's Run, the position at the Forks was seized and held by the Federals, and an advance towards the railroad made. It was repulsed by Rosser."[3]

So sudden and overwhelming was the Federal assault, that masses of infantry poured in between Rosser's division and the main body, and cut off Genl. W. H. F. Lee and Pickett, who were in Rosser's camp at the time, from their commands. Sheridan pressed his advantage, and crowding the Confederates drove them back some miles, the retreat degenerating into a rout.

Pickett, with only 7,000 of all arms, could hardly hope to successfully resist an army of 26,000 men.

That night Rosser's division still remained in the rear of Hatcher's Run, and on the following morning, April 2nd, with difficulty withdrew towards Amelia Court House.

Anderson's division had been sent to aid in holding Five Forks, but taking a circuitous route it did not arrive in time.

[2]Fitz Lee's Report.
[3]Fitz Lee's Report.

Grant, profiting by the weakening of Lee's center, assaulted his works and carried the outer line. The roar of the cannon at Petersburg was heard beyond Hatcher's Run, and the news of Lee's disaster soon spread through the army.

The night of the 2nd Dearing's brigade had encamped near Namozine Church. During the day the Federal pursuit had not been vigorous, for Sheridan with most of his cavalry had turned towards Petersburg.

By daylight on the morning of the 3rd Petersburg was given up, and the whole army of Lee began to fall back. The Federals pressed his rear guard closely, and sent out their numerous squadrons to harass the flanks of the retiring Confederates.

At dawn on the 3rd of April, Dearing's brigade with the rest of the Confederates resumed the retreat.

The news of the disaster at Petersburg had spread through the army and deepened their sorrow for the loss of Five Forks. Now, for the first time, some began to lose confidence in the star of Lee. Though they still deemed him invincible in battle, they could not repress the apprehension, that even his genius might prove powerless against those grim allies of Grant, famine and general want.

On the march, at first, Rosser's division constituted the rear guard of the column under Fitz Lee. A continuous skirmish with the enemy was kept up. The road was muddy and the wagons dragged heavily. At points of advantage a stand was made. Sometimes the men dismounted and fired from under cover, at others a dashing charge was made, and the confident foe was taught, by the fierceness of the onset, to beware of valor inspired by despair.

The Federals, however, pressed on with numerous squadrons.

A regiment of infantry, Colonel Tabb's of Wise's brigade, now aided the rear guard, and the column fell back slowly in the direction of Tabernacle Church, the enemy keeping at a respectful distance.

Upon nearing Deep Creek a regiment of Rosser's division was sent out to occupy and hold the bridge. But a Federal force had already been despatched on the same errand. Within a mile of the bridge it was encountered and a sharp fight ensued, in which the Confederates were worsted.

The whole of Rosser's division and Wise's brigade of infantry now came to the rescue. The Federals stubbornly resisted for a while, but were forced to retire after suffering serious loss.

After crossing Deep Creek the cavalry went into camp near Tabernacle Church.

"To give a check to the enemy's rapid advance, at Deep Creek the command was placed in line of battle to take advantage of the defensive position there offered."[4]

In the battle that ensued the Eleventh Regiment, under Col. M. D. Ball, and the Twelfth, under Major Knott, participated gallantly, repulsing the advance along their front.

From Deep Creek Rosser's division moved back to the Devil's Bridge Road, with orders to cover the rear of the wagon trains belonging to the main army of Genl. Robert E. Lee.

---

[4]Lee's Report.

Over Devil's Bridge the bulk of Lee's army had crossed the Appomattox River to the right bank, and from this point on the line of retreat, the Federal pursuit grew daily more vigorous. The wagon trains were a favorite object of Sheridan's cavalry, as being next in importance to barns, stack-yards, and mills, which had suffered so much at Sheridan's hands. The same old policy of destroying Lee's means of subsistence was kept up to the end.

Not a few of Lee's wagons, however, were burned by his own orders, the knowledge of which had quite a discouraging effect on his soldiers.

To aid in protecting the trains, Rosser's division was ordered to take position near Pleasant Oaks, on the left of a heavy infantry force under General Anderson.

All night long the Federals threatened an advance, but the most serious result of their menace, was the loss of sleep it entailed on the part of the Confederates.

On the morning of the 5th Dearing's brigade, the old Laurel, with the rest of the division moved towards Amelia Court House. The suffering of the men for the want of food and rest were now almost unbearable, and their spirits were depressed by the exaggerated rumors of disaster to the infantry columns, which spread quickly through the ranks.

Intense bodily distress, and a prospect of impending disaster, filled the minds of many with gloomy forebodings, and over the hearts of even the bravest there flitted the shadows of despair. Yet no outward sign of discouragement was given, only the weary troopers marched on, with an intensified desire for the relief of battle depicted in their grim and care-worn countenances.

The hopeful ones, however, were easily encouraged, and the promise of better cheer at the next halting place, in a measure sustained their spirits, though like the phantom waters of the desert, the good cheer failed to be overtaken. It was now said that there was an abundance of food and forage at Amelia Court House, and with gladdened hearts the starving Confederates moved on. Upon arriving there some corn-meal was gotten for the men, but there was nothing whatever for the horses.

After a short halt the march was resumed. An order had come for the division to move at once towards Amelia Springs, near which place the Federals were engaged in burning Lee's trains. Moving at a trot the command soon reached Shank's Farm. There were the blackened ruins of the wagons, but the Federals were gone. Fitz Lee, with a cavalry force, had gotten there ahead of Rosser, but too late to prevent the burning of some of the wagons. He had ridden on in hot pursuit, leaving orders for Rosser to join him, following on the road to Amelia Springs. The jaded horses were spurred into a gallop and Fitz Lee was soon overtaken.

Upon nearing the Springs the enemy was discovered drawn up on a high ridge. "Ride over them!" was Rosser's order to General Dearing after a momentary inspection of the hostile force. Dearing did not wait for a second command, though the enemy greatly outnumbered him. "Forward! Gallop. March!" he cried, and waving his hat he led the way, the gallant spirits of the foremost squadron eagerly contending with him for the post of honor.

The Federals were strongly posted, splendidly armed and mounted, and flushed with victory. Against them came a greatly inferior force, both horses and men weak from want of food and sleep. Their ammunition was nearly exhausted, but their trusty sabres were sharp and gave a steady gleam as the charging column approached the summit of the ridge.

The Federals with solid front and stubborn courage received the assault. The Confederates did not pause, but with fiery eagerness dashed onward, piercing the hostile line and using their sabres with great effect; and the nearest foemen, appalled at the fury of the onset, began to give way and turn their backs. The disorder spread and soon the whole Federal force broke and fled. Like an avenging nemesis the grey troopers rode among them, doing bloody execution. With great spirit the Federal officers attempted to stem the tide, but the onward rush of the victors seemed resistless.

Along with Dearing rode many of the choice spirits, officers, and men of the brigade, for as in the charge so in the pursuit, there was a noble emulation of valor. Among the foremost were Captains James Rutherford, Hugh McGuire, and Fox Dangerfield. There, too, with many others were the lions of the horse artillery, Majors James Thompson, James Breathed, and Col. R. P. Chew.

In the charge the leading regiment was the Eleventh, under Colonel Ball, the foremost company that of Capt. Hugh McGuire.

The Federals in their retreat, when climbing the hill near Jeters house, were so closely pursued that they left the road and turned into the pines and escaped.

The Confederates now halted and began to form, in anticipation of a hostile movement from Jetersville, for a large body of Federal cavalry was posted there. Soon from this direction a heavy column approached. The odds were great, but once more the grey troopers, McGuire's company in front, dashed forward and turned back the Federal column, driving it pell-mell.

The violence of the assault gave no opportunity to reform, and the superior numbers of the enemy only made the unwieldy mass an easier prey for slaughter. The Confederates rode among them sabring at will and chased the fugitives back into Jetersville.

In this action the Federals lost heavily. The loss to the Confederates was small in numbers, but two of their best officers were mortally wounded, Capt. Hugh McGuire of Company E, Eleventh Virginia, and Capt. James Rutherford of General Dearing's staff. "Two of my best and bravest officers," wrote Genl. Fitz Lee. "Two unusually promising men and most superb soldiers." wrote General Rosser.

By the men of the brigade the loss of Capt. Hugh Holmes McGuire was especially lamented. Being in the early flower of manhood, only twenty-three years of age, of splendid form, of genial and winning disposition, and rashly brave in battle, there were united in him the qualities that never fail to win the admiration and affection of men.[5]

The fight was over for that day at least; the trains were rescued and the Federals heavily punished, though the cravings of hunger were still unappeased. Perhaps the pain

---

[5]Among the wounded were General Dearing, and Maj. James W. Thompson of the horse artillery, each in the arm, and Capt. Foxhall Dangerfield of the Seventh Virginia Cavalry, through the thigh. All of whom, with their wounds bandaged, participated in the next day's fighting, in which the two former met death.

of long abstinence had much to do with the fierceness of the
Confederate charge at Jetersville.

Says Fitz Lee in his report, "In this encounter thirty of
the enemy were killed, principally with sabres, and 150
wounded or captured. The gallantry of General Dearing in
leading the charge of his command was conspicuous."

This bloody little victory greatly encouraged the men of
the brigade, and though they passed a restless night, spending much of it in search of food and forage, and in caring
for their wounded, they arose at dawn stirred with new
hope. Little did they think that to many of their bravest
that day would be the last.

During the night of the 5th Grant's army had been
marching in all directions in the endeavor to encompass
Lee, who had his main body in and around Amelia Court
House. It was Grant's plan, first, to prevent Lee from
moving southward and uniting with the army of Johnston,
and next, if possible, to end the matter before Lee could
move further west.

The Federals were full of enthusiasm, each man wishing
to participate in the overthrow of an army that for four
long years had been crowned with victory.

A part of the plan to head off Lee was to destroy High
Bridge over the Appomattox River. For this purpose a
considerable body of infantry under General Reid, and a

Maj. John Locher Knott, of the Twelfth Virginia Cavalry, was
captain of Company D of the Twelfth Virginia Cavalry, and was
promoted to the rank of major. He was killed at the desperate fight
at High Bridge. He was greatly admired and beloved by the men of
the regiment. No truer patriot nor braver soldier served in the Confederate cause.

squadron of cavalry under Colonel Washburn, had been despatched on the morning of the 6th.

Rosser with his own division and parts of W. H. F. Lee's and Munford's divisions had been ordered by Genl. Fitz Lee to move to Rice's Station, on the Southside Railroad, and report to General Longstreet. As nearly all the roads were occupied by trains and artillery moving in the same direction, the march thither had to be mainly through fields and woods. By means of efficient guides the march was accomplished, and in good time, too, for there was memorable service to be rendered there that day by the cavalry.

On the part of the Federals General Ord had been directed to take possession of all the roads southward between Burkeville and High Bridge.

"On the morning of the 6th Ord sent Colonel Washburn with two infantry regiments, with instructions to destroy High Bridge and return rapidly to Burkeville station."[6]

Intelligence of the movement reached Longstreet's headquarters shortly after the arrival of Rosser with the cavalry, and with Longstreet's consent Rosser, after having established his pickets, and leaving a regiment to support them, marched with the rest of his command to overtake and capture this audacious body of Federals.

About one o'clock P. M. they were discovered near Watson's Farm before they had reached High Bridge. Notified of Rosser's approach, General Reid posted his men in a strong position along the edge of a forest behind a high fence.

It was of supreme importance that Rosser should attack at once, and the Confederates advanced to the assault.

---

[6]Grant's Memoirs.

Munford's division as well as Rosser's had been greatly reduced by the constant fighting and marching, and Rosser's whole force hardly numbered more than 1,200 men. The strength of the enemy is unknown, but was less numerically than the Confederate; but their infantry made it stronger in point of fact.

Munford's division, dismounted, advanced through a body of pines to the edge of a field, on the opposite side of which slightly to the right of Munford's front was General Reid's command, behind a high fence in the edge of the woods.

Across this field the dismounted men charged under a heavy fire of the enemy's infantry. At the same time the mounted brigades of McCausland and Dearing assaulted the Federal right flank. Against them boldly advanced a body of infantry and cavalry under Colonel Washburn. The approaching columns as they drew near each other did not slacken speed, but rushed on with reckless daring, eager for the trial of strength.

Washburn, gallantly leading his command, was met with equal gallantry by General Dearing, and now all along the battle front, there was the clash of steel, and the cries of furious combatants mingled with the sound of small arms. The two foremost leaders of either side, Dearing and Washburn, closed in a hand-to-hand encounter, supported each by brave followers, who rushed to the rescue of their chiefs, and fought around them with determined valor. Dearing and Washburn had been old schoolmates at West Point, but did not recognize each other. In the general mix-up they were separated before either had hurt the other, but a moment afterwards Washburn fell pierced by a bullet.

Dearing, too, fell near by, mortally wounded by a bullet supposed by him to have come from his own men, but more generally believed to have come from the enemy. Such was the confusion and fury of the conflict the truth cannot be established.

Dearing fell while in the act of discharging his pistol at General Reid, another schoolmate, who was killed by the shot, neither having recognized the other, and around these fallen officers the waves of battle surged to and fro, until the Federals of the charging column were all either killed, wounded or captured.

The number of prisoners taken, according to the report of Genl. Fitzhugh Lee, amounted to 780. These were taken over by the proper officers, and the brigade, now under the command of Col. E. V. White, better known as "Lige," of the Thirty-fifth Battalion, went with Rosser back to Rice's Station.

Among those who fell in this fight, in the early part of it, was the gallant Major Knott of the Twelfth Virginia, a modest, brave and efficient officer, exceedingly popular among the officers and men, and whose loss was a sad blow to the cause.

There also fell the gallant Maj. James W. Thompson of the horse artillery, whose guns being retarded by the impassability of the roads, had for two days been fighting with the cavalry and participated in this desperate engagement; the day before, near Amelia Springs he was wounded in the arm. He fell while pursuing fugitives after the onset at High Bridge, wounded in several places, his death wound being through the vertebra of the neck.

The hand-to-hand conflicts, in this fierce encounter, engaged in by many brave privates as well as officers, are worthy of special mention, which space here forbids.

From High Bridge Rosser returned to Rice's Station and took position on the right of Longstreet's line, which was in position to resist a threatened advance of the Federals. The night passed without a battle, though throughout its weary hours it was constantly expected.

The tired soldiers, many of whom were suffering from wounds, slept on their arms. Indeed, during those seven days of retreat sleep was snatched, at odd times, whenever the column halted, and often the exhausted riders yielded to the demands of nature astride their horses in the marching column.

On the night of the 6th the position at Rice's Station was abandoned, and the cavalry under Genl. Fitz Lee moved in the rear of Longstreet towards Farmville, having a rear guard fight with the enemy's advance in the streets of that town; the effort of the enemy having been to prevent Fitz Lee from crossing the Appomattox. Their efforts were so far successful, that Rosser was forced to move up the river about two miles before he could cross, while Fitz Lee with the remainder of his force crossed the bridge of the Cumberland Court House Road.

Having gotten successfully over, Rosser moved down the river to effect a junction with Fitz Lee. Near the Cumberland Plank Road he found the enemy about to assail the division under General Munford, and took part in the successful defense made by Munford. As the Federals pressed on the Laurels, now under White, dashed forward and struck the enemy in flank.

The other brigade of Rosser's division, McCausland's, came gallantly on and joined in the fight. The wooded and broken country soon made the engagement a desultory one, in which detached parties and squadrons charged and fought with mutual loss. The Federals, in the confident expectation of a general victory near at hand, exhibited unusual spirit, charging boldly. But the Confederates, though depleted in numbers, fought with the energy of despair.

In one of the Federal charges Genl. J. Irvin Gregg, their gallant leader, was unhorsed and captured by one of the Seventh Virginia Regiment.

"The march of the cavalry," says Genl. Fitzhugh Lee in his report, "was resumed towards Appomattox Court House in rear of Longstreet's corps, and continued that

---

Foxhall A. Dangerfield was born in Rockingham county, Virginia, at "Westwood," February 8th, 1839. He was descended from distinguished colonial ancestors, his father and mother being cousins, were both grandchildren of Richard Parker, Judge of the General Court of the Colony of Virginia, and later of the Supreme Court of Appeals of Virginia.

He was the youngest son of eleven children, and removed with his parents to Bath county at an early age; was educated in most part at the semi-military school of George P. Terrill and at Lewisburg Academy, studied law in the office of his brother-in-law in California, from which State he returned home to defend his native State in the John Brown raid. Later he studied at the law school—now Washington and Lee University.

In 1861 the law class disbanded, and after taking his legal examination at Staunton, he joined the cavalry company commanded by Capt. A. T. Richards of Bath county, and in 1862, at the reorganization, was elected captain of that company, which was soon after transferred to Ashby's command, as a company of the Seventeenth Battalion, which afterwards was merged into the Eleventh Virginia Cavalry.

Captain Dangerfield participated in all the engagements of his regiment except when absent from wounds or imprisonments. He was wounded at Orange Court House August 2nd, 1862, receiving a severe

order of march throughout the 8th, followed by a portion of the Federal infantry. Their cavalry, and the remainder of their infantry, pursued the line of railroad from Farmville to Appomattox station.

"During the evening of April the 8th I received orders to move the cavalry corps to the front, and to report in person to the commanding general.

"Upon arriving at his headquarters I found General Longstreet there, and we were soon joined by General Gordon. The condition of our situation was explained by the commanding general to us, as the commanders of his three corps, and the correspondence between General Grant and himself, as far as it had then progressed, was laid before us. It was decided that I should attack the enemy's cavalry at daylight."[7]

---

sabre wound and taken prisoner to the Old Capitol, Washington. Being soon exchanged, and before his wound was healed, he was again in command of his company.

In the twelve days' fighting in the Wilderness the Bath Squadron, commanded by him, lost heavily. He was severely wounded at Sapony Church.

In the two days' fighting at Trevilians his squadron was actively engaged and lost heavily. He was shot through the thigh at Amelia Springs, and fought next day in the desperate charge at High Bridge.

After Appomattox he rode home—230 miles—notwithstanding his painful wound.

After the retiring of Col. O. R. Funsten, by seniority M. D. Ball became entitled to the rank of colonel, E. H. McDonald of lieutenant-colonel, and Foxhall A. Dangerfield of major of the Eleventh Cavalry.

He was known throughout the brigade as a brave and sagacious officer.

Maj. Holmes Conrad said of him, "The sum of his virtues and graces is just that he wore the white flower of a blameless life, and they that knew him best can appreciate the fragrance and beauty of that life in all its symmetry and perfection.

[7]Last Official Report of Genl. Fitz Lee, War Records, Series I, Vol. XLVI, page 1298.

At daybreak on the 9th the cavalry corps, about 2,400 men, took position on the right of Gordon's infantry, on the Lynchburg Road, a short distance west of Appomattox Court House, Rosser's division in the center.

"The attack was made about sunrise and the enemy's cavalry quickly driven out of the way, with a loss of two guns and a number of prisoners."[8]

Rosser's division participated in this the last cavalry charge of the war, the Laurel Brigade led by the dauntless "Lige" White,—and when the Lynchburg Road was reached wheeled about for the purpose of attacking the enemy moving towards Appomattox.

But soon in the distance white flags were seen, and from the mingling of the blue and grey which followed, it became evident that all was over.

Rosser now rode off with his command to Lynchburg. The Laurel Brigade—the remnant of it,—upon reaching Lynchburg was disbanded by Colonel White, who informed the men that Lee had surrendered, and that the men of the Laurel Brigade were at liberty either to accept the terms of surrender or to make an effort to join the army of Joseph E. Johnston; as to which, each man would have to decide for himself.

A considerable part of the Twelfth Regiment under command of Lieut. Wm. F. Anderson of Company G, which had participated in the last charge, did not escape with the brigade towards Lynchburg, but surrendered at Appomattox, according to the special terms agreed upon by Generals Lee and Grant, for the cavalry of the Army of Northern Virginia.

---

[8]Lee's Report.

INDEX